Setting Up an Internet [Site] For Dummies®

COMPUTER BOOK SERIES FROM IDG

W9-CEJ-416

Cheat Sheet

Site Information

Supply the information in the second column.

Service	Address
Home Page URL	_____
POP Server Address	_____
List Server Address	_____
FTP Server URL	_____
IRC Server Address	_____
E-mail Information Server	_____
Internet BBS Address	_____
NNTP Server URL	_____
Gopher URL	_____

Emergency Contact Information

Type	Contact Name	URL
Police	FIRST Forum of Incident Response and Security Teams	http://www.first.org/first/
Fire	US Fire Administration	http://www.fema.gov/netc/usfa.htm
Medical	McAfee Associates	http://www.mcafee.com/
Network	Access Provider	_____
Network	Service Provider	_____
Network	Service Provider	_____
Family	Mom and Dad	_____

Useful Keywords for Internet Queries

- Setting up an Internet Site
- Creating an Internet Site
- Setting up Shop on the Internet
- Internet Publishing
- Providing Information on the Internet
- Internet Programming
- WinSock
- MacTCP
- Internet Commerce
- Internet Security
- Internet Servers
- Server Software
- Internet Advertising
- Internet Presence

IDG BOOKS WORLDWIDE

. . .For Dummies: #1 Computer Book Series for Beginners

COMPUTER
BOOK SERIES
FROM IDG

Setting Up an Internet Site For Dummies®

Cheat Sheet

Domain Information

Supply the information in the second column.

Domain Name	_____
IP Address	_____
Primary DNS Server	_____
Secondary DNS Server	_____
Technical Contact Name	_____
Technical Contact E-mail Address	_____
Technical Contact NIC Handle	_____
Administrative Contact Name	_____
Administrative Contact E-mail Address	_____
Administrative Contact NIC Handle	_____
Billing Contact Name	_____
Billing Contact E-mail Address	_____
Billing Contact NIC Handle	_____
SMTP Relay Host	_____
Default Internet Gateway	_____

Resources for Site Developers

Resource	URL
SCIENCE.ORG™ Internet Site Page	http://www.science.org/internetsite/
Web66 Internet Server Cookbook	http://web66.coled.umn.edu/Cookbook/contents.html
Apple Computer Internet Provider Site	http://www.solutions.apple.com/apple-internet/
Building Internet Servers	http://www.charm.net/~cyber/
WinHTTPd/WebSite Central	http://website.ora.com/
MacHTTP Home Page	http://www.starnine.com/software/
WinSMTP Home Page	http://www.seattlelab.com/
Internet Servers for Macintosh	http://www.freedonia.com/ism/
The InterNIC	http://www.internic.net/

. . .For Dummies: #1 Computer Book Series for Beginners

SETTING UP
AN
INTERNET SITE
FOR
DUMMIES®

SETTING UP AN INTERNET SITE FOR DUMMIES®

by Jason Coombs and Ted Coombs

IDG BOOKS WORLDWIDE

IDG Books Worldwide, Inc.
An International Data Group Company

Foster City, CA ♦ Chicago, IL ♦ Indianapolis, IN ♦ Braintree, MA ♦ Southlake, TX

Setting Up An Internet Site For Dummies®

Published by
IDG Books Worldwide, Inc.
An International Data Group Company
919 E. Hillsdale Blvd.
Suite 400
Foster City, CA 94404

Library of Congress Catalog Card No.: 96-75120

ISBN: 1-56884-335-6

Printed in the United States of America

10 9 8 7 6 5 4 3

1E/TR/QV/ZW/IN

Distributed in the United States by IDG Books Worldwide, Inc.

Distributed by Macmillan Canada for Canada; by Computer and Technical Books for the Caribbean Basin; by Contemporanea de Ediciones for Venezuela; by Distribuidora Cuspide for Argentina; by CITEC for Brazil; by Ediciones ZETA S.C.R. Ltda. for Peru; by Editorial Limusa SA for Mexico; by Transworld Publishers Limited in the United Kingdom and Europe; by Al-Maiman Publishers & Distributors for Saudi Arabia; by Simron Pty. Ltd. for South Africa; by IDG Communications (HK) Ltd. for Hong Kong; by Toppan Company Ltd. for Japan; by Addison Wesley Publishing Company for Korea; by Longman Singapore Publishers Ltd. for Singapore, Malaysia, Thailand, and Indonesia; by Unalis Corporation for Taiwan; by WS Computer Publishing Company, Inc. for the Philippines; by WoodsLane Pty. Ltd. for Australia; by WoodsLane Enterprises Ltd. for New Zealand.

For general information on IDG Books Worldwide's books in the U.S., please call our Consumer Customer Service department at 800-762-2974. For reseller information, including discounts and premium sales, please call our Reseller Customer Service department at 800-434-3422.

For information on where to purchase IDG Books Worldwide's books outside the U.S., contact IDG Books Worldwide at 415-655-3021 or fax 415-655-3295.

For information on translations, contact Marc Jeffrey Mikulich, Director, Foreign & Subsidiary Rights, at IDG Books Worldwide, 415-655-3018 or fax 415-655-3295.

For sales inquiries and special prices for bulk quantities, write to the address above or call IDG Books Worldwide at 415-655-3200.

For information on using IDG Books Worldwide's books in the classroom, or ordering examination copies, contact the Education Office at 800-434-2086 or fax 817-251-8174.

For authorization to photocopy items for corporate, personal, or educational use, please contact Copyright Clearance Center, 222 Rosewood Drive, Danvers, MA 01923, or fax 508-750-4470.

is a trademark under exclusive license to IDG Books Worldwide, Inc., from International Data Group, Inc.

About the Authors

Jason Coombs and Ted Coombs

Jason Coombs (jasonc@science.org) and Ted Coombs (tedc@science.org) lead a science and engineering research think-tank called SCIENCE.ORG (http://www.science.org/). Together they have co-authored several books about computers including three in the *...For Dummies* series published by IDG Books. When not writing books and magazine articles, Ted and Jason relentlessly pursue scientific and technical innovation. They live and work near the ocean in Encinitas, California, where they surf, SCUBA dive, and ocean kayak with the local dolphins.

ABOUT IDG BOOKS WORLDWIDE

Welcome to the world of IDG Books Worldwide.

IDG Books Worldwide, Inc., is a subsidiary of International Data Group, the world's largest publisher of computer-related information and the leading global provider of information services on information technology. IDG was founded more than 25 years ago and now employs more than 7,700 people worldwide. IDG publishes more than 250 computer publications in 67 countries (see listing below). More than 70 million people read one or more IDG publications each month.

Launched in 1990, IDG Books Worldwide is today the #1 publisher of best-selling computer books in the United States. We are proud to have received 8 awards from the Computer Press Association in recognition of editorial excellence and three from Computer Currents' First Annual Readers' Choice Awards, and our best-selling ...*For Dummies*® series has more than 19 million copies in print with translations in 28 languages. IDG Books Worldwide, through a joint venture with IDG's Hi-Tech Beijing, became the first U.S. publisher to publish a computer book in the People's Republic of China. In record time, IDG Books Worldwide has become the first choice for millions of readers around the world who want to learn how to better manage their businesses.

Our mission is simple: Every one of our books is designed to bring extra value and skill-building instructions to the reader. Our books are written by experts who understand and care about our readers. The knowledge base of our editorial staff comes from years of experience in publishing, education, and journalism — experience which we use to produce books for the '90s. In short, we care about books, so we attract the best people. We devote special attention to details such as audience, interior design, use of icons, and illustrations. And because we use an efficient process of authoring, editing, and desktop publishing our books electronically, we can spend more time ensuring superior content and spend less time on the technicalities of making books.

You can count on our commitment to deliver high-quality books at competitive prices on topics you want to read about. At IDG Books Worldwide, we continue in the IDG tradition of delivering quality for more than 25 years. You'll find no better book on a subject than one from IDG Books Worldwide.

John J. Kilcullen

John Kilcullen
President and CEO
IDG Books Worldwide, Inc.

WINNER
*Eighth Annual
Computer Press
Awards 1992*

WINNER
*Ninth Annual
Computer Press
Awards 1993*

IDG BOOKS WORLDWIDE

IDG Books Worldwide, Inc., is a subsidiary of International Data Group, the world's largest publisher of computer-related information and the leading global provider of information services on information technology. International Data Group publishes over 250 computer publications in 67 countries. Seventy million people read one or more International Data Group publications each month. International Data Group's publications include: **ARGENTINA:** Computerworld Argentina, GamePro, Infoworld, PC World Argentina; **AUSTRALIA:** Australian Macworld, Client/Server Journal, Computer Living, Computerworld, Digital News, Network World, PC World, Publishing Essentials, Reseller; **AUSTRIA:** Computerwelt, PC TEST; **BELARUS:** PC World Belarus; **BELGIUM:** Data News; **BRAZIL:** Annuário de Informática, Computerworld Brazil, Connections, Super Game Power, Macworld, PC World Brazil, Publish Brazil, SUPERGAME; **BULGARIA:** Computerworld Bulgaria, Networkworld/Bulgaria, PC & MacWorld Bulgaria; **CANADA:** CIO Canada, ComputerWorld Canada, InfoCanada, Network World Canada, Reseller World; **CHILE:** Computerworld Chile, GamePro, PC World Chile; **COLUMBIA:** Computerworld Colombia, GamePro, PC World Colombia; **COSTA RICA:** PC World Costa Rica/Nicaragua; **THE CZECH AND SLOVAK REPUBLICS:** Computerworld Czechoslovakia, Elektronika Czechoslovakia, PC World Czechoslovakia; **DENMARK:** Communications World, Computerworld Danmark, Macworld Danmark, PC World Danmark, PC World Danmark Supplements, TECH World; **DOMINICAN REPUBLIC:** PC World Republica Dominicana; **ECUADOR:** PC World Ecuador, GamePro; **EGYPT:** Computerworld Middle East, PC World Middle East; **EL SALVADOR:** PC World Centro America; **FINLAND:** MikroPC, Tietoverkko, Tietoviikko; **FRANCE:** Distribuitique, Golden, Info PC, Le Guide du Monde Informatique, Le Monde Informatique, Reseaux & Telecoms; **GERMANY:** Computer Business, Computerwoche, Computerwoche Extra, Computerwoche Focus, Electronic Entertainment, GamePro, I/M Information Management, Macwelt, PC Welt; **GREECE:** GamePro, Macworld & Publish; **GUATEMALA:** PC World Centro America; **HONDURAS:** PC World Centro America; **HONG KONG:** Computerworld Hong Kong, PCWorld Hong Kong, Publish in Asia; **HUNGARY:** ABCD CD-ROM, Computerworld Szamitastechnika, PC & Mac World Hungary, PC-X Magazine; **INDIA:** Computerworld India, PC World India, Publish in Asia; **INDONESIA:** InfoKomputer PC World, Komputek Computerworld, Publish in Asia; **IRELAND:** ComputerScope, PC Live!; **ISRAEL:** PC World 32 BIT, People & Computers; **ITALY:** Computerworld Italia, Computerworld Italia Special Editions, Lotus Italia, Macworld Italia, Networking Italia, PC Shopping, PC World Italia, PC World/Walt Disney; **JAPAN:** Macworld Japan, Nikkei Personal Computing, SunWorld Japan, Windows World Japan; **KENYA:** East African Computer News; **KOREA:** Hi-Tech Information/Computerworld, Macworld Korea, PC World Korea; **MACEDONIA:** PC World Macedonia; **MALAYSIA:** Computerworld Malaysia, PC World Malaysia, Publish in Asia; **MEXICO:** Computerworld Mexico, GamePro, Macworld, PC World Mexico; **MYANMAR:** PC World Myanmar; **NETHERLANDS:** Computable, Computer! Totaal, LAN Magazine, Macworld, Net Magazine; **NEW ZEALAND:** Computer Buyer, Computerworld New Zealand, MTB, Network World, PC World New Zealand; **NICARAGUA:** PC World Costa Rica/Nicaragua; **NIGERIA:** PC World Africa; **NORWAY:** Computerworld Norge, Computerworld Privat, CW Rapport Klient/Tjener, CW Rapport Nettverk & Telecom, CW Rapport Offentlig Sektor, IDG's KURSGUIDE, Macworld Norge, Multimedia World, PC World Ekspress, PC World Nettverk, PC World Norge, PC World's Produktguide, Windows Spesial; **PAKISTAN:** Computerworld Pakistan, PC World Pakistan; **PANAMA:** GamePro, PC World Panama; **PARAGUAY:** PC World Paraguay; **P. R. OF CHINA:** China Computerworld, China Infoworld, Computer & Communication, Electronic Product World, Electronics Today, Game Camp, PC World China, Popular Computer Week, Software World, Telecom Product World; **PERU:** Computerworld Peru, GamePro, PC World Profesional Peru, PC World Peru; **POLAND:** Computerworld Poland, Computerworld Special Report, Macworld, Networld, PC World Komputer; **PHILIPPINES:** Computerworld Philippines, PC Digest, Publish in Asia; **PORTUGAL:** Cerebro/PC World, Correio Informático/Computerworld, Mac•In/PC•In Portugal; **PUERTO RICO:** PC World Puerto Rico; **ROMANIA:** Computerworld Romania, PC World Romania, Telecom Romania; **RUSSIA:** Computerworld Rossiya, Network World Russia, PC World Russia; **SINGAPORE:** Computerworld Singapore, PC World Singapore, Publish in Asia; **SLOVENIA:** MONITOR; **SOUTH AFRICA:** Computing S.A., Network World S.A., Software World; **SPAIN:** Computerworld España, COMUNICACIONES WORLD, Dealer World, Macworld España, PC World España; **SWEDEN:** CAP&Design, Computer Sweden, Corporate Computing, MacWorld, Maxi Data, MikroDatorn, Nätverk & Kommunikation, PC/Aktiv, PC World, Windows World; **SWITZERLAND:** Computerworld Schweiz, Macworld Schweiz, PCtip; **TAIWAN:** Computerworld Taiwan, Macworld Taiwan, PC World Taiwan, Publish Taiwan, Windows World; **THAILAND:** Thai Computerworld, Publish in Asia; **TURKEY:** Computerworld Monitör, MACWORLD Turkiye, PC WORLD Turkiye; **UKRAINE:** Computerworld Kiev, Computers & Software Magazine, PC World Ukraine; **UNITED KINGDOM:** Acorn User, Amiga Action, Amiga Computing, Amiga, Appletalk, CD Powerplay, CD-ROM Now, Computing, Connexion, GamePro, Lotus Magazine, Macaction, Macworld, Open Computing, Parents and Computers, PC Home, PC Works, The WEB; **UNITED STATES:** Cable in the Classroom, CD Review, CIO Magazine, Computerworld, Computerworld Client/Server Journal, Digital Video Magazine, DOS World, Electronic, InfoWorld, I-Way, Macworld, Maximize, MULTIMEDIA WORLD, Network World, PC World, PUBLISH, SWATPro Magazine, Video Event, WebMaster; **URUGUAY:** PC World Uruguay; **VENEZUELA:** Computerworld Venezuela, GamePro, PC World Venezuela; and **VIETNAM:** PC World Vietnam
10/17/95

Acknowledgments

We'd like to first thank Amy Pedersen, Anne Marie Walker, Madhu Prasher, Karen Muldrow, and Heidi Steele for helping us through the first couple versions of this book. We hope you like how it turned out. We're also grateful to Matt Wagner at Waterside Productions `http://www.waterside.com/` (our faithful agent).

Having had the pleasure of writing several books now, it's become clear to us that the most important person on the team is the project editor. Without their unflagging attention to detail, we doubt if many books would ever be printed. So, thank you, Barb Terry. Even though your house burned down in the middle of this book, you hung in there. Amazing! We'd also like to thank our partners who pitched in when times got tough, John Hovis and Don Brewer. We can't thank you enough. As always, we'd like to thank many members of the team we sometimes only know by their initials in our edited manuscripts. Thanks for all your hard work getting this book done, and done so well. We want to thank everyone at IDG `http://www.idgbooks.com/` for believing in this book enough to let us rewrite it over and over and over as everything kept changing. And to Patrick McGovern, wherever you are, thanks.

Many other people have helped us get this book done. We certainly want to thank Bill Blue and Morgan Davis of CTS `http://www.cts.com/`, the best Internet access provider in San Diego. Thanks to Chris Schefler at Web Communications `http://www.webcom.com/` for the great Web publishing account. We want to thank the folks at U.S. Robotics `http://www.usr.com/` for their support.

Special thanks to Alun Jones, Jack De Winter, Mikael Hansen, Michele Fuortes, Gunter Hille, Peter Lewis, Chuck Shotton, Peter Tattum, Martin Hall and Robert Denny, whose pioneering Internet software efforts have made it possible for the average person to set up an Internet site.

Publisher's Acknowledgments

We're proud of this book; please send us your comments about it by using the Reader Response Card at the back of the book or by e-mailing us at feedback/dummies@idgbooks.com. Some of the people who helped bring this book to market include the following:

Acquisitions, Development, & Editorial

Project Editor: Barb Terry

Acquisitions Editor: Tammy Goldfeld

Product Development Manager: Mary Bednarek

Copy Editors: Leah Cameron, Charles A. Hutchison, Julie King, Shannon Ross, Kathy Simpson

Technical Reviewer: John Munnell

Editorial Managers: Kristin A. Cocks, Mary Corder

Editorial Assistants: Constance Carlisle, Chris H. Collins, Kevin Spencer

Production

Associate Project Coordinator: Debbie Sharpe

Layout and Graphics: Shawn Aylsworth, Linda M. Boyer, Cheryl Denski, Jill Lyttle, Jane Martin, Ron Riggan, Anna Rohrer, Kate Snell, Marti Stegeman, Gina Scott, Angela F. Hunckler

Proofreaders: Mary C. Oby, Joel Draper, Christine Meloy Beck, Gwenette Gaddis, Dwight Ramsey, Carl Saff, Robert Springer

Indexer: Sherry Massey

General & Administrative

IDG Books Worldwide, Inc.: John Kilcullen, President & CEO; Steven Berkowitz, COO & Publisher

Dummies, Inc.: Milissa Koloski, Executive Vice President & Publisher

Dummies Technology Press & Dummies Editorial: Diane Graves Steele, Associate Publisher; Judith A. Taylor, Brand Manager; Myra Immell, Editorial Director

Dummies Trade Press: Kathleen A. Welton, Vice President & Publisher; Stacy S. Collins, Brand Manager

IDG Books Production for Dummies Press: Beth Jenkins, Production Director; Cindy L. Phipps, Supervisor of Project Coordination; Kathie S. Schnorr, Supervisor of Page Layout; Shelley Lea, Supervisor of Graphics and Design

Dummies Packaging & Book Design: Erin McDermitt, Packaging Coordinator; Kavish+Kavish, Cover Design

◆

The publisher would like to give special thanks to Patrick J. McGovern, without whom this book would not have been possible.

◆

Contents at a Glance

Cartoons at a Glance

By Rich Tennant

page 7

page 16

page 53

page 142

page 169

page 180

page 297

page 232

page 279

page 213

Table of Contents

Part V: Preparing for the Future *279*

Chapter 15: The Second Wave 281

Chapter 16: The Interactive Global Village 287

Introduction

∙ ∙

*T*he Internet represents a fundamental social change of immense proportion. Media coverage of the Internet attempts to identify and explain just what makes the Internet special. Terms such as *interactive* and *global* are common elements of such explanations. *Interactive television* and *GATT* attract interest directly from this publicity as people conclude that anything *interactive* or *global* will yield exponential Internet-style growth.

This book was written because one obvious explanation of the popularity of the Internet is often overlooked: the Internet is special because it enables normal people to do extraordinary things. Unlike other communications technologies such as TV or radio, you don't need expensive equipment, a costly broadcasting license, and years of on-the-job training to provide information on the Internet. We wrote this book to help you create your own Internet site so that you can participate in shaping the future of this exciting new technology.

When we began doing research for this book, we believed in the ideal of the World Wide Web. The Web was supposed to integrate Internet information resources and provide a single, easy-to-use interface to them all. The Web promised to deliver a seamless, interconnected, global library of online resources and, for the first time, make the Internet accessible to everyone, not just the scientists and engineers who created it.

Well, an entire year has gone by since we started writing this book, and we're still waiting for the ideal to be realized. In the meantime, the World Wide Web of the past (circa 1995) emerged as one of the largest time-consuming inventions ever devised, especially for the information provider. Countless people and companies have poured time and money into creating Web sites and turning them into a competitive advantage or a profit-making venture. Few have succeeded to any reasonable degree.

The reason is that in the rush to commercialize the Internet and get as many people connected to it as possible, the more challenging, idealistic goals of the Web were put on hold. This delay is understandable and necessary, if unfortunate. Only now that the Internet is firmly established as a viable economic enterprise have companies turned their attention back to the original intentions set forth by the creators of the World Wide Web.

The Web is rapidly approaching the end of its infancy. For that matter, so is the Internet. If you're like many people, you got swept away by the gold-rush fever of this new frontier and, before you knew it, weird-sounding things like HTML and TCP/IP started to seem important, even interesting. We're here to remind you that they're not. They're boring technical details that you need to understand only because the technology is brand-new, uncooked, and immature.

Luckily, this is all changing. Soon, thanks to the efforts of companies like Netscape and Microsoft, the Internet will be an information appliance that's easier to use than your VCR. Surfing the Internet will no longer require painful, endless hours of mouse-clicking and page-switching. As a user, the Internet will become your gateway to the rest of the world. Banking, commerce, work, shopping, government, and just about every other facet of your life will be enhanced, simplified, and (hopefully) made more efficient and more enjoyable.

Publishing information on the Internet will be as simple as using your favorite word processing program or shooting a home movie. Today, a Web site is as much a burden and a liability as it is an essential business tool. If you already have a Web site, you probably spend your time updating the HTML in your Web pages over and over again in order to provide a "compelling" experience for other Internet users. Or, like us, you've grown tired of wasting your time with HTML, so you stop updating your Web pages and they quickly become stale and outdated.

The ideal solutions to these problems aren't here just yet or you wouldn't be holding this book. There are, however, many things that you can do today to turn the Internet into a truly useful and viable resource for yourself and for others. The ideal course of action during this transition period is to analyze the Internet technology currently available, learn how it works and how to set it up, and then decide which technology is appropriate for you. *Setting Up an Internet -Site For Dummies* shows you how to implement a sensible Internet strategy that won't become a burden or a disappointment.

And the best part is that you don't need to learn complex programming languages, spend hours struggling with a technical manual, or even leave the comfortable and familiar environment of your personal computer.

About This Book

This book is designed to meet the needs of three types of readers:

- ✔ People who already use the Internet and want to turn it into a more useful tool
- ✔ Anyone who wants to provide information on the Internet for a business or for themselves
- ✔ Experienced Web publishers who realize the limitations of the World Wide Web and need to take their Internet site to the next level

This book assumes that you are an experienced computer user. It makes no attempt to explain files, icons, using your mouse, or any other basic computer concepts. If you're new to computers, then you'll need some basic training before this book will make much sense.

And What about You?

Setting Up An Internet Site For Dummies is the ideal book for anyone who wants to create a permanent Internet presence or to set up his or her own site on the Internet. Whether you're an experienced (or travel-weary) Internet navigator or just beginning to explore what the Internet can do for you, this book will be a valuable guide.

Above all, this book is for people who believe that providing interactive resources on the Internet should be simple, effective, and fun — not technical, time-consuming and dull. Buy this book if you want to do something with the Internet. Take a cruise to some distant island if you're just looking for entertainment.

How This Book Is Organized

This book is organized. We promise that it is. In fact, it's so organized that we were able to divide it into parts, chapters, sections, paragraphs, and sentences . . . just to keep everything from spilling out all over the place. Here are the six parts that you'll find in this book:

Part I: Laying the Foundation of an Internet Site

Anyone building a structure knows that it needs a solid foundation. Setting up an Internet site is no different. The better your foundation, the more effective your site. Part I guides you away from weak materials and toward those that will make your Internet site strong and vibrant.

This part also presents the basic concepts you'll need to understand as you prepare to follow the instructions found in this book. As a provider of Internet resources, you need to know some things that the average Internet user doesn't. This part also walks you through the first two steps that everyone needs to take when setting up an Internet site: getting a domain name and creating a Web home page.

Part II: Equipping Your Site with the Right Tools

This part shows you how to set up the most important enabling resources. As you'll discover throughout this book, good software tools turn your Internet site into something very special. The tools covered in this part include:

- ✔ File Transfer Protocol (FTP), which enables you to receive files from other Internet users
- ✔ E-mail information servers and automated interactive mailing lists, which turn e-mail into a useful interactive tool
- ✔ Internet Bulletin Board Systems (BBSs), which enable you to create powerful, electronic work environments, to build a private communications resource for your company's internal use, or to provide a public members-only Internet resource

Part III: Setting Up Other Useful Internet Resources

This part focuses on other Internet tools that can be useful as part of your Internet presence. Topics covered in this part include real-time communications software such as the Internet Phone, global conferencing software known as Usenet News, and an old, yet reliable service called Gopher.

Part IV: The Essentials of Life Online

Life on the Internet is what you make it. This part gives you the basic skills that everyone who runs an Internet site should have. Things that we all take for granted and are comfortable with in real life work differently on the Internet. Every site developer should know how to obtain publicity for Internet resources and create a secure environment in which to conduct electronic commerce.

Part V: Preparing for the Future

Part V reveals the important changes shaping the future of the Internet and shows you how to prepare for these changes today. This part shows you exciting multimedia presentations, new Internet software tools, and a simpler, yet more powerful approach to Internet publishing that is replacing the old World Wide Web technology.

Part VI: The Part of Tens

The Internet is a happenin' place. Its software and sites change rapidly and drastically. The chapters in this part present ten important topics that serve as launching pads into other related subjects. You'll find our ten favorite Internet add-on applications and more than ten places to go for more information.

Icons Used in This Book

This book has icons in the margins. Pay attention to them. They'll guide you to the points that can make your Internet site work, your work fly, or keep everything from sinking.

When you see this icon, you'll find information about the software or hardware that you need in order to do the things described in this book. If you've got the "Right Stuff," there's no limit to what you can accomplish.

This icon suggests ways in which the technology described in this book can be used to start an Internet business. The Internet is an evolving landscape of opportunity. New products and services are already emerging that use Internet technology or that help other users. Many such businesses exist only on the Internet, having no real-world business location.

This icon points out the hidden wisdom of Internet veterans. Beside this icon, you'll find insights and war stories from the electronic frontier so that you might benefit from the experiences of others.

Watch out! The Information SuperHighway is still under construction, and it has a few potholes. This icon points them out to help you avoid trouble.

Sometimes we forget things, so we use this icon to jog our memories. You probably won't forget things, but humor us when you see this icon.

Most of the technical stuff in this book appears in a simple, readable, and entertaining format in the main text. You can read it, or you can skip it — without hurting our feelings.

Part I

Laying the Foundation of an Internet Site

The 5th Wave   By Rich Tennant

"Awww Jeez— I was afraid of this. Some Internet addict, bored with the usual chat lines, starts looking for bigger kicks, pretty soon they're surfin' the seedy back alleys of cyberspace, and before you know it, they're into a file they can't 'undo'. I guess that's why they call it the Web. Somebody open a window!"

In this part . . .

This part introduces you to the basics of setting up an Internet site. Chapters 1 and 2 prepare you for action by covering key concepts and introducing the Internet strategy featured throughout this book. Chapter 3 shows you how to begin creating your site by registering a new domain name and setting up a Web site. You are about to discover the new world of Internet technology. Get ready to change forever the way that you think about and use the Internet.

Chapter 1

Putting the Internet to Work for You

B y now, you probably know that surfing the Internet until your skin is as wrinkled as a prune's won't get you a date. What a way to start a book! It's true, though. Like ocean surfing, Internet surfing is fun, but it really doesn't accomplish much. Beyond simple Web publishing, the Internet is perhaps one of the greatest enabling technologies since the first wheel rolled off the assembly line. In this book, you'll discover two important things:

✔ Why the Net is far more than an endless interconnection of Web pages

✔ How easily you can set up your own high-performance Internet site

In this chapter, we give you a glimpse of how you may be using the Internet in the future. Throughout this book, we help you understand why you may want to set up your own Internet site, and we help you develop a strategy for using the Internet to its maximum potential. We don't want you to get stuck in the Web when you have so many more options available for turning the Internet into a useful tool. You can choose from hundreds of programs that will help you do everything from telecommute to form your own Internet business to enhance the quality of your family life.

Old Things Get Better

One of the first, and still the most important, applications on the Internet is electronic mail. Often forgotten in the hype of the World Wide Web, we use e-mail more than any other Net application. E-mail keeps us in touch with work associates on a daily, sometimes minute-by-minute, basis. Family members hear from us far more often than ever before, as do distant friends. For example, you may want your Aunt Mable to know you're thinking about her without having to listen to her go on and on about her lumbago. You can't pick up the phone and shout, "Hi, Aunt Mable!" and then make crackling sounds as if your cellular phone just lost its connection. Well, maybe you can, but even Aunt Mable will catch on after a while. With e-mail, you can jot a quick, "Hi. How are you?" and that's that.

E-mail is also the answer to the 30-second voice mail limitation. In a world where very few people actually answer their phones at the office, e-mail allows you to leave detailed information, attach documents, and edit what you want to say. The recipients can pick up your e-mail messages and handle them at their convenience. They don't have to worry that you are fast asleep on the other side of the world when they want to communicate with you.

Information, please!

You can do more with e-mail than simply send text messages to and fro. You can use a type of program we refer to as an *e-mail information server,* which allows you to provide information to other people through e-mail. Chapter 5 discusses these information servers in more detail.

E-mail is the one application you can be fairly certain that everyone has. So providing information through e-mail is definitely one of the most practical ways you can begin to do more with the Internet.

What kind of information are we talking about? If you run a bus company, you can provide your bus schedule. If you're a teacher, you can provide a list of homework assignments so that parents actively involved in their child's learning can send e-mail and receive the day's assignments. The list goes on and on. You can use e-mail information servers for everything from technical support to baseball card prices. If you already use e-mail today, then you have everything you need to start providing information in this way.

Automated electronic mailing lists

A type of software known as an *automated electronic mailing list* (sometimes called a *listserver*) allows people to subscribe to an electronic mailing list. You can use this list to distribute e-mail to everyone who has subscribed to the list.

Two basic types of electronic mailing lists are available: one type of software distributes any e-mail message sent by anyone on the list to the entire group; the other type uses a person, often called a *moderator,* to send messages that are distributed to the entire list.

We use a listserver software package to run a mailing list for people who use Netscape products to write software. People subscribe to our list and then send messages to the entire group asking for help, giving answers, or just informing the group of important information. We also subscribe to lists run by other people, such as mailing lists devoted to scientific research or Internet programming.

Ways to Work Together

E-mail information servers, regular e-mail, and listservers are just a few of the ways the Internet helps people work together. All types of new software (sometimes referred to as *collaborative* software) are now available that make working together or communicating over the Internet simple. Who knows? Even video-conferencing may soon be available on every desktop.

Today you can get software known as *electronic whiteboards* that allows people to work together online — drawing, circling, and doing all the other things you do with a whiteboard without the awful smell of the markers. All over the world, Internet work groups use electronic whiteboards and similar software. Whiteboards have become standard equipment for meeting rooms.

An electronic whiteboard is not the only type of software that allows people to communicate and work together over the Internet. Some of the hottest applications on the Internet are the Internet phone packages. With a sound card, some software, and a microphone, you can talk to others all over the world without the long-distance charges. Phone software is in its early stages of development, and the sound quality needs some improvement. When the technology is more fully developed, it will be an important money-saving business tool.

Phone software is now being coupled with video hardware and software to create true video-conferencing. Now, full-motion color video pictures can accompany your Internet phone conversations. Imagine a desktop where you have several windows containing video images of work associates. In another window, a shared whiteboard allows each of you to express thoughts visually while you're conducting a meeting over the Internet. This is the way in which you might use the Internet in the future.

Telecommuting

With traffic congesting most major cities, some companies allow their employees to work at home, or to *telecommute*. With Internet technologies, you can do everything you do in the office right in your home — except hang out by the coffee pot. In fact, telecommuting is so easy that many companies no longer need to move people from distant cities to hire them. Now, companies can simply set up people in remote home offices. Men and women are finding it easier to stay home with their children rather than ship them off to a day-care center. Studies now show that, even with children around, workers actually increase productivity by working at home.

Setting up an Internet site at home can make telecommuting simple and fun. You can share information with people throughout your company or with Internet users around the world. You can accept electronic payments, hold Internet conferences, publish World Wide Web pages, and much more.

Groupware is a special type of office software that allows people to share information, create group schedules, and perform many other common workplace functions. Companies that sell groupware products such as Lotus Notes or SoftArc's FirstClass software are now adapting them to run over the Internet. The use of these products will greatly enhance the telecommuting capability of the next generation of "knowledge workers" — people who work in technical or educational fields and aren't tied to a factory or office work environment.

Virtual companies

Small, dynamic organizations are joining together to create virtual companies online. The virtual-company organization can be long-term, each group performing its specialized functions, or the companies can work together on individual projects and then go their own ways at the end of the project. Communication is one of the most important capabilities within a virtual company. Unlike traditional companies in which everyone usually is under a single roof, virtual companies must set up a telecommunications backbone that allows them to carry on business as if the employees were all in the same building.

The Internet has made forming virtual companies much simpler and cost-effective. Using electronic mailing lists, Usenet newsgroups, World Wide Web servers, and the other software mentioned earlier, virtual companies are actually more efficient than their traditional Internet-impaired counterparts. Going to meetings that never start on time, playing phone tag, and carrying on business through pink message pads now seem foreign and clumsy to us. The enabling technologies available today on the Internet and those just over the horizon are exciting.

The Internet and Your Family

The Internet is on its way to every home in the world — at least this is the dream of most Internet-related companies. Many people sign on with an Internet provider without really knowing what the Internet is going to do for them or their family. The following sections present a few ways that having Internet access and your own Internet site can involve your entire family.

The kids

Your kids can have international pen pals through e-mail. Swapping e-mail every day with kids all over the world expands their horizons far beyond the once-a-month pen pals shared in the past. This capability prepares your kids for the global culture in which they are growing up. Having an international Internet pen pal may not be a bad idea for you, too.

Your children also can entertain themselves with Internet multiplayer games, or they can play games against a computer on the other side of the world. With most of these games online and free, your kids won't have to bug you every time they grow bored with their current games. The Internet provides a nearly endless set of games and new players to challenge them.

If you have your own Internet site, your kids may find that having their own home page gives them a sense of global identity. We're never surprised to learn about kids who have mastered the art of producing interesting Internet magazines or who have learned to use all the tools on their parents' Internet site. With Internet-related job opportunities skyrocketing, we can't think of a better skill for children to develop early than global interactive communications.

Some people say that the world is a horrible place, waiting to pervert your children; others say that being alive is wonderful. Because the Internet gives your kids access to the world, it gives them the same opportunity for finding wrong as it gives them for finding good in learning, entertainment, exploration, and global friendships. Parents must guide their children through the maze without giving into fear of the unknown. The Internet genie is out of the bottle and is a force shaping the future. We believe it's important to involve your kids in setting up the family Internet site.

Education

The Internet is perfect for educational use. Teachers have already begun reporting assignments electronically in some areas. Parents can log in to find their children's assignments for the day. Teachers can correspond directly with parents in a way that is convenient for everyone. Electronic correspondence between parents and teachers is also more reliable than sending a note home with the student.

The Internet can be much more than a message tool, though. It is one of the greatest libraries in the world. Information, usually with full-color graphics, is available on almost every topic imaginable. Even more exciting is that this information doesn't become stale, as it can when you buy books that become outdated or just don't capture kids' imaginations. On the Internet, children can read about science as it is created and, in some cases, can even correspond with the scientists.

In fact, the Internet may eventually create the global classroom. Who knows, you may be working in one room of your house while your kids go to school in another. We should also mention that busy professionals can use the Internet to continue their own education. In a world that changes as quickly as ours, lifelong education becomes a must. Some universities offer fully accredited classes through the Internet. So whether you are working toward a degree or just keeping up with your career specialty, the Internet can be an invaluable tool.

The Internet family

Your family can publish its own Web pages. You, too, can bore people with pictures of family vacations and home-movie clips — without having to wait for parties. Now you can simply say, "Hey, Uncle Marty, we got those pictures back from our fishing trip. Check them out on our home page." Your parties will be much more interesting when you can set up a conference with your relatives in Germany, France, and Thailand, using the Internet phone.

Parents can keep in touch easily with their kids away at college. Many colleges now offer e-mail accounts for their students. In fact, in today's busy world, parents can use e-mail to keep in touch with family members living in the same home. You can even use groupware to plan and schedule family outings!

We find that we keep in touch with cousins, aunts, and uncles more frequently than we used to. Sending e-mail is simpler than writing a letter. The best part is that you can just say, "Hi, thinking about you," and zap your message off in seconds. Sending an electronic message is a lot easier than sitting down and writing a letter on a piece of paper, folding it, sticking it in an envelope, addressing it, sticking a stamp on it, and then walking out to the mail box.

Business on the Internet

Because you can do business on the Internet in so many ways, listing them all is difficult. The Internet is becoming a central figure in the Global Marketplace. Soon, buying and selling on the Internet will be a common global activity. As businesses expand their understanding of the Internet and discover ways in which to put it to use, several key products and services will become very important:

- Package delivery
- Electronic file transfer
- Credit card processing services

    ▸ Permanent network connections

    ▸ Multimedia authoring tools

What follows are some thoughts on two of the industries that are already being affected dramatically by the Internet. Both the publishing industry and the computer software industry are being revolutionized by Internet technology. Your industry might not experience the level of change that these two will, but it does illustrate the Internet's potential for serious business.

Publishing

Running a storefront is only one way to do business on the Internet. Magazine and newspaper publishers are finding entirely new audiences. In addition to cutting printing costs, publishers find that their material is more timely and interactive. Scientific journals are distributed globally when they once had a small readership.

Books are now becoming available online. The idea of reading books at your computer may not seem as comfy as curling up in your bed with a good book. But online books are now the rage. Being able to research texts by doing key-word searches has brought many of the classics back to life. Many technical books are now coming with either a disk or an online value-added Internet site. Now, when you buy a book, your investment can live on as the Internet site continues to keep your book up-to-date.

Software

The Internet is the hottest thing to hit the software industry since, well, since the invention of the personal computer. Companies such as Microsoft have begun to make all their applications Internet-ready. This trend continues as the idea of *Internet appliances*, low-cost Internet tools that might be sold like televisions and radios, gains momentum.

The Internet creates a new possibility for the software industry. People will be able to borrow or rent software on an "as-needed" basis. Why buy hundreds or thousands of dollars' worth of software that you may only need a few times in your life? Why not rent the software each time you need it? This way, you can keep your hard drive free of old programs. You'll also never have to worry about upgrades or new technologies making your old software obsolete. Software rental sites on the Internet may become like video stores are today, offering a range of titles that you borrow for a short time instead of purchasing your own copy.

The 5th Wave By Rich Tennant

"Mona, come on outta the closet. This is no way to handle your surfing addiction."

Chapter 2

The Anatomy of the Internet

*H*as your perspective about the Internet changed? The Internet is more than just a bunch of computers tied together; it is a living and breathing organism that has the power to alter life as we know it today. (Okay, that description is a little melodramatic. But go along with us on this tangent for a while.)

As a living and breathing organism, the Internet has an anatomy that anyone who is thinking about making the switch from Net surfer to site developer must understand. When you're a surfer on the Net, the nuances that make up the various parts of the Internet make little difference to your Net experience. When you're a site developer, however, those nuances can make the difference between a successful site and one that gets lost in mediocrity. This chapter dissects this beast to show what makes it work from a site developer's perspective.

Explaining the Internet

First, what is the Internet? Simply put, the Internet is nothing more than a worldwide wiring *infrastructure* — a bunch of fiber, twisted-pair cable, and the like, left over from the Cold War era, put to better use by individuals and businesses all over the world.

As a person who is interested in setting up an Internet site, you can think of the Internet as being the capillaries, veins, and arteries that transport data — the lifeblood of this organism — to and from site developers and Internet surfers.

This analogy leads you to the next lesson in your Internet anatomy class. Connected to the veins and arteries that make up the Internet are specialized Internet software products. These products come in two flavors: server and client packages.

Providing information with Internet server software

The *server software* on the Internet does just what the name implies: serves or gives out information to those who request it. This information may be in the form of Web pages, mail, file-transfer procedures, or any number of things discussed later in this book. Server software packages play a critical role in setting up an Internet site. Because you use this software to deliver the information to the surfer, understanding server systems is important to you as a site developer.

When you have information ready to be served, you must provide a way for surfers on the Net to access that information, which is where the client software packages come into play. *Client software* is what people on the Internet use to search, transfer, retrieve, and otherwise handle data provided by site developers. Understanding the features and limitations of a client package is important for anyone who is interested in setting up an Internet site.

You have an organism with veins and arteries and data flowing through it. What's the next step in the anatomy of the Internet? The Internet access provider.

The Internet access provider (commonly referred to as service provider) is the way to plug in to the veins and arteries of the Internet. An access provider usually is a group that has rented access to the Internet and then turns around and leases its rented bandwidth to individuals and businesses.

Hold on, now. We just introduced a word that is batted around the Internet quite a bit: bandwidth. What does this word mean to the prospective site developer?

Bandwidth refers to the size of the "pipe" that connects you (or, in this case, the access provider) to the Internet. (We talk more about bandwidth issues, as they relate to the individual user, later in this chapter.) The larger the bandwidth that your Internet access provider has, the less likely that you, the site developer, will face unhappy customers as a result of performance problems due to heavy use at your site.

But bandwidth is not the only issue that the prospective site developer needs to address with the Internet access provider. The access provider can be a rich source of services that may make developing, launching, and maintaining your site that much easier.

Most access providers also rent the computers, server software, disk storage space, and security systems needed to host various applications on the Internet. Unlike the price of bandwidth, the prices of these services can vary widely from provider to provider. As a site developer, you need to shop around for the best combination of services and bandwidth that suits your particular needs.

When you have an Internet access provider, the next layer is the Internet access software. This access software is your computer's passport to the Internet. When connecting to the Internet, your computer must be able to speak to other computers using a common language (*protocol*). The access software enables your computer to communicate with other computers using this protocol, allowing the computer to send and receive information sent in small information packets.

With Internet access software, your computer can tap directly into the Internet. As a site developer, all you need to know about Internet access software is that it simplifies communication between computers that usually speak very different languages by introducing a common communication interface called TCP/IP (Transmission Control Protocol/Internet Protocol).

Many different TCP/IP software packages are used on the Internet. Many of these packages are shareware products, available as try-before-you-buy. You need to get a TCP/IP package that is designed for your computer's operating system. Windows, DOS, and Macintosh versions are readily available on the Net. Your service provider probably can provide a tried-and-true package for you to install on your computer.

TCP/IP is the protocol used by all computers on the Internet to send and receive data. This protocol is important because it greatly reduces the difficulties that usually arise when computers with different operating systems attempt to communicate with one another.

When the Internet access software is in place, the next layer is the actual connection to the Internet — typically, a modem connected to a telephone line. After you're connected, your next concern is how much information you can send back and forth across the phone line. This is known as *bandwidth,* a major issue for Internet site developers.

Why should you be concerned about bandwidth? As a provider of information on the Internet, you must understand the limitations that your customer may have. An Internet surfer who is using a modem of 14.4 baud or less and a typical analog phone line will become frustrated quickly if your World Wide Web site is full of large files that must be downloaded each time a user visits.

The various connection options available today play an important role in the site-development process. Chapter 3 talks more about considering your target audience and the bandwidth issues that they may face when you design a site.

Now we get down to the lowest common denominator on the Internet: the computer platform. The TCP/IP protocols make all computer platforms on the Internet fairly equal. People visiting your Internet site won't know or care whether you are using a PC, a Macintosh, or a supercomputer. There's a joke going around that "On the Internet, no one knows you're a Mac."

Your computer runs *server* software that provides information on the Internet. People who contact your site use *client* software to access your information. TCP/IP becomes the universal translator between all machines on the Internet providing a common language, or protocol, spoken by both server and client programs.

We've introduced some of the inner workings of the Internet and the various connections and components that make it possible — important stuff for a site developer to understand. By knowing what it takes for the surfer to actually get to your site, you can eliminate many of the problems that can occur as you communicate on the Internet.

Getting There from Here

You can't go anywhere on the Internet without knowing what a URL is. *URL* stands for *Uniform Resource Locator*. Sounds more like something you would use to find your laundry at the dry cleaners than a computer term, doesn't it? The comparison isn't too far off.

The URL is the key to uniquely identifying your site and the information stored there. The URL is much more than just a name, though. Simply giving each resource on the Internet a name isn't good enough, because names are not always unique. (The authors just discovered that the world has other Jason and Ted Coombs'.)

For Net surfers, URLs may seem to have little reasoning behind them. But for site developers, understanding the makeup of a URL is critical. This section takes a close look at URLs and their makeup.

Each bit of information on the Internet is known as a *resource,* and resources are stored in many formats. Some of the information is stored in files used on the World Wide Web, called *HTML files.* Other information is stored in documents on special servers such as Gopher or FTP. The list of file types and how they're served over the Internet is endless.

Files that contain information are not the only type of resource on the Internet. Resources also include interactive programs, searchable databases, games, and other types of software.

Each resource is given a URL, which specifies the following:

- ✔ The type of resource (the protocol and server used to provide it)
- ✔ The computer on which the resource is located
- ✔ The name of the resource

By using a resource's type, location, and name, developers can build a unique address for every resource on the Internet. Each chapter in this book explains the anatomy of the URL used to locate the specific type of resource discussed in that chapter.

Using the URL to identify resources

You may have heard that URLs identify resources on the World Wide Web. You see them all over the place, on billboards and in newspaper ads and magazines, and you hear them in radio announcements. More than simply identifying Web resources, URLs have become the shorthand way to identify almost every bit of information on the Internet. Including URLs in your advertising or on your business cards to identify your important Internet resources is more than just a great idea; it's almost expected.

As an information provider, you must understand the different parts of a URL, if you don't already. The first part of a URL describes the type of server software used to handle this resource. You can access Web pages, FTP sites, and Gopher servers, for example. For each resource, the URL begins with an abbreviation or word that describes the type of server. Following are a few of them.

- ✔ `http://`   World Wide Web
- ✔ `ftp://`   FTP
- ✔ `gopher://`   Gopher
- ✔ `news://`   Usenet news

The next part of the URL includes a very important part of the addressing scheme: the name of your computer (*domain name*) where your resource is located. You may have to ask your Internet service provider for this information if you're using a special Internet information publishing service.

The domain name typically is followed by a forward slash (/). After this slash come the specific directories and subdirectories where the individual files that make up the URL resource are located. To help clarify the structure of a URL, look at the address `http://pk1.pk.com/pcrf/`, which is the address of the Planetary Coral Reef Foundation (see Figure 2-1). The SCIENCE.ORG computer has a directory named `pcrf`, containing information about the Planetary Coral Reef Foundation.

The address tells you that the site named in the URL is a Web resource — signified by `http://`. The domain name is `pk1.pk.com`. The subdirectory on the Web server that houses the information is `pcrf`.

Now look at a URL for an FTP site, and check out the naming convention:

```
ftp://ftp.science.org/pub/win31/gatt_1.zip
```

This URL tells you where you can go to download the text of GATT (Global Agreement on Tariffs and Trade) for Microsoft Windows. Without getting into the political side of the Internet, the following paragraphs examine the URL of this site to show what you can learn from its address.

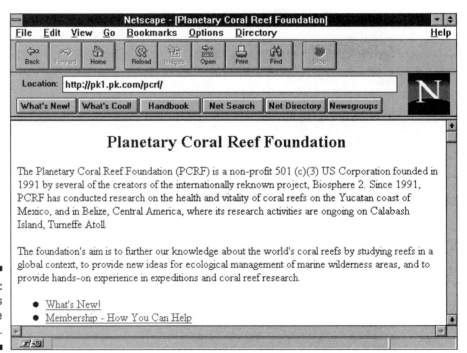

Figure 2-1:
Examine this
sample
Web site.

The first part of the URL, `ftp://` tells you that the resource is an FTP site. The next part, `ftp.science.org`, is the domain name of the computer running the FTP server. Next comes the directory path where the information is stored. For this example, the directory path `/pub/win31/` is where you can find the file `gatt_1.zip`.

Want to know more about GATT? Follow these steps to download the document from this site:

1. **Open your Web browser and locate the dialog box that allows you to enter a URL.**

2. **Type the URL as follows:**

   `ftp://ftp.science.org/pub/win31/gatt_1.zip`

3. **Tell the computer where you want to store the file on your machine.**

4. **Sit back and watch those bytes fly down your phone line.**

URLs are fairly simple to understand; they provide the surfer and site developer with a great deal of information about the resources that are being delivered on the Internet. In this book, we will help you gain a better understanding of URLs and show you how to best use the syntax of this information locator to help maximize your site's effectiveness.

Domain names and IP addresses

The section on URLs rushed past domain names. Now you need to focus on what a domain name is and why it's important for the site developer.

As you learned earlier, the Internet is a global network of computers. This network uses a special address, called an *IP address,* to identify every computer on the network. You may be familiar with networks (sometimes called *LANs,* for local-area networks) in your office. Your entire network can be connected to the larger Internet; the word *Internet* actually means *between networks.*

Each network that is connected to the Internet often is referred to as a domain, and each domain can have a name. In many cases, a single computer connected to the Internet has a domain name. You can apply for a domain name through the organization that manages them: the InterNIC — Network Information Center, the central Internet authority that governs domain-name registration. For a complete description of the services offered by the InterNIC, open your Web browser and enter the URL `http://www.internic.com/`

When you first obtain an Internet account, you'll probably use your access provider's domain name. The access provider knows how to route information to your computer by using your computer's *IP address* (the number assigned to each computer on the Internet).

A domain can be a single computer or a network of computers, which is like saying, "I live at 1515 Elm Street." This address could be a private house or a huge apartment complex. Our main computer, science.org, is the network server for several personal computers. It acts like a mailman, delivering the right information packets to the correct machines.

Each computer on the network is identified by an IP address (or *IP number*), which is a little like a phone number. An IP address is a set of four numbers separated by periods, or dots (also called a *dotted quad*). An IP address looks like this:

```
204.94.74.209
```

Each number of the dotted quad contains significant information about where a computer on a network is located. Every computer has an IP address. These facts are all you really need to know about IP numbers, because your access provider will assign you a number.

IP numbers aren't user-friendly. An easier way of referring to computers without having to memorize meaningless numbers is to give the computer a name. If your computer is on a network, each computer on that network can have a name. The individual computer's name, added to the domain name, is known as the computer's *fully qualified domain name*. The domain of our network is `science.org`; the fully qualified domain name of one of the machines on our network, titanium, is `titanium.science.org`. These names are managed by a utility known as the *Domain Name System* (DNS). Your service provider has the DNS running on a machine so that network traffic is directed to your computer correctly.

Computers on the Internet communicate with each other computers only by using IP addresses — domain names mean nothing to a computer. To communicate with other computers, client software (such as Web browsers) must contact the DNS software and ask what IP number is associated with a particular computer's name. The software then sends information to a particular IP address without your having to know anything more than the domain name of the computer.

IP numbers are allocated according to geographic location, to simplify network routing. The InterNIC assigns each area blocks of numbers, which are reallocated to access providers and then to you. If you move or change service providers, you have to change your IP address.

That's the anatomy of a domain name. Choosing a name (and getting that name assigned to you) is a process that the site developer must understand clearly. The next chapter covers this process in more detail.

Using the Goodies on the Internet

After you have your computer firmly connected to the Internet and have ways to route traffic from your computer to the rest of the Net, you need some software. (You wouldn't throw a party and not have something to eat, would you?) Well, the type of software you're going to be most concerned with is called *server* software. Just like it sounds, this software "serves" information.

Each type of Internet service has a server program. Today, most of the servers have been around for many years. But, hold on to your hats. New server software is being created every day. Some of the standard server programs you'll want are:

- ✔ HTTP Server to provide World Wide Web pages
- ✔ FTP to provide file transfer services
- ✔ E-mail to provide e-mail to yourself or others on your network
- ✔ Gopher to provide text-based information
- ✔ News to provide Usenet news groups

Developers currently are working on server programs that go far beyond the capabilities of these servers. The new programs will enable multimedia content to be served, new and easier kinds of file transfer, and direct peer-to-peer communications.

The World Wide Web

Internet users can easily become convinced that the World Wide Web *is* the Internet. After all, World Wide Web users can access nearly every Internet resource through one graphical interface, called a *World Wide Web browser*. Although the World Wide Web is an important tool for an Internet user, it's only one of the many goodies that you will want to consider when setting up your Internet site.

The Web was designed to provide a seamless, simple-to-use, graphical interface to the various other tools on the Internet. Unfortunately, this lofty goal has not yet been reached. Although the Web is an exciting and powerful tool, the site developer must be aware of certain limitations to take full advantage of this aspect of the Internet.

One limitation is that you currently cannot transfer a file from a client's computer to a server through the Web browser. For someone to send you a file, that person must open an FTP client software program and transfer the files to your FTP server. This situation is only one in which the Web's objective — seamless access to Internet resources — is not met.

In this book, we discuss the Web in great detail. As a site developer, you want to learn as much as you can about the World Wide Web, its advantages, and the limitations that you need to work around.

FTP

FTP (file transfer protocol) is one of the foundation resources of the Internet. Most of the other programs and resources online use FTP to move files, share files in an archive, and provide files to people over the Internet. Gaining an understanding of what FTP is, how it's used, and how to provide this service on your Internet site is an important first step. You will see how other programs on the Internet use FTP to move files, and you'll say, "I know why they do that!"

E-mail

Learning how to use electronic mail is an important step in setting up your Internet site. Understanding e-mail is a lot like knowing how to use the telephone effectively. Mailing lists have long been used to find customers in the business world; now you can use them to your advantage to provide information or sell your products on the Internet. Special software allows you to provide information to anyone who wants it via electronic mail. In Chapters 5 and 6, we explain how to deliver information through electronic mail.

Gopher

Gopher was the first popular search utility on the Internet. This resource allows you to share files on the Internet in a mystical place called *Gopherspace*. People can find and read the information on the Internet that they want by using gopher clients. Gopher still is used extensively today as an integrated part of the World Wide Web. Being able to provide information via Gopher is still important because quite a bit of archival information is stored in Gopherspace. Also, Gopher enables site developers to provide many types of information without running many types of server programs. Chapter 9 discusses Gopher more completely.

News

Usenet news provides a way for you to disseminate information to millions of people who choose to use this Internet tool every day to find what's new. This book provides information on how you can run your own news server and create news groups on every subject under the sun. You also can contact services that will carry your newsgroup.

Knowing What You Need

It's a common misconception that you need to be a UNIX guru to provide information on the Internet. This is far from true. Today's server software brings all the capabilities formerly available only on UNIX machines to your PC or Macintosh. We've gone one step further in this book. We also explain how to create your own Internet site without owning a computer at all. It's important to some people to have an Internet presence. By using Internet service providers, you can design an impressive presence and never know how to turn on a computer. All the discussions about server software, providing information, and marketing yourself on the Internet will still apply when using a service provider.

Many Internet service providers are already in business, and new ones are springing up every day. With the help of this book, you can decide what services you want or need. You may find that it doesn't make sense to run one, or any, of the server programs described in this book on your local computer. In such a case, you want to use a service provider. Our service provider is CTSNET in San Diego, which offers all the services discussed in this book. For more information, contact them at: `http://www.cts.com`

Handy utility programs

You probably will use a variety of utility programs to handle information on the Internet. One of the most common types of utility programs is *file-compression programs,* which compress files so that they can be transferred over the Net quickly. You need to use some (or all) of these utilities to decompress the files that you download from the Internet. Some of the most common are:

PKZIP

StuffIt

GZIP

COMPRESS

For every compression utility, there is an equally wonderful *decompression* utility that returns compressed files to their original size. All the utilities discussed in this book are commonly available (mostly as shareware). Chapter 11 describes how to use each utility.

Chapter 3

The First Steps to a Useful Internet Presence

• •

In This Chapter

▶ Registering a new domain name

▶ Creating your own World Wide Web presence

▶ Setting up a permanent World Wide Web site by using a service provider

▶ Installing a World Wide Web server on your personal computer

• •

*N*o matter what type of Internet presence you want to develop, the process starts with the domain name. This chapter provides tips on choosing, searching for the availability of, and registering a domain name. We also discuss the steps that a site developer might follow to set up his or her own World Wide Web presence.

Just like your name, the domain name gives your site the character and identity that are needed to set your site apart from the rest. A great deal of effort may go into selecting a domain name for your site. Getting that domain name registered, however, can be a simple process. Read on to learn more about domain names and the details that will help you develop your Internet site.

Choosing a Domain Name

Choosing a domain name is like naming a child; it's usually a laborious process of "How about this one?" or "How about that one?" This part is the most fun.

A domain name has two parts. The first is the wonderful part that you get to create; the second is an extension that identifies the type of organization to which you and your computer belong. This extension is known as the *top-level domain.* Table 3-1 identifies some of the top-level domains.

Table 3-1	Top-Level Domains
Extension	**This computer belongs to**
.COM	A commercial company
.ORG	A not-for-profit organization or other noncommercial entity
.EDU	An educational institution
.GOV	A government organization
.MIL	A military institution
.NET	A larger network
.US	Regional two-letter extensions, such as .US (for United States), identify the geographic locations of Internet sites. The extension for the United Kingdom is .UK. .CL is for Chile, .CA is for Canada, and so on.

If your company makes peanut brittle, for example, you may want to use the domain name `peanutbrittle.com`

Because all domain names in the world must be unique, the first step is finding out whether the name has already been taken. To check the availability of a domain name, you need to go to a Web site hosted by InterNIC — Network Information Center, the central Internet authority that governs domain-name registration. Follow these steps to check the availability of a domain name:

1. **Open the Web site** `http://rs.internic.net/`**, which is the InterNIC Web site.**

   This site houses a great deal of useful information. As you develop and administer your site, you will refer to the InterNIC page time and time again. Figure 3-1 shows the opening page for the InterNIC site.

2. **Go to the Registration Services page by selecting the Registration Services link.**

3. **Scroll down the page to the Registration Tools section.**

4. **Select the Whois Query Form option (see Figure 3-2).**

5. **Type the name** `peanutbrittle.com` **in the space provided.**

6. **Press Enter to begin the search.**

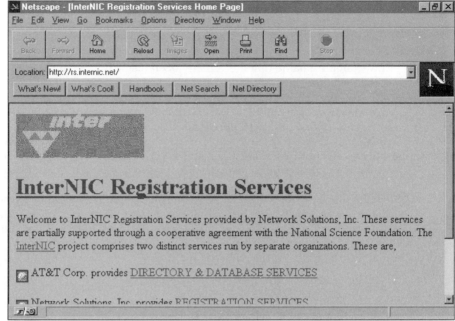

Figure 3-1:
Contact the
InterNIC
Web site to
check the
availability
of a new
domain
name.

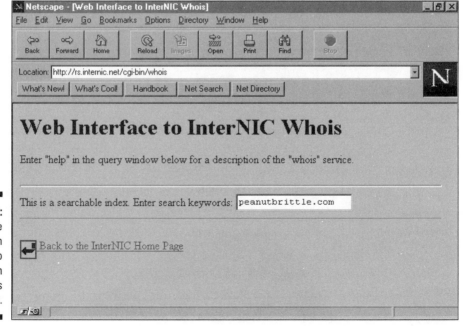

Figure 3-2:
Enter the
domain
name to
check in
the whois
query form.

As you see when you complete this task online, `peanutbrittle.com` is available for use (as of the printing of this book). If the name that you want is available, you are ready to move to the registration process.

Now examine a name that has already been taken. Follow the preceding steps to check the name `science.org`. Figure 3-3 shows the result of the search.

A great deal of information is provided about who owns the name. Names, addresses, phone numbers, and IP addresses are given for domain names that are already registered. What you do with this information depends on how badly you want the domain name. In some cases, you may want to contact the owner of a name to find out whether he or she is willing to release it to you.

If a domain name registered by someone else potentially violates a trademark that you own, contact the InterNIC for assistance. Also contact the InterNIC if you find that the person or organization listed as the owner of the domain name is unreachable through the information provided in the whois query; the owner may have abandoned the name.

Sometimes, a person and/or organization no longer wants to maintain a registered domain name. InterNIC wants to free unused domain names. To do so, it needs to know which names are no longer supported by the registered applicant. By taking a few more minutes to follow up a whois query on a domain name that appears to be registered, you may be able to gain control of that name if it is no longer in use.

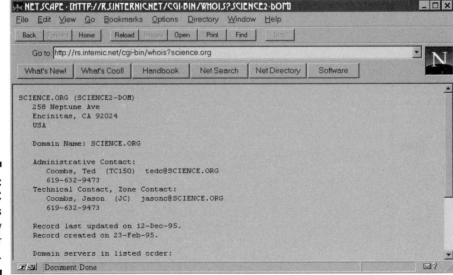

Figure 3-3:
The InterNIC
Web whois
query
results for
science.org.

When you know that your domain name is available, you can register it.

You can be very creative with your domain name. The name can be up to 24 characters long but can't contain spaces. Domain names are not case-sensitive, so you could have a domain name like `WE_LOVE_PEANUTBRITTLE.COM`

Registering your domain name

To register a domain name, you may once again be dealing with the InterNIC. Quite often, however, this service is made available by your local service provider as part of the fee for managing your domain name.

If you decide to register the name yourself, you need to contact the InterNIC Web site again. To register your domain name via the Web, follow these steps:

1. **Using your Web browser, go to the InterNIC Web site located at** `http://rs.internic.net`

2. **Scroll down the page, and select Registration Services.**

3. **Scroll down the page to Registration Information, and select Templates (WWW).**

4. **Select New to register a new domain name.**

   You now see a caution screen. InterNIC has introduced a policy of charging $100 to register a domain name. This fee covers two years of ownership. After two years, you will be charged $50 per year. Charging to register domain names helps offset the cost of managing the monumental task of keeping track of all the domain names on the Internet.

5. **If you are ready to register the domain name, move to the application form shown in Figure 3-4.**

   Follow the instructions provided, and be sure to fill in all the information. (Some tips on how to find the necessary information are provided. See the following section "Getting the necessary information.")

6. **Submit that thing!**

   Your filled-out form will be sent to you via e-mail. Forward the e-mail to `hostmaster@internic.net` to complete the submission process. Keep a copy for your records.

By submitting the form to the InterNIC, you are saying that you want the name and have the items in place to use the name at an Internet site. The InterNIC will notify you by e-mail when the name is registered.

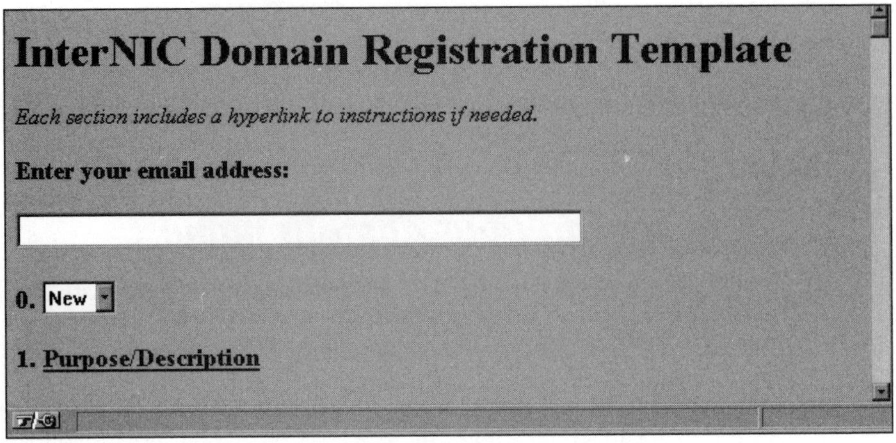

Figure 3-4:
Register
your new
domain
name by
filling out the
InterNIC
domain-
name
registration
form.

InterNIC Domain Registration Template

Each section includes a hyperlink to instructions if needed.

Enter your email address:

[   ]

0. [New ▾]

1. **Purpose/Description**

Getting the necessary information

If you are making the application to the InterNIC yourself, you should gather the following information before creating your application:

- ✔ The top-level domain from Table 3-1.
- ✔ The full domain name of your choice.
- ✔ The name and postal address of your organization. (This information will be available publicly.)
- ✔ The contact information (or *NIC handle*) for the person who is the adminis-trative head of your organization. (See the sidebar in this section, "You and your NIC handle," for more information.)
- ✔ The contact information (or NIC handle) for the technical contact for your organization.
- ✔ Information about your service provider's servers. Ask your service provider to identify its two unique domain-name servers. The provider should give you the names and IP addresses of both machines. The InterNIC requires a primary and a backup name server.
- ✔ A brief description of your organization.

Registering a domain name with the InterNIC does not give you any legal right to that name. To guarantee your right to a domain name, you must trademark it. When you perform your search to find out whether a domain name has been taken, you also should find out whether the name has been trademarked. When you apply to the InterNIC, you will have to certify that, to the best of your knowledge, the name you want to register is not trademarked by another person or company.

You and your NIC handle

Administrative and technical contacts are identified in the InterNIC database by a special alphanumeric code known as a *NIC handle*. If the person whom you identify as your administrative or technical contact does not have a NIC handle, you must submit detailed contact information for that person along with your application. The InterNIC then will issue a NIC handle to the person.

You don't have to wait for the NIC handle to be issued to submit the application; the handle will appear in your organization's NIC information record automatically. You can see this record by doing a whois search.

After you (or someone in your organization) has been given a NIC handle, that handle stays with you forever. Whenever you move, you should update your NIC handle information with your new mailing address. If you give your new NIC handle in an application and include detailed contact information, the InterNIC will update your record. This corrected information will appear in all domain-name records that include your NIC handle.

Making the application

Many times, you can simply have your Internet access provider submit the domain-name registration for you. If you want to register the name yourself by using the steps outlined earlier in this chapter, first contact your Internet service provider. The provider will need to have your domain-name service ready to go when the new domain name is registered. If the domain-name service is not set up to recognize your application, the InterNIC may reject the application automatically when you submit it.

Make sure that the contacts in your application have e-mail addresses. It is important that the InterNIC be able to reach you by e-mail.

You should receive an automatic reply to your message, indicating that it has been received by the InterNIC. If you don't, something went wrong, and the InterNIC didn't receive your message. Try again until you receive an acknowledgment. You will be notified when your application has been processed.

It's a good idea to occasionally do a whois search on your domain to make sure that your record has not been changed accidentally (it happens).

What Is the World Wide Web?

The World Wide Web is a deceptively simple mechanism. The Web is simpler than your computer, and a computer is just electrons flowing into a hunk of material that manipulates them to perform calculations. Like your computer, the World Wide Web seems to be much more complicated than it truly is because of the wonderful things it does.

Although it is not inherently difficult to understand, the World Wide Web can be confusing if it's not explained clearly. So we will do our best to make this discussion straightforward and free of unnecessary jargon.

The World Wide Web is based on a communications protocol. This protocol is called *HyperText Transfer Protocol* (HTTP). Remember that a protocol is a set of commands sent by a client program to a server program. HTTP is the set of commands that a World Wide Web client uses to make requests of a World Wide Web server program. You're probably familiar with the most common type of client program: the World Wide Web browser. The most popular Web browser is Netscape Navigator.

Which protocols the Web accepts

One of the most important things to know about World Wide Web browsers is the fact that they are well versed in many protocols, not just HTTP. To display text and graphics, a Web browser contacts an HTTP server and has an HTTP conversation. In Figure 3-5, however, the Web browser doesn't contact an HTTP server. Instead, the browser uses File Transfer Protocol (FTP) to contact an FTP server.

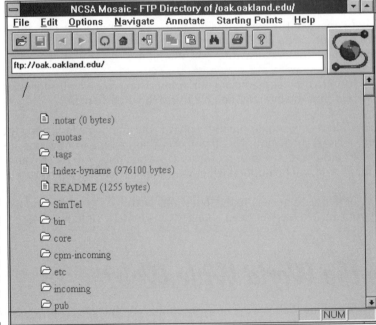

Figure 3-5:
World Wide
Web
browsers
also speak
File Transfer
Protocol.

This fact may surprise you. If the World Wide Web is based on the protocol HTTP, how do other protocols, such as FTP, fit into the picture? Are you really using the World Wide Web when you access an FTP server from your World Wide Web browser, or is your browser simply acting like a glorified anonymous FTP client program?

How the Web works

The World Wide Web is an idea within a concept within a language within a standard. The *idea* is that every Internet resource of every kind should have a simple, consistent address structure, called a Uniform Resource Locator (URL). As you read in Chapter 2, the URL for an FTP server looks like this:

```
ftp://ftp.science.org/
```

Further, the idea includes the goal that every one of these resources should be accessible from a single easy-to-use, familiar interface. Your World Wide Web browser acts as this interface.

The *concept* is called *hypertext* — text with links. The hypertext concept has been around for ages. Ever since the first person decided to place a reference to another work within his or her own creation (see the cave paintings in Vallon, Pont-d'Arc, France), people have been placing references to other writings within their own.

What makes hypertext in the World Wide Web different from simple cross-references is that with hypertext, instead of simply referring to another document, you can actually create a link to it. You aren't limited to text documents; you can create links to images, sounds, movies, searchable databases, FTP servers . . . anything at all. Because URL syntax is used to create the link, a World Wide Web hypertext link can point to any Internet resource of any kind. The term *hypermedia* sometimes is used to refer to the diverse resources that are linked via World Wide Web hypertext, which allows you to access many forms of media beyond simple text.

The *language* is called *HyperText Markup Language (HTML)*. HTML is a special text-formatting language that World Wide Web browsers read to display a document, along with its links to other Internet resources. Creating HTML documents is the key to joining the World Wide Web.

The *standard* is HyperText Transfer Protocol. HTTP enables a World Wide Web browser or other HTTP client program to retrieve HTML documents from an HTTP server. Any images, sounds, or other files associated with an HTML document also can be retrieved through HTTP. Software was created that combined the URL idea with the hypertext concept, the HTML language, and the HTTP standard. The World Wide Web was born.

What this fact means is that although FTP technically isn't part of the World Wide Web, you can still use the World Wide Web to access FTP resources. When you use a Web browser to contact an FTP server, your browser temporarily becomes a glorified FTP client program that allows you to talk to that FTP server. Your browser will do this even if you access an FTP server through a URL link in a hypertext document. Thus, the World Wide Web allows you to access both World Wide Web hypertext documents and other resources that aren't a true part of the Web.

In this way, all the resources on the Internet can be integrated through the World Wide Web. Ideally, the Web is to be a single user interface to all Internet resources that are available to surfers on the Net. Although this goal has some way to go to full implementation, Internet users already rely on Web browsers to access popular Internet services such as FTP, Gopher, and (to some extent) mail and newsgroups.

To recap the highlights of working with the Web:

- HyperText Transfer Protocol (HTTP) is a communications protocol that allows a server program to send hypertext documents and other files to a client program.
- HyperText Markup Language (HTML) is the text-formatting language that uses URL syntax to create links to other Internet resources.
- A World Wide Web browser is a program that speaks many Internet protocols and languages, including HTTP and FTP, allowing a World Wide Web user to access many types of Internet resources with a single program.
- HyperMedia is the integration of hypertext and other forms of communications media, such as images and sounds.

With this new understanding, you're ready to join the World Wide Web without getting stuck.

Setting up a World Wide Web Home Page

Now we get down to the heart of the matter. You have information that you want to make available on the Web. What's next? You need two things to set up your World Wide Web home page:

- At least one HTML document to publish
- A World Wide Web (HTTP) server through which to publish your HTML documents and other files

You can either set up your own HTTP server on your personal computer or subscribe to a World Wide Web publishing service on the Internet. Unlike setting up an FTP server, there is no obvious advantage to setting up your own HTTP server on your personal computer, aside from the fact that you'll avoid paying fees to a World Wide Web service provider. Even this advantage may be offset, however, by the cost of the dedicated Internet connection that you need if you want your HTTP server to be accessible to other users at all times.

Also keep in mind that the World Wide Web is evolving rapidly; standards are changing, and new technologies are being created all the time (to allow you, for example, to conduct true electronic financial transactions by using the World Wide Web). If you set up your own HTTP server, you may need to keep up with these changes and continue to update your HTTP server software or buy add-ons to take advantage of these new technologies. On the other hand, if you're using a World Wide Web service provider, the provider should do all these things for you; if it doesn't, you should change service providers.

Most World Wide Web service providers charge by the number of bytes that you publish and/or by the amount of network traffic that your publishing generates. More people reading your World Wide Web material means more work for your service provider, so it passes on the cost to you. You may reach a point at which it's more cost-effective to set up your own HTTP server than to pay a World Wide Web publisher. You'll have to balance your needs against your resources to decide on the best approach.

Whether you set up your own HTTP server or subscribe to a publishing service, you need to create at least one HTML document to publish on the World Wide Web before you consider other options for expanding your presence on the Web.

Writing a World Wide Web hypertext document

In this section, you find out how to start creating hypertext documents without learning the entire HTML language. Think of this section as your traveling English-to-HTML book of useful phrases in which you learn how to ask for the rest room or request political asylum. Chapters 15 and 16 discuss writing World Wide Web documents with HTML. If you're interested in learning more about HTML, check out *HTML For Dummies* (IDG Books Worldwide, Inc.).

The basic HTML language is quite simple, and you can use any text editor to write in HTML. Use a text editor to create a new file so that you can experiment as you read on. If you use a word processing program such as WordPerfect or Microsoft Word to create your HTML document, be sure to save the file in text-only format when you finish editing it. World Wide Web browsers can read only text documents; they can't read files saved in a word-processing format.

Use your World Wide Web browser to view your HTML document as you experiment. You don't need an HTTP server to see what your HTML document will look like when it's published. In fact, if you're connected to the Internet, you can even click on the links you create to make sure that they work!

Each World Wide Web browser is different when it comes to viewing local documents. In Mosaic, you can use the Open Local File option in the File menu. In Netscape, use the Open File option, also located in the File menu. When you open the local HTML document, your browser displays that document's contents just as it would any other World Wide Web page. If you are using CompuServe or America Online's browser, you will find similar menu selections.

Working with text in your HTML document

Text and text formatting are the most basic components of an HTML document. To add normal text to your HTML document, simply type it as though you were writing a letter. The text automatically word-wraps in the browser, depending on the user's window size. Carriage returns (pressing Enter at the end of a line) are ignored. Even a text-formatting feature as simple as a carriage return must be added with special HTML codes, called tags.

To spice up the text a bit, you can use HTML text-formatting tags. To turn a segment of text into a major heading, for example, you can use the following:

```
<H1>This text will appear as a level 1 heading</H1>
```

The <H1> tag means "start a level-1 heading." The </H1> tag means "end a level-1 heading."

HTML tags generally come in pairs; you might call HTML the Noah's ark of the Internet. To create bold text, use the following tags:

```
<B>This text will appear in bold</B>
```

The <B> tag means "begin bold text," and the </B> tag means "end bold text."

You create italics and underlines with the following tags:

```
<I>This text will appear in italics</I>
<U>This text will appear underlined</U>
```

The <I> tag means "begin italic text," and the </I> tag means "end italic text." (Are you seeing a pattern yet?) The <U> and </U> tags function the same way for underlining.

For a more complete guide to creating World Wide Web pages with HTML, see *HTML For Dummies*.

To save time, you can convert existing text documents to HTML-formatted documents. Simply add HTML formatting tags in appropriate places in your text document, and be sure to save the document in text-only format. When you save the file, give it either an .HTM or .HTML file extension.

Give your document a title

Each HTML document should have a title. Your Web-page title appears in the title area of the Web browser window, not in the document itself. Using a title serves two purposes:

- ✔ It provides users an informative label that describes the document.
- ✔ It gives the document a meaningful name by which other people can refer to it.

In addition, many World Wide Web browsers allow you to create a list of your favorite documents so that you can get back to them easily. Lists such as these usually are organized by document title. These lists are sometimes referred to as *bookmark lists* because you use them to mark a place on the World Wide Web.

To add a title to your HTML document, use the <TITLE> and </TITLE> tags. A good title describes the content of the document, so that when a user searches through a list of Web page titles, he or she instantly knows what the document is about. The following title is very specific:

```
<TITLE>Dimercaptan-polyaniline composite electrodes for
              lithium batteries with high energy density</TITLE>
```

A title that doesn't mean anything out of context is less effective:

```
<TITLE>Technical specifications in three languages</TITLE>
```

You can use only one title per document. The title is placed in the beginning of the file.

Add some graphics to bring your document to life

You can embed a graphic directly in an HTML document by referring to it with a special tag. This tag makes it possible to mix text with graphics on the same World Wide Web page. To display a graphic image in an HTML document, use the following:

```
<IMG SRC="http://www.science.org/science.gif">
```

Like other HTML tags, the <IMG> tag tells Web browsers to add the picture located at the following URL. As you can see from the example, you begin with IMG SRC=, which means "begin embedded image." Think of the IMG as being IMAGE and the SRC as being the SOURCE of the image. Follow the IMG SRC tag with the URL of the image file. Enclose the URL in quotation marks, and place brackets around the entire thing, as you would any HTML tag. Notice that HTML has no "end embedded image" tag to match the IMG tag.

The <IMG> tag embeds an image in your document. When someone loads the Web page into his Web browser, he sees the picture instantly. Not all World Wide Web browsers handle embedded images correctly — or at all. If the image is important to your HTML document, a better idea is to create a *link* to the image instead. The image won't appear immediately in your document when users open it, but clicking on the link allows all users to view the image. This way, even users who have text-based browsers can see the images after downloading them by clicking on the links. The next section shows you how to create a link.

Drop an anchor to create a link to another Internet resource

The elements used to designate hypertext links are known as *anchors*. Someone viewing your Web page will see an anchor as highlighted text. Think of anchoring one document to another using this highlighted text. Clicking on this text loads the new Web page to which you've linked. To add an anchor to your HTML document, begin by typing the following:

```
<A HREF=
```

This tag means "begin a new anchor." Now type the full URL of the Internet resource to which the link is to be created, and enclose it in quotes. End the link tag with the closing bracket (>). You could type the following code to create a link to the HTTP server at www.science.org:

```
<A HREF="http://www.science.org">
```

This tag means "begin a new anchor, linking this document to http:ww. science.org." The tag marks the beginning of an HTML formatting instruction.

If you've ever gone boating, you know that simply dropping the anchor isn't enough; the anchor has to be set before it does any good. The same is true of a hypertext anchor; it needs to be attached to something to work properly. To attach an anchor, place the reference to the text or image file to which you want to attach it immediately after the "begin anchor" tag, like this:

```
<A HREF="http://www.science.org">SCIENCE.ORG Web Server
```

Finally, use the "end anchor" tag </A> to mark the end of the anchor, as follows:

```
<A HREF="http://www.science.org">SCIENCE.ORG Web Server</A>
```

This example places the text SCIENCE.ORG Web Server on your Web page in the form of a hypertext link. World Wide Web users can select this text in their browsers to follow the link.

You can attach an anchor to something other than text; you can use an image instead. To attach the anchor to an image instead of text, use an image reference, as in the following example:

```
<A HREF="http://www.science.org"><IMG SRC="http://
```

This example places a graphic image in your HTML document in the form of a hypertext link. To follow the link, a user simply clicks on the image. The only difference between this link and the last example is a visual one. Instead of displaying SCIENCE.ORG Web Server on the page, the link displays a graphic image.

Learning how to perform Web-page programming with HyperText Markup Language opens the door to an interesting business idea. Consider providing Web-page-programming services to people and organizations that want to establish an Internet presence by means of the World Wide Web.

Using a service provider for World Wide Web publishing

Rather than run your own server, you can subscribe to a Web publishing service, which means that your Web pages will reside on someone else's computer. That computer is attached to the Internet full time and runs the server program. This arrangement means that your documents are available through the Web all the time, normally over a fast Internet connection.

When you subscribe to a World Wide Web publishing service, your service provider gives you at least two things:

- A user ID and password
- A directory in which to place your files so that they'll be available on the Web

Your service provider also gives you instructions that show you how to log in with your user ID and password and how to send files to your World Wide Web directory. To publish your HTML documents, simply follow your service provider's instructions to send the files to your directory.

You should create a special HTML document named `index.html` and place it in your directory. This file is the one that World Wide Web users see initially when they access your directory. You will have to refer to your World Wide Web provider's documentation to find what you should name this file. Most Web servers look for a file called `index.html` by default, but this is not the case with every server. Some servers look for the file `welcome.html` by default.

The `index.html` file (or other default file that you create) is commonly called the *home page*. Your home page is most often used as a guide to the other pages on your Web site. In this way, the home page becomes sort of a menu to the other pages. If you have no other pages, put anything on your home page that tickles your fancy.

Telling other people how to access your World Wide Web site

There is only one practical way to tell other people how to access your World Wide Web site: give them your site's URL. The syntax for your URL probably will be similar to the following:

```
http://serverdomainname/~youruserid
```

Not all Web servers use the tilde (~) before the user name. The URL is determined by the administrator of the World Wide Web server. The administrator will tell you what your home page's URL is. Following is a sample URL for a World Wide Web home page.

```
http://www.science.org/jasonc
```

The beginning of the URL identifies the resource as an HTTP server, as follows:

```
http://
```

The domain name of the HTTP server follows `http://`, identifying which computer to contact on the Internet to access the HTTP server. In our example, that domain name is the following:

```
www.science.org
```

After the domain name comes the name of the directory to access on the HTTP server, such as the following:

```
/jasonc
```

If your World Wide Web directory doesn't contain a default file, simply giving out the name of your directory may not be enough; you'll need to include the filename of your main HTML document. Because typing the entire filename is less friendly for people who are trying to access your home page, creating a default file is a good idea.

The URL for an HTTP resource can include a filename. The following URL points to a page called `writing.html` in the `jasonc` directory on the HTTP server `www.science.org`:

```
http://www.science.org/jasonc/writing.html
```

Some computers don't have domain names like `www.science.org`. For this reason, you can use a computer's unique IP address (such as `204.94.74.209`) in place of its name. Following is a valid URL:

```
http://204.94.74.209/directory/file.html
```

Spinning Your Own Web Server

We've discussed the idea of using someone else's machine to publish your Web pages. As part of setting up an Internet site, you may want to run your own server software. The next few sections provide detailed instructions on setting up an HTTP server on your Macintosh or Windows-based personal computer.

What do you get if you cross an Apple with a spider?

An excellent Macintosh HTTP server is available from BIAP Systems, Inc. The software, called MacHTTP, was written by Chuck Shotton. The software usually is distributed as a StuffIt archive, so your first step is to obtain the software and unStuffIt onto your hard drive.

To use MacHTTP, you must have System 7 (or later) and MacTCP version 1.1 (or later) on your Macintosh. You also need some kind of TCP/IP Internet access so that Internet users can access your HTTP server. For more information on getting a TCP/IP connection to the Internet, see *The Internet for Dummies* (IDG Books Worldwide, Inc.).

After installing MacHTTP, execute the program by double-clicking on the MacHTTP program icon. MacHTTP appears on your screen, as shown in Figure 3-6. This figure shows the MacHTTP status window, which reports the status of the running software.

```
┌──────────────────  MacHTTP 2.0 Status  ──────────────────┐
│ Connections : Total 0  Max 10  Listening 6  Current 0  High 0  Busy 0  Denied 0  Timeout 0 │
│ Free Memory : Max 427808  Current 427728  Min 427696  Sent:  0.0K  Up Since : 02/15/95:18:12 │
│                                                                        ⇧ │
│ MacHTTP 2.0, Copyright ⓒ1994 Chuck Shotton,                            │
│ BIAP Systems, Inc. All rights reserved.                                │
│                                                                        │
│ Loading MacHTTP.config...                                             │
│ 680x0 (CW) Server is running on port 80.                              │
│                                                                        │
│                                                                        │
│                                                                        │
│                                                                        │
│                                                                        │
│                                                                     ⇩ │
└──────────────────────────────────────────────────────────┘
```

Figure 3-6:
Launch
MacHTTP to
begin World
Wide Web
service.

After you have a server running, you should test it to make sure that it's
working. The Web server and the browser that you use to test it can be on the
same machine. Use your World Wide Web browser to connect to the server.
(Using Web browser software to connect to a particular server is often known
as *pointing your browser*.) You need to know the name of your Macintosh or its
IP address to do this. If your IP address is 204.94.74.209, for example, point your
browser at the following:

```
http://204.94.74.209/
```

When you connect to the server, the `Default.html` file displays, as shown in
Figure 3-7.

`Default.html` is a special file that MacHTTP reads by default when a World
Wide Web user connects to the MacHTTP server. (As we mentioned earlier in
this chapter, not all default HTML files are called `index.html`.) Your home page
should have the name `Default.html`. MacHTTP loads this file by default.

Spinning a web in Windows

Touted as being "your chalkboard for the World Wide Web," Windows Httpd is a
very good HTTP server for Windows, written by Robert B. Denny. Although
Denny doesn't ask for payment if you use the software for noncommercial
purposes, we strongly suggest paying what you can anyway to help support the
development of future versions.

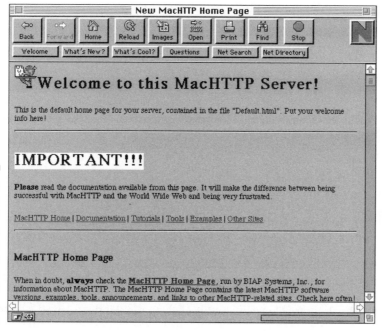

Figure 3-7:
Connect to
your World
Wide Web
server to
make sure
that it's
ready and
working.

To run Windows Httpd, you must be running Windows 3.1 with a TCP/IP communications program that is compatible with Winsock 1.1 (or a later version). You need TCP/IP access to the Internet for other Internet users to access your server.

The first step is to obtain the Windows Httpd software, which usually is distributed in PKZIP format, and then unzip it onto your hard drive. Be sure to use the -d parameter when you unzip the file. (Follow the instructions in Chapter 11 for unzipping your file.) Detailed instructions on downloading (and tips for launching) the Windows Httpd product are available at the Windows Httpd Web site http://www.city.net/win-httpd/. Be sure to read the instructions at this site carefully when you install your copy of this server package.

To create an icon for Windows Httpd in your Windows Program Manager, follow these steps.

1. **Start Windows, if you haven't already. In Windows 3.1, choose New from the File menu.**

   The New Program Object dialog box appears.

2. **Click on the Program Group radio button.**

3. **Click on the OK button.**

   The Program Group Properties dialog box appears.

4. **Type the following in the Description field:**

   Windows HTTP Server

5. **Leave the Group File field blank.**

6. **Click on the OK button.**

   The Windows Program Manager window appears.

7. **Choose New from the File menu again to display the New Program Object dialog box.**

8. **Click on the Program Item radio button.**

9. **Click on the OK button.**

   The Program Item Properties dialog box appears.

10. **In the Command Line field, type the full DOS path to the HTTPD directory, followed by the executable name (HTTPD.EXE), as follows:**

    ```
    c:\httpd\httpd.exe
    ```

11. **Click on the OK button to accept the new program item.**

From the Program Manager, double-click on the Windows Httpd icon to start the application. Windows Httpd initializes (see Figure 3-8) and then disappears into the background. Press Alt+Tab to switch to Windows Httpd if you want to see the startup screen again.

Figure 3-8: Launch the Windows Httpd program to begin serving Web documents over the Internet.

After you run the Windows Httpd program, your World Wide Web server is ready to be used. Point your browser at the server, using the name or IP address of your computer. As with the Mac, the server and browser can be on the same machine. If your computer's IP address is 204.94.74.209, use the following URL in your browser program:

```
http://204.94.74.209/
```

The document shown in Figure 3-9 displays in your World Wide Web browser. This file, named index.htm, is the HTML document that displays by default when a user contacts your Windows HTTP server.

The index.htm file is located in the \HTTPD\HTDOCS directory. Your home page, or the page that you want to appear by default, should be named index.html.

Figure 3-9: Use your browser to contact the Windows HTTP server.

Figuring Out What to Do with Your HTTP Server

More than any other Internet resource, an HTTP server opens a huge array of possibilities. If you use the Macintosh or Windows HTTP servers identified in this book, you may want to consider several tools and add-ons.

For a Macintosh, go to the official MacHTTP page at `http://www.biap.com/`. At this page, you will find a link to Tools for use with MacHTTP — information for the Mac site developer who wants to add more functionality to his or her Web presence.

For a Windows machine using Windows HTTPd, consider checking out the Windows HTTPd page where you download the server file (`http://www.city.net/win-httpd/`). Read the "Tips and Tricks" section, and check out the tools that are available.

The following sections provide a few other ideas that may be useful to you.

Set up other Internet utilities to make your site more useful

Nearly all the remaining chapters of this book show you how to integrate other Internet resources with your HTTP server. Although you can set up and use each of these resources independently, when you integrate them and provide a single user interface through the World Wide Web, your Internet site becomes a valuable Internet resource.

Publish creatively to lower costs and improve performance

Graphics, sounds, and other binary files take up much more storage space than hypertext documents do, and they're often less important than the text that they enhance. Therefore, consider one of the following possibilities to reduce your costs when you get started with the World Wide Web:

- Establish FTP service with an FTP service provider that gives you a large amount of storage space for a small monthly fee and doesn't charge by the amount of network traffic that your FTP service generates.

- ✔ Place your graphic files on this FTP server and create links to them in your HTML documents, using an FTP URL.

- ✔ Set up World Wide Web service with another service provider (or the same one, if you want) and publish your HTML documents only through this service.

- ✔ Relax and enjoy yourself as users of your World Wide Web site receive a true HyperMedia experience and your bank-account balance doesn't plummet as you make your World Wide Web service provider rich.

You also can create links to other people's image and sound files on the Internet instead of creating your own. This practice is especially useful if you set up your own HTTP server on your personal computer but have a slow modem connection to the Internet. Instead of transferring graphics and sounds from your computer over your modem, users of your World Wide Web site can transfer images and sounds from other computers on the Net that have faster connections.

If you expect people in other countries to use your World Wide Web site frequently, you can set up publishing services with providers in those countries. Copy your HTML documents and other files to each of your World Wide Web directories around the world. Then create links to each of those sites in the beginning of your home page, so that users can choose the sites closest to them for faster response time.

Today, joining the World Wide Web is the single most important way to establish your presence on the Internet. The site developer, however, must balance the desire to be on the Web against the challenges of working with the Web's limitations and drawbacks. The key to making the Web work for you (instead of the other way around) is having a carefully considered Internet strategy. How will you use the Web to provide your resources? What updates are you willing to perform on a regular basis? How much time do you have to dedicate to site maintenance and update? What other Internet resources will you create and maintain? Taking time to consider how the Web will be used can reduce complications down the road.

Part II
Equipping Your Site with the Right Tools

The 5th Wave   By Rich Tennant

"HOW SHOULD I KNOW WHY THEY TOOK IT OFF THE LIST? MAYBE THERE JUST WEREN'T ENOUGH MEMBERS TO SUPPORT AN 'AIREDALES FOR ELVIS' BULLETIN BOARD."

In this part . . .

An Internet site is much more than just a World Wide Web home page. The Internet's open nature means that your site is limited only by the type of server software that you use, and Internet software companies are producing at a surprising rate new server programs that enable everything from video conferencing to virtual worlds.

The key to turning your Internet site into a competitive advantage, a functional virtual workplace, or a useful public relations tool is to add enabling server software. To communicate with others automatically through e-mail, set up an automated e-mail server. To form a cohesive community surrounding a special interest (even if that special interest is you), create a new automated electronic mailing list or run your own Internet BBS. To exchange files easily and securely with others, set up your own FTP server. And if you're serious about making your Internet site something special, learn about options available to you other than the World Wide Web.

You're going to invest lots of time and money in your Internet site; it should be at least as easy to set up and maintain as using your favorite word processing program. The enabling tools discussed in this part make an effort to do just that.

Chapter 4

Exchanging Files on the Internet

. . . .

In This Chapter

▶ Understanding how FTP works

▶ Providing files to others on the Internet

▶ Receiving files from others by using FTP

▶ Setting up a permanent FTP site

. . . .

*T*he Internet is the ultimate in diverse computing environments. When you connect to the Internet, you join a computer network that integrates everything from Cray supercomputers to computerized Coke machines. This diversity works because all the computers speak the same set of languages to transfer and store executable and data files.

Transferring files is an important function of the Internet. If your computer cannot transfer files, you can't get the latest software programs or send files to your associates. An important aspect of almost any program that runs on the Internet is the way that it transfers files. Many programs use an Internet set of commands designed just for transferring files, called *File Transfer Protocol* (*FTP*).

Understanding How FTP Works

By setting up your own FTP server, you can send files to and receive files from other people on the Internet. Anyone who uses a World Wide Web browser, such as Netscape Navigator, can access files on your FTP server. However, to send files to your server, users need a special FTP program.

FTP is a protocol (a set of standardized instructions) that allows computers to transfer files over the Internet. An *FTP client program* (or *FTP client*) sends a request to an *FTP server program* (or *FTP server*), asking to exchange information and transfer files. The server then verifies that the user is authorized to send or receive files and responds to the request accordingly. Normally, World Wide Web browsers support the part of FTP that enables files to be retrieved, but not sent.

One very desirable feature of FTP is the fact that it maintains the original formatting of the file. Unlike other file-transfer techniques, such as attaching a file to an e-mail message, FTP doesn't require the user to decode received files before they can be used.

Using the FTP client

Numerous graphical FTP client software packages are available as freeware or shareware. One of the best FTP clients available on the Internet is WS-FTP (available as either a 16-bit or 32-bit application); you can find it on the Web at http://www.tucows.com/

The top of the screen illustrated in Figure 4-1 begins with the fill-in box for the Profile Name, which is simply the name of the connection that is to be established. You can use anything for the Profile Name; the name is for your benefit only and doesn't affect the function of FTP. For simplicity, just type the same name that is used for the Host Name as the Profile Name.

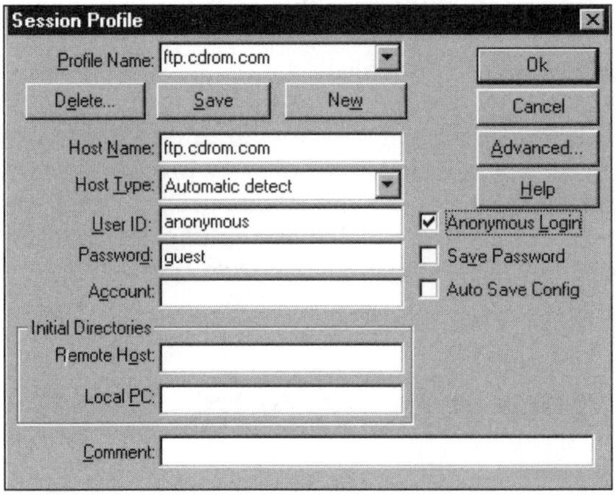

Figure 4-1:
Connecting
to an FTP
server using
the WS-FTP
client
program.

The Host Name can be either a registered Internet domain name or an IP address of an FTP server. In Figure 4-1, the Host Name of the FTP server is ftp.cdrom.com.

Enter the appropriate User ID and Password (or check the Anonymous Login box to fill in these spaces) and then click on OK to launch the client and establish the connection.

Anonymous FTP

Can you imagine handing out a password to every single person who wants access to your FTP site? You probably won't know most of the people who send or receive files through your FTP server, and you certainly won't have time to give all of them personal accounts with passwords.

Many FTP server programs use a special login account called *anonymous FTP* to allow anyone on the Internet to log in and transfer files. Users can enter the word **anonymous** as the user ID and then enter their e-mail address or the word **guest** as the password. Does this mean that the Internal Revenue Service can access financial records on your computer to see how accurate your tax return is? No. You can set up FTP server software so that the public can access only those files that will not compromise your computer or your private information. (Whew!)

After a successful connection to the desired FTP server, the screen in Figure 4-2 should appear. The screen shows the local system that is running the FTP client and the directories existing on the FTP server that has been contacted.

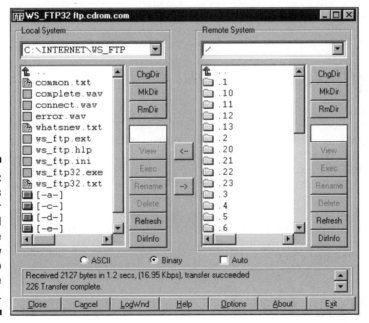

Figure 4-2: Select files to send or receive and click on the arrow buttons to begin the transfer.

Uploading and downloading files at this point is quite simple. The user simply clicks on the files in the desired directories located in either system and then clicks on one of the appropriate arrows to begin the transfer of the files.

Deciding if FTP is right for you

Something strange is happening on the Internet that we don't fully understand. In the rush to create new Internet products, many companies seem to be overlooking the basics, as though all the electronic trees are obscuring the view of the forest. One of the best examples of this is Internet file transfer technology. While FTP works well for some people, the majority of us need a better file transfer tool. So far, no company has stepped forward to offer one.

One scenario in which FTP works well is when you need to exchange files with a friend or colleague on a regular basis. You don't want just anyone to be able to retrieve the files that you send, so putting the files up on your Web site is out of the question. Even if your Web site were an option, you still wouldn't have any way to receive files from your friend or colleague. Running your own FTP server is the answer here because you can create a password-protected user account just for the person with whom you need to exchange files.

You may find other times when FTP is an acceptable solution for Internet file transfer, though the best way to find out if it's right for you is just to start using it. You may encounter situations in which FTP lets you down, as in the case of sending files to a brand-new Internet user who doesn't understand and can't figure out how to use FTP. Be on the lookout for better file transfer technology that will allow you to send files directly to anyone on the Internet.

Providing Files by Using FTP

The potential uses of FTP are limitless. Some companies use an FTP server to provide customer support; other companies use FTP for communicating with employees at remote sites. A construction company, for example, can use FTP to transfer construction drawings back and forth from remote construction sites. When the foreman in Montana requests a drawing change, he can use FTP to transfer the file to the home-office FTP site. The home office then makes the change and places the corrected drawing on the FTP site for him to download.

You can easily find numerous needs that could be fulfilled by providing files by FTP to the general public or specific people. The applications are endless. The answer is simple: FTP.

Using an Internet FTP service provider

The simplest, quickest, and least painful way to provide files by FTP involves using an existing FTP service provider. FTP service providers come in all shapes and sizes. Nonetheless, all providers have a few things in common:

> ✔ Their Internet connections probably are faster than yours.
>
> ✔ They enable you to provide files on the Internet through their FTP server, so that you don't have to set up and maintain your own.
>
> ✔ They like it when you pay them.

Using an FTP service provider should allow you to bypass many initial hassles and set up a good FTP site immediately. This method is the suggested way to go if you currently have limited resources, such as a low-bandwidth Internet connection, or are not connected to the Internet 24 hours a day, 7 days a week.

The company that you use to connect to the Internet may also offer FTP service. If not, you can always subscribe to an FTP service provided by another organization. Some service providers even give you a graphical interface to make setting up and maintaining your FTP service easy (although having a graphical interface certainly isn't essential).

Your FTP service provider will tell you two important things when you set up FTP service:

> ✔ Which directory to store files in so that they can be accessed through anonymous FTP. This directory is called your *anonymous FTP directory*.
>
> ✔ How to put files in your anonymous FTP directory.

Your anonymous FTP directory will be something like this:

```
/pub/youruserid
```

The *pub directory* (short for public directory) is a standard directory set up by FTP administrators as part of anonymous FTP sites. The next directory establishes where you can find files associated with you; service providers typically name this directory with your user ID. When you see this directory and subdirectory, you usually can find publicly accessible files and directories there. Any files that you put in this directory are available to others on the Internet, and users who contact this directory can download the files therein.

UNIX shell account

When you request FTP service from an Internet service provider, you also can request a UNIX shell account that can be accessed by any computer with a telnet client. This account makes maintaining the files in your FTP directory simpler, assuming that you are familiar with UNIX. A UNIX shell account also is useful for many of the other services discussed in this book. If you aren't familiar with UNIX, you should check out *UNIX For Dummies*, which is an excellent resource (IDG Books Worldwide, Inc).

Putting files in your FTP directory

You generally have two ways to put a file into your anonymous FTP directory:

- ✔ Beg and plead to get your FTP service provider to do it for you. (Don't forget to make the provider show you how.)
- ✔ Send it, using FTP. From your local computer, log in to the FTP server with your user ID and password; then send the file to your anonymous FTP directory.

If your FTP service provider set everything up correctly, you can transfer files into and out of your FTP directory. You can have special security set up that allows you alone to upload files to your FTP directory and that allows other users only the capability to download files. The next few sections explain how to do this as well as how you can create directories designed specifically for allowing public uploads.

Removing files from your anonymous FTP directory

To remove a file from your anonymous FTP directory, simply delete it. If you're logged in to the FTP server, your FTP client program has a Delete option. The standard UNIX text-based FTP client, for example, understands the following command:

```
delete filename
```

In your UNIX shell account, files can be removed from the anonymous FTP directory with this command:

```
rm filename
```

Receiving files from others

Your FTP service provider probably will give you a special subdirectory called incoming. The full name of the directory usually is something like this:

```
/pub/youruserid/incoming
```

FTP users can send files to the incoming directory, but they can't get files from it. This arrangement gives you a secure way to receive files from other users through FTP. Our service provider (CTS.COM), for example, calls this directory an *FTP drop-box;* it's also referred to as your *incoming directory* or your *FTP inbox.*

Checking the security of your incoming directory

Some FTP server programs allow people to get files out of an incoming directory if they know the exact name of the files. This setup is not very secure, because anyone who guesses the name of a file in your incoming directory can get a copy of that file. To find out whether your incoming directory behaves this way, follow these steps:

1. **Use your FTP client program to connect to your FTP server.**

2. **Log in as anonymous.**

Creating an incoming directory using your UNIX shell account

If your service provider doesn't give you an incoming directory, and you have a UNIX shell account along with your FTP service, you can create your own incoming directory by following these steps:

1. Log in, using your UNIX shell account.

2. Change to your anonymous FTP directory, as follows:

```
cd /pub/youruserid
```

The name of your anonymous FTP directory may be a little different when you access it with your UNIX shell account. Instead of `/pub/youruserid`, for example, the name might be more like `/usr/spool/ftp/pub/youruserid`. Your service provider will clarify this for you.

3. Create a new directory named `incoming`, as follows:

```
mkdir incoming
```

4. Change the permissions for the new directory.

The following UNIX command allows the owner to read, write, and access files in the directory (everyone else can only access the directory and transfer files to it):

```
chmod 733 incoming
```

Even if you already have an incoming directory, you can follow the preceding steps to create another one that has a different name. Any directory can act as an incoming directory, as long as you set the permissions to 733. Having multiple directories allows you to use different incoming directories for several purposes. You might want an incoming directory specifically for customers to send files for customer support, for example.

3. Send a file to your incoming directory.

4. Try to get the file out of the incoming directory, using the filename.

If you can get the file, anyone else on the Internet also can get the file if they know (or can guess) the filename. Your incoming directory has a minor security hole, although it may be one that you can live with.

If the incoming directory in your FTP service comes with the security hole described in this section, you can use the hole to your advantage. When you need to give files to a particular person, you can place the files in your incoming directory and then tell the other person the specific names of the files so that he or she can get them out of the incoming directory. You'll probably want to create an incoming directory called *outgoing* if this method seems to be a useful way to control access to certain files on your FTP server. This approach is a much simpler way to control access to sensitive files than creating a new user account for each authorized accesser.

Telling others how to access your anonymous FTP directory

You can tell other people how to access your FTP directory in one of two ways:

- Write out a Uniform Resource Locator (URL).
- Say it in English.

A URL looks like the cat's been walking across your keyboard, as the following example shows:

```
ftp://ftp.science.org/pub/internetsite/
```

The English explanation goes something like this:

Connect to the FTP server at `ftp.science.org`, and log in as `anonymous`. Then go to the directory `/pub/internetsite/`

Setting up Your Own FTP Server

Although using an FTP service provider is convenient, we think that nothing can beat setting up your own FTP server. With your own FTP server, you can set up user accounts so that business associates and friends can log in to your FTP site securely. You can receive files from other users directly rather than through a third party, and you can provide files to others simply by copying those files to your FTP directory.

Uniform Resource Locator (URL) review

Uniform Resource Locators are standardized addresses used to refer to Internet resources. The first three letters in the URL identify the resource as an FTP server. The domain name of the FTP server follows ://. The domain name identifies which computer to contact on the Internet to access the FTP server. After the domain name comes the name of the directory that you want to access on the FTP server, such as the following:

`/pub/internetsite/`

The URL for an FTP resource also can include a filename. The following URL points to a file called

gatt.zip in an anonymous FTP directory on the FTP server named ftp.science.org:

```
ftp://ftp.science.org/pub/
    internetsite/gatt.zip
```

Some computers on the Internet don't have domain names, but all computers on the Internet have a unique address called an *IP address*. You can use the IP address in place of a domain name. The following is a valid URL:

`ftp://192.188.72.27/pub/`

Setting up your own FTP server has one drawback: your FTP server is available only while you're connected to the Internet. If you don't have a permanent 24-hour connection, you probably should use an Internet FTP service provider. This approach is a great way to establish a permanent FTP site on the Internet; it's also much less expensive than establishing your own permanent connection and requires less maintenance.

If your computer can communicate with the Internet by using TCP/IP, you can set up and run your own FTP server. All you need is access to the Internet and FTP server software that works in the operating system that you're using. Most FTP server software is very straightforward; just install it, and away you go.

The next few sections provide detailed instructions on setting up FTP server software for either a Macintosh or Windows-based personal computer.

Macintosh FTPd server

The best shareware FTP server software available for your Macintosh computer is FTPd, by Peter N. Lewis. The price is $10, and it's worth every penny. The software usually is distributed as a StuffIt archive, so your first step is to obtain the software and unStuffIt onto your hard drive.

Computer daemons

We encountered an interesting account about the origin of the term *daemon*. Rob Beckers, the author of an FTP server program for Windows called Serv-U, writes, "The term daemon comes from ancient Greek mythology. There, the Daemons were half-gods, acting as messengers between the people on Earth and the gods."

Rob likens the daemons of Greek mythology to the software daemons of today, but instead of acting as messengers between people on Earth and the gods, software daemons act as messengers between people on Earth and the computer.

FTPd is short for *FTP daemon*. The term *daemon* refers to a server program that is available all the time — a program that never rests. You can download a copy of FTPd from:

```
http://www.science.org/internetsite/
```

To use FTPd, your Macintosh must have System 7 (or later) and MacTCP version 1.1 (or later), and must have File Sharing enabled. To enable Internet users to access your FTP server, you need some kind of Internet IP access, such as PPP or (if you're special) a direct network connection.

Checking security

Before you install FTPd, you should check the security on the computer system. Follow these steps to prepare for the installation of the FTPd server on your computer and to check the computer's security:

1. **Make sure that you have File Sharing enabled (use the Sharing Setup control panel, as shown in Figure 4-3).**

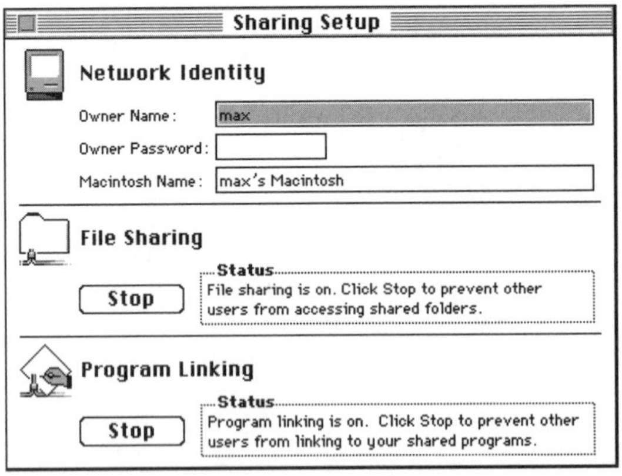

Figure 4-3:
Use the Sharing Setup control panel to enable File Sharing.

Sharing Setup

Network Identity
Owner Name: max
Owner Password:
Macintosh Name: max's Macintosh

File Sharing
Stop
Status
File sharing is on. Click Stop to prevent other users from accessing shared folders.

Program Linking
Stop
Status
Program linking is on. Click Stop to prevent other users from linking to your shared programs.

2. **Configure sharing for your drives and folders by using the Finder to locate and click on a drive or folder icon, and then choose Sharing from the File menu.**

A sharing configuration window like the one shown in Figure 4-4 appears.

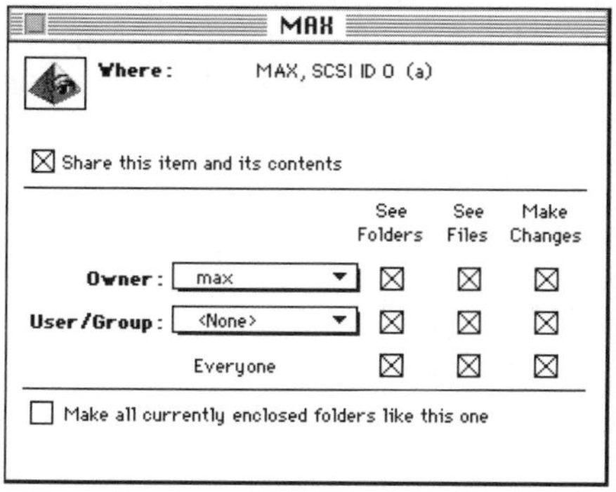

Figure 4-4:
Set up
access
permissions
for folders
and drives
to establish
security.

```
┌──────────────────────── MAX ──────────────────────┐
│ ▛                                                  │
│   ◆   Where :      MAX, SCSI ID 0  (a)             │
│                                                    │
│  ☒ Share this item and its contents                │
│  ─────────────────────────────────────────────    │
│                              See   See   Make       │
│                            Folders Files Changes    │
│         Owner :  [ max      ▼ ]  ☒    ☒    ☒        │
│      User/Group : [ <None>  ▼ ]  ☒    ☒    ☒        │
│                    Everyone      ☒    ☒    ☒        │
│  ─────────────────────────────────────────────    │
│  ☐ Make all currently enclosed folders like this one│
└────────────────────────────────────────────────────┘
```

3. **If you don't want anonymous FTP users to access a particular drive or folder, be sure to clear each of the three check boxes to the right of the word** Everyone.

You can change all your folders at the same time by selecting the Make all currently enclosed folders like this one check box at the bottom of the sharing dialog box shown in Figure 4-4.

Installing FTPd

Now that you have checked the security on your computer, you can install the FTPd server. When you install FTPd on your Mac, you see several program icons in the FTPd folder:

- ✔ FTPd
- ✔ FTPd (Background)
- ✔ FTPd Setup

Don't click on any of these icons yet; just admire their beauty. The FTPd Setup program allows you to configure FTPd. FTPd and FTPd (Background) both start the actual FTP server program. The only difference between the two is the fact that FTPd (Background) runs the FTP server without displaying the log of connections and transfers.

You should do a few things before configuring FTPd. The following four steps show you how to prepare your Macintosh to run FTPd.

1. Run the Internet Config program.

The Internet Config program is located in the FTPd folder. When the Internet Config program is run, as shown in Figure 4-5, it allows you to determine the general settings for use in many Internet applications, including FTPd. You don't have to click on each of the boxes in the Internet Preferences window — just the interesting ones. The important thing is that you run the application at least once, so that the Internet Config extension gets installed. FTPd will use the Internet Config extension later.

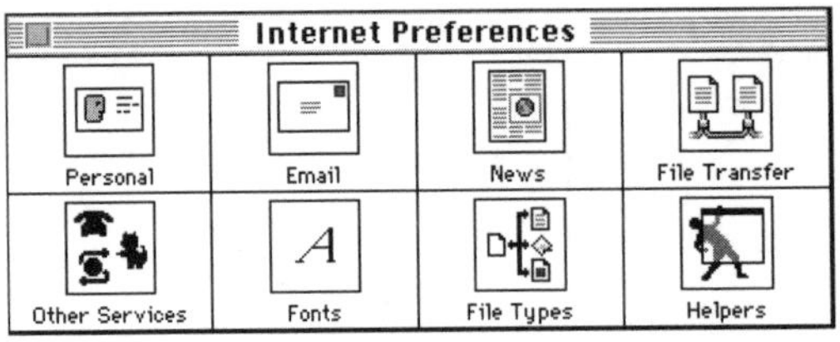

Figure 4-5:
Configure your Internet preferences with the Internet Config extension.

2. At some point, run the Register program to register and pay for FTPd (see Figure 4-6).

Be sure to look at the neat payment methods!

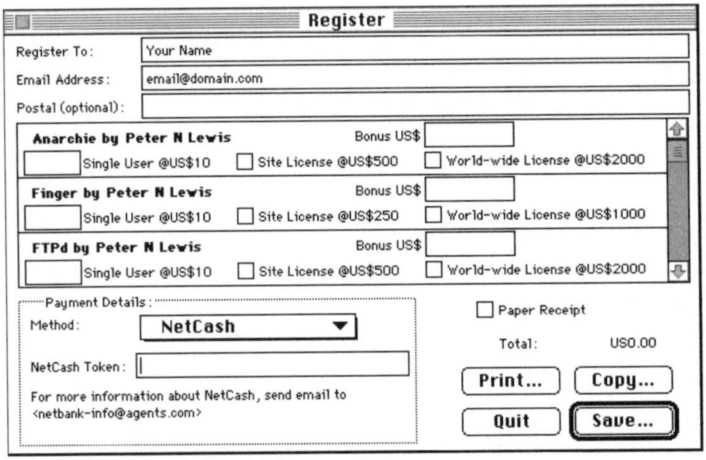

Figure 4-6:
Register and pay for FTPd — one shareware program that you'll definitely use.

3. If you want to allow anonymous FTP logins, use the Users & Groups control panel to set up the <Guest> user and enable File Sharing for <Guest> (see Figures 4-7 and 4-8).

Figure 4-7:
Set up a
<Guest>
user in the
Users &
Groups
control
panel to
enable
anonymous
FTP logins.

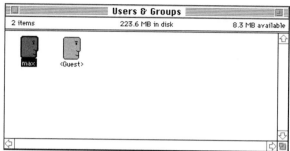

Figure 4-8:
Click on the
File Sharing
check box
to allow
guests to
connect.

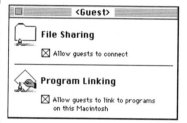

4. Double-click on the FTPd Setup icon to get started with FTPd.

The window shown in Figure 4-9 appears, telling you a little about the program. Close this window by clicking on the close box in the upper-left corner.

Figure 4-9:
Learn a little
about FTPd.

Configuring in the FTPd Setup window

After the FTPd server has been installed, you must configure the FTPd server properly, using the FTPd Setup window (see Figure 4-10).

Figure 4-10:
Use FTPd
Setup to
configure
your FTP
server.

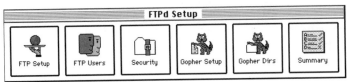

To configure general FTPd settings, click on the FTP Setup box in the FTPd
Setup window. The FTP Setup window, shown in Figure 4-11, appears.

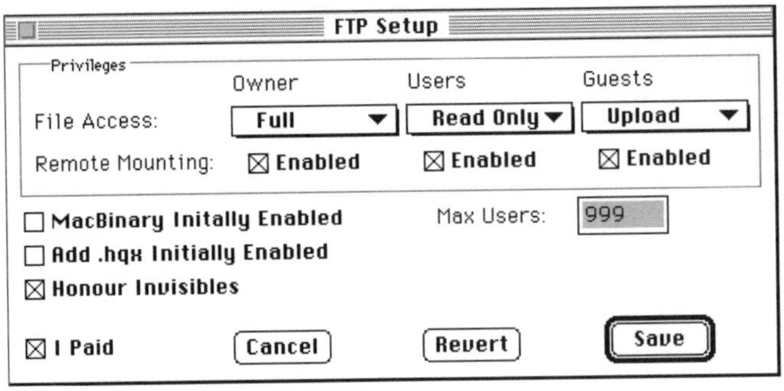

Figure 4-11:
Set access
privileges in
the FTP
Setup
window.

The most important settings in this window are the File Access privileges,
which offer four levels of access:

- ✔ *None:* no access
- ✔ *Read Only:* receive files only
- ✔ *Upload:* send and receive only
- ✔ *Full:* send and receive files, and delete, rename, or modify files and folders

You can set the access privileges independently for each of the three types of
users:

- ✔ *Owner:* the user whose name appears in the Sharing Setup control panel as
  the owner of the Macintosh
- ✔ *User:* any other user defined in the Users & Groups control panel
- ✔ *Guest:* anyone who uses anonymous FTP to access the FTP server

Choose an access-level privilege for each of the user types by making selections
from the drop-down lists.

Another important setting in the FTP Setup window is Remote Mounting, which allows an FTP user to access shared file systems on other Macintosh computers on your network. To access file systems on other computers, the FTP user sends a command like this from an FTP client program:

```
quote smnt MacFileServer
```

To enable Remote Mounting, check the Enabled check box in the appropriate user-type column. Remember that you should enable Remote Mounting only if you have a good reason to do so. Typically, you will disable Remote Mounting.

Enabling Remote Mounting for guests is dangerous if you have an AppleTalk network. If you enable Remote Mounting for guests, anyone on the Internet can get files from any Macintosh on your network. If you don't have a good reason to enable Remote Mounting, disable it by clearing the Enabled check boxes.

Otherwise, the defaults should be fine for the other settings in the FTP Setup window. Click on the Save button when you're done making changes.

Now check the default login directory for FTP users by clicking on FTP Users in the FTPd Setup window. The FTP Users window appears, allowing you to set up the Login Directory and Login Commands for each FTP user. You also can set up defaults that apply for every FTP user (see Figure 4-12).

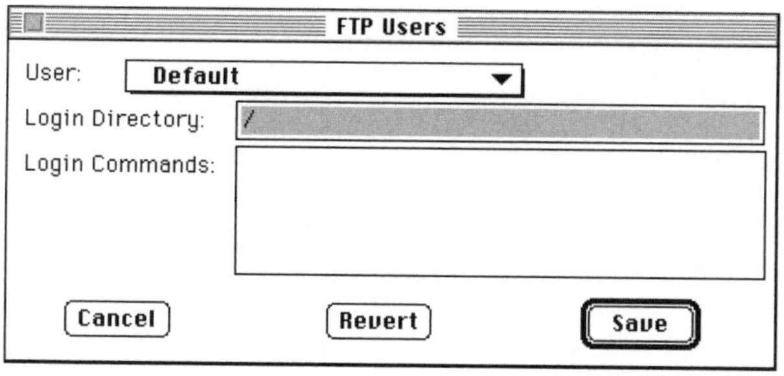

Figure 4-12:
Establish
Login
Directory
and Login
Command
defaults
with the FTP
Users
window.

☐	FTP Users

User: **Default** ▼

Login Directory: `/`

Login Commands:

[Cancel]   [Revert]   [Save]

Login Directory is the drive or folder that you want FTP users to see initially when they connect to your FTP server. If you want the Macintosh Desktop to appear first when a user connects to your FTP server, set the Login Directory to a single forward slash (/).

The Login Commands box allows you to define commands to execute when a user logs in. This option enables users to do such things as mount remote shared folders and drives automatically or display usage statistics. You can include any SMNT or SITE command in the Login Commands box; see the FTPd documentation for details.

Creating an anonymous FTP directory

Your FTP server will be easier for others to use if you create a /pub directory. To create a /pub directory, follow these steps:

1. **Use the Finder to create a new folder called pub.**

2. **Create the pub folder on the Desktop, or place an alias to the pub folder on the Desktop.**

3. **Click on the pub folder, and choose Sharing from the File menu.**

4. **Check the box labeled Share this item and its contents (refer to Figure 4-4).**

5. **Change the owner of the folder, if necessary.**

   Changing the owner is handy if a user other than the owner of the Macintosh is responsible for maintaining the FTP server.

6. **Clear the Make Changes check box for Everyone and for each User/ Group as desired.**

7. **Close the window by clicking on the close box in the upper-left corner.**

8. **Start FTPd Setup, and click on FTP Users.**

9. **Change the Login Directory for Default user to /pub.**

10. **Click on the Save button.**

Now put some files in the pub folder. Remember that some computer operating systems don't allow spaces in filenames. It's a good idea to avoid using spaces in the names of the files that you make available through your FTP server. This will allow everyone on the Internet to access the files without trouble.

Creating special files

FTPd allows you to create special files to help FTP users find the files that interest them (you have to give these special files specific names). You can create a file named !Folder Info in any folder, for example; the contents of this file will appear automatically when an FTP user enters the folder. Then you might create a !Folder Info file in the pub folder, containing this message:

```
This is the pub folder. In this folder, you'll find files and
folders that you might want to get. If you need help, send
mail to help@domain.com. Don't blame us if your computer
blows up when you use files from this folder. Enjoy!
```

You also can create a Startup file — another type of special file that appears when an FTP user logs in to the FTP server. You must store Startup files in a Startup Messages folder, which you have to put in one of two places:

- The FTPd folder
- The FTPd Preferences folder, located in the System Preferences folder

You can create a default Startup file, as well as Startup files for each type of user. FTPd would display a file named Anonymous Startup, for example, when an anonymous FTP user logs in to the FTP server. If FTPd doesn't find a Startup file for a particular user type, it displays the file named Default Startup (if one exists).

All special files, including !Folder Info and Startup files, should be text-only. Also, you should press Enter at the end of each line in the file rather than use word-wrap. Some FTP client programs don't perform word-wrap properly, so you have to do it for those programs in your file.

Try to keep these special files small to improve performance. If you have a good idea of which files your FTP users will be most interested in, provide simple, direct instructions on retrieving those files. These instructions make your FTP server much easier to use.

Configuring security settings

The Security window of FTPd Setup (shown in Figure 4-13) controls several security settings. Click on the Security button in the FTPd Setup window.

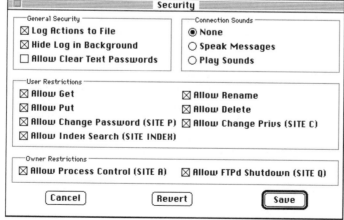

Figure 4-13: Configure additional security settings with the Security window.

You may want to disable (or clear) any of the following three Security settings, because the average user doesn't need them:

- ✔ *Allow Change Password (SITE P):* allows users to change their passwords
- ✔ *Allow Change Privs (SITE C):* allows users to change their file privileges (file-level security restrictions)
- ✔ *Allow Process Control (SITE A):* allows the owner to control processes

The rest of the settings are optional. Enabling Connection Sounds can be helpful if you plan to be nearby when people connect to your FTP server. Connection sounds can be annoying in a busy office, though.

Checking the setup

The last step in the setup process is clicking on Summary in the FTPd Setup window. If you need to do anything else, the Summary window informs you. If everything is set up correctly, your Summary window should look something like Figure 4-14.

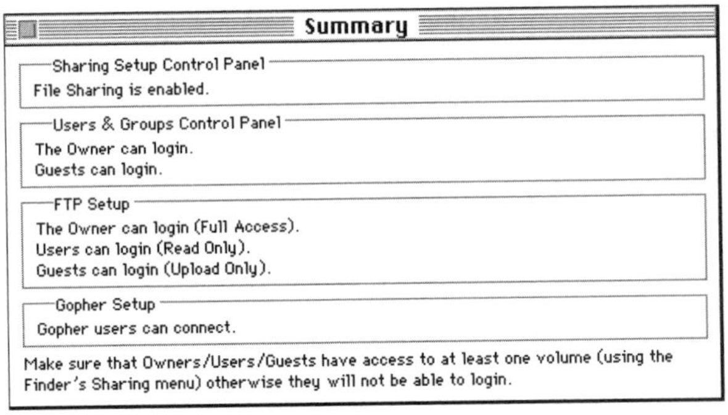

Figure 4-14:
Always
check the
Summary
window to
make sure
that your
configuration
is correct.

```
                          Summary
 ┌─Sharing Setup Control Panel──────────────────────────┐
 │ File Sharing is enabled.                              │
 ├─Users & Groups Control Panel─────────────────────────┤
 │ The Owner can login.                                 │
 │ Guests can login.                                    │
 ├─FTP Setup────────────────────────────────────────────┤
 │ The Owner can login (Full Access).                   │
 │ Users can login (Read Only).                         │
 │ Guests can login (Upload Only).                      │
 ├─Gopher Setup─────────────────────────────────────────┤
 │ Gopher users can connect.                            │
 └──────────────────────────────────────────────────────┘
 Make sure that Owners/Users/Guests have access to at least one volume (using the
 Finder's Sharing menu) otherwise they will not be able to login.
```

Using FTPd

Start the FTPd program by double-clicking on the FTPd icon. This icon starts the FTP server and displays the Log Window. After you use your FTP server for a while, your Log Window should look something like Figure 4-15.

To quit FTPd, start FTPd Setup and then quit FTPd Setup while holding down the Option key. This action closes both FTPd Setup and the active FTPd program.

Windows FTP server

Several good shareware FTP server programs are available for Microsoft Windows. The one to trust is WFTPD by Alun Jones. *WFTPD* stands for *Windows FTP daemon*.

```
                              Log Window
 3:40 PM  2/13/95  198.68.175.194  FTPd 2.4.0   starting up
 3:46 PM  2/13/95  192.188.72.17   coombs@cts.com  1  log in Guest
 3:47 PM  2/13/95  192.188.72.17   coombs@cts.com  1  log out Guest
 4:04 PM  2/13/95  198.68.175.194  FTPd 2.4.0   starting up
 4:04 PM  2/13/95  198.68.175.194  FTPd 2.4.0   shutting down
 4:07 PM  2/13/95  198.68.175.194  FTPd 2.4.0   starting up
 4:11 PM  2/13/95  198.68.175.194  FTPd 2.4.0   shutting down
 3:55 PM  2/15/95  198.68.175.194  FTPd 2.4.0   starting up
 3:58 PM  2/15/95  204.94.74.209   1  refused login   no ftp access allowed
 4:00 PM  2/15/95  204.94.74.209   2  refused login   no ftp access allowed
 4:01 PM  2/15/95  204.94.74.209   anonymous\  3  failed login
 4:01 PM  2/15/95  204.94.74.209   jasonc@pk.com  3  log in Guest
 4:03 PM  2/15/95  204.94.74.209   jasonc@pk.com  3  get file Register
 4:06 PM  2/15/95  204.94.74.209   jasonc@pk.com  3  get file !Folder Info
 4:06 PM  2/15/95  204.94.74.209   jasonc@pk.com  3  get file Documentation
 4:07 PM  2/15/95  204.94.74.209   jasonc@pk.com  3  get file Extra Documentation
 4:07 PM  2/15/95  204.94.74.209   jasonc@pk.com  3  get file Programs
 4:07 PM  2/15/95  204.94.74.209   jasonc@pk.com  3  get file Quick Start
 4:07 PM  2/15/95  204.94.74.209   jasonc@pk.com  3  get file Tutorial by Eric Enwall
 4:08 PM  2/15/95  204.94.74.209   jasonc@pk.com  3  get file Internet Config
 4:09 PM  2/15/95  204.94.74.209   jasonc@pk.com  3  get file Read Me First
 4:09 PM  2/15/95  204.94.74.209   jasonc@pk.com  3  get file User Documentation
 4:11 PM  2/15/95  204.94.74.209   jasonc@pk.com  3  get file Anonymous Startup
 4:11 PM  2/15/95  204.94.74.209   jasonc@pk.com  3  get file Default Startup
 4:11 PM  2/15/95  204.94.74.209   jasonc@pk.com  3  get file Peter Startup
```

Figure 4-15:
Find out
what's been
happening
on your FTP
server by
reading the
Log
Window.

To use WFTPD, you must be running a Windows operating system such as
version 3.1 or Windows 95/NT (a 32-bit version is also available) with a TCP/IP
communications program that is compatible with Winsock version 1.1 or later. If
you want Internet users to be able to access your FTP server, you need some
kind of Internet access, such as PPP or a direct network connection.

Installing WFTPD

The first step in installing WFTPD is obtaining the software, which usually is
distributed in PKZIP format. You can download the WFTPD server program
from the Consummate Winsock Applications site http://www.tucows.com/

You must download the program, unzip it onto your hard drive, and then move
the file CTL3DV2.DLL to the Windows System directory. Follow these steps:

1. **Move the file CTL3DV2.DLL from the folder in which you installed
   WFTPD to the \WINDOWS\SYSTEM folder.**

2. **Delete the CTL3DV2.DLL file in the WFTPD folder.**

   Now that you have copied this file to the Windows System folder, you have
   to remove it from its original location.

3. **Make sure that you don't already have a copy of CTL3DV2.DLL in your
   \WINDOWS folder.**

Now your Windows system should be ready to run WFTPD. To make life simple,
create an icon for WFTPD in your Windows Program Manager. Then you can
double-click on the WFTPD icon to start the application.

Troubleshooting

If WFTPD finds two copies of CTL3DV2.DLL, or doesn't find one at all, it complains, displaying either of the error messages shown in Figures 4-16 or 4-17.

Figure 4-16:
If this error appears, check for the correct installation of the CTL3DV2.DLL file.

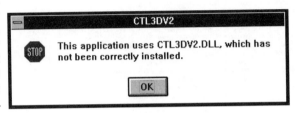

Figure 4-17:
Reinstall CTL3DV2.DLL. We recommend copying it to the \WINDOWS \SYSTEM folder.

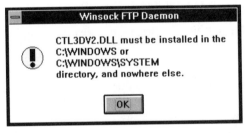

If these messages appear when you run WFTPD, exit WFTPD. Then make sure that you have a copy of CTL3DV2.DLL in your \WINDOWS\SYSTEM folder. Remove any copies of CTL3DV2.DLL that exist in other directories, and try to run WFTPD again.

When you load the WFTPD program, the main WFTPD window should appear (see Figure 4-18).

Setting up WFTPD security

The first and most important thing to do when you get WFTPD is beef up your security. As soon as you started WFTPD, you added a new level of complexity to your Internet presence. Now you need to secure your computer against unwanted intruders. WFTPD doesn't let you down in this regard, because it provides excellent security features.

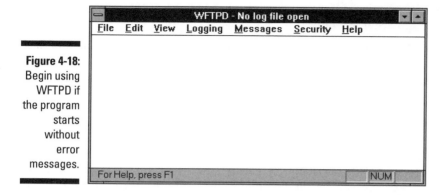

Figure 4-18:
Begin using WFTPD if the program starts without error messages.

To begin establishing general security settings, follow these steps:

1. **Choose General from the Security menu.**

2. **The General Security dialog box (Figure 4-19) appears, allowing you to establish basic security preferences.**

   The most important of these preferences is the Enable Security check box. When you check this check box, every FTP user is required to enter a user name and a password to use your FTP server. Checking the Enable Security check box also means that access restrictions will be enforced according to additional security settings.

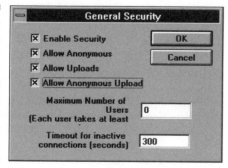

Figure 4-19:
Use the General Security dialog box to establish basic WFTPD security.

If you don't check the Enable Security check box, anyone on the Internet can copy or delete any file on your system. This possibility might be interesting if you're studying psychology or criminal behavior and want to know what Internet users will do when they encounter a defenseless FTP server. If you conduct such a study, intentionally or otherwise, please send us the conclusions.

3. **The other three check boxes are less extreme in their impact, although they still are important:**

    - *Allow Anonymous.* Check this box if you want to allow anonymous FTP access to your FTP server.

    - *Allow Uploads.* Check this box if you want to allow FTP users to upload (send files).

    - *Allow Anonymous Upload.* Check this box if you want to allow anonymous FTP users to upload.

An FTP server accepts two types of users: anonymous users and users who have specific login IDs. Users who have login IDs have password-protected access to files in their home directories or the directories to which you allow them access. The server is like a museum. You allow the public to view, touch, and feel the displays in the public viewing area. Employees, on the other hand, have a key to the back room, where displays are kept that aren't for public viewing.

4. **To limit the number of FTP users who can connect to your FTP server simultaneously, enter a number in the Maximum Number of Users field.**

    A zero in this field means that no limit applies. (If you don't want anyone to connect to your FTP server, don't run it!)

5. **Enter a number in the Timeout for inactive connections (seconds) field.**

    Establishing a time-out period for inactive connections is a good idea. An *inactive connection* is an FTP user who hasn't issued any FTP commands to your FTP server in a while. Rather than allow these inactive connections to sit there consuming memory and processing time on your computer, you can tell WFTPD to boot them off after a certain number of seconds of inactivity. If you enter zero in this field, no FTP users will ever be disconnected, no matter how long they're inactive.

6. **Click OK when you finish setting General Security options.**

Next, you adjust the User Security Settings dialog box (shown in Figure 4-20) to set up FTP user accounts and to control the directories that each user can access. Follow these steps:

1. **Choose User/Password from the Security menu.**

    WFTPD provides one default user name: anonymous.

2. **To change the directories that anonymous FTP users can access, choose anonymous from the User Name drop-down list; enter a directory name in the Home directory field; and check the Restrict to home check box.**

    A user's home directory is the one that he or she sees initially upon logging on to your FTP server. If you restrict users to their home directories (by checking the Restrict to home check box), you prevent those users from accessing files in any directory that is not a subdirectory of the

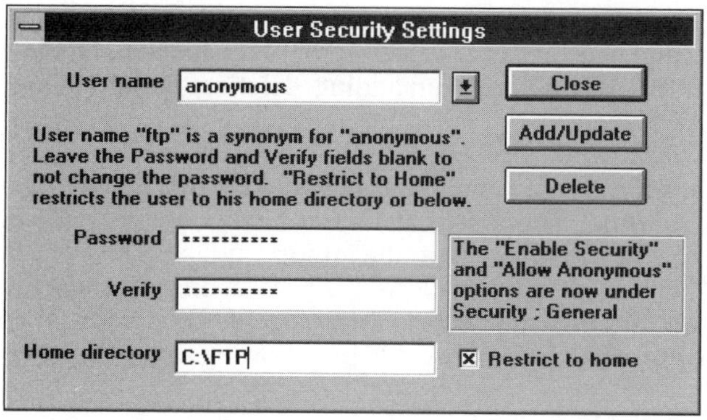

Figure 4-20:
Setup FTP
user
accounts
with the
User
Security
Settings
dialog box.

User Security Settings

User name [anonymous] ▼   [Close]

User name "ftp" is a synonym for "anonymous".   [Add/Update]
Leave the Password and Verify fields blank to
not change the password. "Restrict to Home"   [Delete]
restricts the user to his home directory or below.

Password [**********]   The "Enable Security"
                          and "Allow Anonymous"
Verify [**********]   options are now under
                          Security ; General

Home directory [C:\FTP]   ☒ Restrict to home

home directory. FTP users who are restricted in this way can still access
directories within their home directories. Think of the procedure as being
like grounding your child; you restrict him to home but allow him to
access the refrigerator.

In Figure 4-20, anonymous FTP users are restricted to the C:\FTP directory. This setup protects important files on your computer, but at the same
time allows anonymous FTP users to access files and directories within the
C:\FTP directory.

If you allow anonymous FTP users to connect to your FTP server without
restricting them to a certain directory, anyone on the Internet can access
every directory and every file on your computer.

3. **When you finish making changes for anonymous users, click on the
   Add/Update button.**

You also can add specific users. If you have a company, you may want to
give your employees their own user accounts. These accounts will give them
password-protected FTP access to their files. To add a new user, follow
these steps:

1. **Enter a user name in the User name field.**

2. **Enter a password in the Password field.**

   The password will be hidden as you type.

3. **Re-enter the password in the Verify field.**

   This entry confirms the password that you entered in step 2.

4. **Type a directory name in the Home directory field.**

   This directory is the one that users see first when they log in.

5. **If you want users to have full access to your computer's files and directories, leave the Restrict to home check box unchecked; otherwise, check
   that box.**

6. **Click on Add/Update to save your new FTP user.**

Now that you can add users, you may also want to delete them at some point. To delete an existing user, select the user in the User Name list and then click on the Delete button. When you finish adding, deleting, and updating users, click on the Close button.

As a final level of security, you can deny access to certain hosts or certain networks on the Internet. Suppose that a nasty hacker breaks into your system from IP address 127.0.0.1 and steals some important files. This act upsets you, so you send e-mail to the Computer Emergency Response Team (CERT), informing it about the break-in. You then deny access to anyone on any host or network that begins with the number 127 by following these steps:

1. Choose Host/Net from the Security menu.

The Host Security Settings dialog box appears, as shown in Figure 4-21.

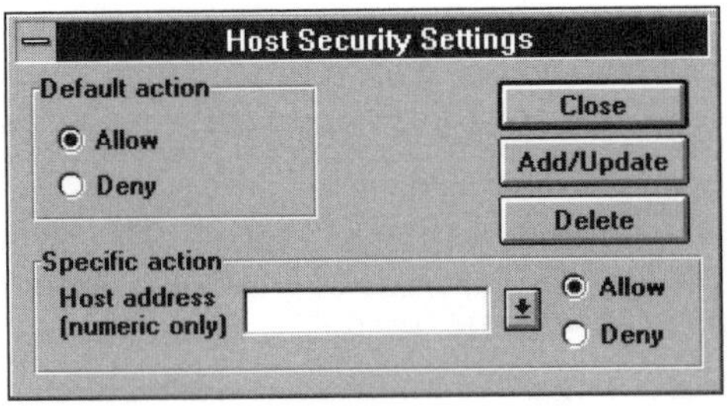

Figure 4-21:
Deny
access to
certain
hosts or
networks
with the
Host
Security
Settings
dialog box.

2. Type the following in the Host address field:

127.*.*.*

3. Click on the Deny radio button to the right of the Host address field.

4. Click on the Add/Update button.

You also can reverse your security approach. Rather than wait until a hacker breaks into your system, you can deny access to *every* host and network by clicking on the Deny radio button in the Default action section of the dialog box. Then you can selectively grant entrance to certain hosts and networks that you trust by entering their IP addresses, one at a time, in the Host address field and then clicking on the Allow radio button next to the field. Be sure to click on Add/Update after you type each address. Click on the Close button when you're done making changes.

Configuring other WFTPD settings

Several WFTPD settings are both interesting and useful. First, look at the Messages menu. The Greeting and Farewell messages have defaults that you can't change until you pay for the software. This situation is your incentive to be honest. (Not that *you* need an incentive, of course, but many people wouldn't pay for the software without some encouragement.) After you obtain the official version of WFTPD, you can change the Greeting and Farewell messages by choosing those options from the Messages menu.

The MESSAGE.FTP option in the Messages menu allows you to turn the display of special messages on or off for each directory. If you check the MESSAGE.FTP option in the Messages menu, for example, the special text file MESSAGE.FTP appears whenever an FTP user changes to a directory that contains this special file. You might create, in your C:\FTP directory, a MESSAGE.FTP file that contains the following text:

```
This is the FTP directory. Here, you'll find several files
that may interest you, as well as a few directories to ex-
plore. If you have questions or need help using this FTP
server, send e-mail to ftphelp@domain.com.
```

The C:\FTP directory then displays this message to any FTP user who accesses it.

Be sure to press Enter at the end of each line when you create your text file. Many FTP client programs don't word-wrap properly, so you have to do it for them.

If you want WFTPD to keep a log of activity on your FTP server, such as logins and files transferred, choose Log Options from the Logging menu. The Logging Options dialog box appears (see Figure 4-22). To turn logging on, check the Enable Logging check box; then check each of the items that you want to have logged. Click on the OK button when you finish.

Figure 4-22:
Configure FTP logging to track activity on your FTP server.

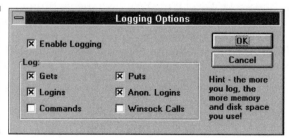

To log activity to a file rather than just to the screen, choose Open Log from the File menu. When the Open dialog box appears (see Figure 4-23), choose an existing log file or type the name of a new one and then click on the OK button.

To close an open log file, choose Close Log from the File menu. To shut down your FTP server, choose Exit from the File menu.

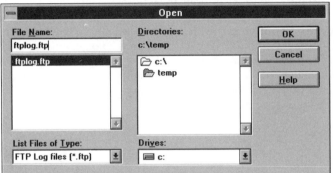

Figure 4-23:
Log to a file
if you want a
more
permanent
record of
activity.

Figuring Out What to Do with Your FTP Server

You can do many things with your FTP server. Whether you set up your own server or subscribe to an FTP service, the possibilities are almost endless. The following sections present some ideas that may not have occurred to you yet.

Providing World Wide Web documents

Yes, you can provide hypertext World Wide Web documents through your FTP server. Although this method isn't a common (or ideal) approach to providing World Wide Web documents on a World Wide Web server, it works in most cases. Create your HTML document and put it in your anonymous FTP directory. Anyone with a Web browser can retrieve and view your HTML document as though they had contaced a Web server.

Providing intracompany file transfer

In addition to providing files to customers, an FTP server can provide the useful function of intracompany file transfer. One of the most useful features of FTP is its capability to limit site access to users who have passwords. This capability allows a company to set up an FTP site that can be accessed only by authorized employees.

An FTP site can be a valuable resource, enabling your employees to transfer files among themselves. The FTP site also can serve as a forum where you can post valuable files — such as employee manuals and general employment policies — that all employees can access and use.

Setting up a public file-exchange area

By giving anonymous FTP users permission to send and receive files through your FTP server, you can create a useful public exchange forum. Swapping files among family members, friends, and strangers around the world has its roots in early bulletin-board systems (BBSs) — online forums, which require user IDs, that existed before the Internet. FTP users can exchange messages and files through your FTP server just as they do by calling a BBS.

If you decide to set up a public file-exchange area, for whatever reason, consider talking to a lawyer about your potential liability. A lawyer can help you create a good disclaimer that makes it clear to all users of your exchange area that they use it at their own risk and that you do not control the content or tolerate illegal activity.

Currently, no better tool exists for transferring files on the Internet, for personal or business purposes, than FTP. Depending on your requirements and skill level, you can provide FTP service in two ways: by using a service provider or by running your own server on a Mac or Windows machine. The FTP system is a very valuable tool and usually essential to setting up an Internet site.

Chapter 5

Providing Information through Electronic Mail

*A*lthough the World Wide Web dominates the media about the Internet, the basic tools available to Net surfers and site developers are what bring the Internet to life. This chapter looks closely at another Internet tool that you should consider whenever you develop an Internet site.

More people use electronic mail, also known as *e-mail*, than they use any other Internet utility. Current estimates place the number of e-mail users in the tens of millions. All commercial online services — such as CompuServe, America Online, and Prodigy — provide Internet e-mail to their customers. Furthermore, organizations of all sizes are creating links between their internal e-mail systems and the Internet.

E-mail isn't as fancy as the World Wide Web, but in many ways, e-mail is a more practical and useful way to distribute information — especially when your site may appeal to Net surfers who cannot support the additional bandwidth demands of the Web.

Consider international visitors to your site. In some countries, the Web is not available to users on the Internet because their communications network simply cannot handle the flow of graphics through the system. You must make allowances for delivery of information even when the Web is not appropriate.

Knowing that the Web is not available to everyone on the Internet makes e-mail an even more interesting tool for the Internet site developer. Keep in mind that even though e-mail is not as glamorous as the World Wide Web, it is the single most widely used tool on the Internet. On the Net, new users and old-timers alike know and understand e-mail, and they use it every day.

The enormous number of people who use e-mail as part of their businesses makes the number of World Wide Web users seem insignificant. If you want to reach as many people as possible and provide information in a way that works for the average user, e-mail is the answer.

Many forward-thinking companies have already realized the important role that e-mail plays in communicating with other Internet users. Qualcomm, a tele-communications engineering company, uses e-mail to distribute information about job opportunities. Anyone who wants information about Qualcomm jobs can send e-mail to `jobs@qualcomm.com`. This special e-mail address illustrates several advantages of e-mail compared with other Internet information resources:

- ✔ The address is easy to remember.
- ✔ It's simple to advertise.
- ✔ It's accessible to every person who has e-mail access.
- ✔ It's less complicated to use than Gopher, FTP, and the Web.

Another common use for e-mail is providing contact information and a basic introduction to Internet users who want to know more about an organization. Companies often use a special e-mail address, such as `info@informational virtualcorporation.com`, for this purpose. The info and jobs e-mail addresses are excellent examples of the power and importance of e-mail.

By providing information through special e-mail addresses, you can target a specific audience for a specific purpose. Other information resources, such as the World Wide Web, are like your storefront and large-scale advertising efforts, whereas communicating with people through e-mail is like having a conversation on the telephone or giving somebody your business card.

If you have plenty of time on your hands, the only thing that you need to provide information through e-mail is an e-mail account of your own. You can respond manually to each piece of incoming e-mail and send whatever information is required, but this approach is unwieldy, especially if you receive a large number of e-mail messages. One of the primary reasons to provide information through e-mail is to automate the process of communicating directly with people over the Internet. Without automation, providing information through e-mail is little better than using the telephone to talk with each caller personally.

It's tempting to think that manually replying to each e-mail request provides a bit of class and a human touch, and initially, when you and others are new to business on the Internet, it does seem to be classy. What this strategy really says, however, is that you're lagging behind other people when it comes to using your resources effectively. You have better things to do than to send your electronic brochure to every college student on the planet. Automate your responses to repetitive e-mail requests.

Providing information through your existing e-mail account

E-mail accounts are like opinions: everyone has one, and they're all different. Because e-mail accounts vary so greatly in terms of what they offer and how they work, we've decided to ignore the possibility that your existing e-mail account with CompuServe, America Online, Prodigy, or MCI, or your e-mail account at work, gives you the capability to respond to incoming e-mail automatically. This doesn't mean that you should ignore this possibility; it just means that

giving detailed instructions for non-Internet e-mail systems is beyond the scope of this book.

Regardless, you don't need to give up your existing e-mail account. If you're like most people, you've already added your e-mail address to business cards and stationery. You can obtain a new e-mail service to provide information on the Internet, but keep your existing account for your personal e-mail.

You can provide information through e-mail in three ways:

- ✔ Reply automatically, with a predefined message, to incoming e-mail.
- ✔ Use an Internet e-mail information service to fulfill specific information requests.
- ✔ Set up your own e-mail server on your personal computer.

Of the three options, automatically replying to e-mail possibly is the most important. This method is simple yet powerful and can be set up very quickly. The next section shows you how.

Replying Automatically to Incoming E-Mail

If you ever sent e-mail that never reached its destination or that wasn't replied to for weeks, you know firsthand how useful an automatic reply can be. An automatic reply tells people who send you e-mail that their mail has been received. The reply also can contain references to other information sources or tell people how to contact you in other ways.

An automatic reply is especially useful as a way to communicate with customers. If you run a store with walk-in business, you can use an e-mail address that sends an automatic reply as a way to tell people what your hours of operation are and to give directions. Add your automatic-reply e-mail address to your advertising, especially to your ad in the phone book.

You can create an automatic-reply e-mail address in three ways:

- ✔ Subscribe to an automatic-reply e-mail service on the Internet.
- ✔ Use a mail client program that has new mail filtering capability.
- ✔ Set up a UNIX shell account with an Internet service provider.

Responding automatically to e-mail through a service provider

If you subscribe to an automatic-reply e-mail service, you need only follow these steps:

1. **Create a text file of the message that you want to send as the automatic reply.**

   You can use any text editor or word processing program to create this document, as long as you save it as a text-only file.

2. **Send the text file to your service provider.**

   Your provider will give you instructions for this process. All providers are different. Some accept the message through e-mail; others allow you to fax the message to them and then retype it for you.

3. **Give out the e-mail address that the provider assigns to you.**

If you have access to e-mail, test the automatic reply by sending a message to the e-mail address yourself.

Your service provider should ask whether you need to save the e-mail that is sent to your automatic-reply account. If you choose not to save the e-mail, be sure to mention in your reply message that no human being will read the sender's original e-mail. Otherwise, people may assume that a human will get around to reading their messages eventually, even though they received an automatic reply.

If you decide to keep the e-mail that is sent to your reply account, it's important to find out from your service provider exactly where the incoming e-mail goes after the automatic reply is sent. If you already have another e-mail account, most service providers can forward these e-mail messages to that account. If you prefer, you can ask your service provider to keep the messages in a separate mailbox. Your service provider can tell you how to access those messages.

Whether you save or discard the e-mail sent to your automatic-reply account ultimately depends on the way in which you use the service. If you create a simple text file that contains your store's hours of operation and gives directions to your customers, you can safely discard every message that is sent to the automatic-reply account. On the other hand, if you use your automatic-reply account as a first contact for potential clients, you most likely will want to save the e-mail that is sent to the automatic-reply account so that you can follow up later with a more involved e-mail message — one that answers any questions posed in the original e-mail and takes your marketing effort the next step with each client.

Creating a do-it-yourself automatic reply e-mail account

This section describes two options for creating your own automatic-reply e-mail account. One option is to use a mail client program that has new mail filtering capability; the other option is to use a UNIX shell account.

New mail filtering is the capability to have your e-mail client program figure out what to do with your incoming mail, based on your instructions. Not all e-mail client programs have this capability. A popular e-mail client program for Windows that has new-mail filtering capability is called Pegasus. A version of Pegasus is available for the Macintosh as well. Also, the popular e-mail program Eudora supports new mail filtering in the commercial version. You may want to read the following section anyway, however, because it will give you a good idea of what to look for in an e-mail client program.

The *Setting Up An Internet Site* World Wide Web page always has the most up-to-date information on e-mail client programs and anything else that affects your Internet site. If you need to find an e-mail client program for your PC, this site is an excellent Internet resource. The address is:

```
http://www.science.org/internetsite/
```

Replying automatically with a large, winged horse

Pegasus, a mail client written by David Harris, is one of our favorite Windows-based e-mail client programs. The program has the capability to filter and respond to new mail as it arrives in your mailbox when you define mail-filtering rules. A *rule* is a directive that you give to your computer, as you would give an instruction to an assistant. You might tell someone, "If Bob calls, tell him I went golfing." A mail-filtering rule is similar: "If you get mail from George, file it under New Business." You don't get to type the rule in plain English, but constructing rules for handling your e-mail is very simple in Pegasus.

1. **Choose New Mail Filter from the File menu in the Pegasus program to bring up the Filtering Rules dialog box (see Figure 5-1).**

   This dialog box lists any existing rules or is empty (if you have not added rules). In this dialog box, you can edit, add, or delete rules.

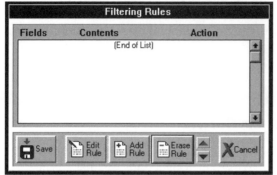

Figure 5-1:
The Filtering
Rules dialog
box.

2. **To create a new rule, click on the Add Rule button.**

   The Edit Rule dialog box appears, allowing you to define or change rules. Your rule can tell Pegasus to look for text in either the header or body of the mail message.

3. **Click on either the In these headers check box or the As an expression check box (see Figure 5-2).**

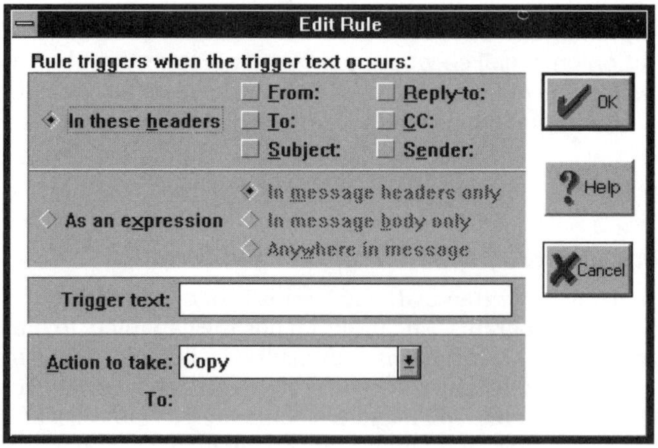

Figure 5-2:
Create rules
with this
simple
dialog box.

By checking the In these headers check box, you tell Pegasus to look for key words in the areas shown. When mail is received, Pegasus automatically looks for the words that you specify in the From, To, Subject, Reply-to, CC, or Sender headers. You can check more than one box to have Pegasus look for the text that you identify in any of the areas that you indicate.

If you check the As an expression box, you give Pegasus permission to look for information in a more global manner. Depending on what item you check, Pegasus looks for information In message headers only, In message body only, or Anywhere in the message.

4. In the Trigger text field, enter the text that will trigger the rule.

This text could be someone's name, a product name, or some key word or command that is unique enough for your computer to answer appropriately. Try to choose words that you're sure are going to appear only in the messages in which you expect them to appear. You should avoid words that are too generic or that have multiple meanings. If you tell your computer to send love letters whenever it sees the word *Sue* in the body of the message, for example, you might get an interesting reaction from an unfriendly lawyer.

5. Now tell the computer what action to take by selecting an action from the Action to take drop-down list.

Pegasus can do many things with the incoming e-mail, including move messages to a particular folder, delete them automatically, or reply to them automatically. To create an automatic-reply filter, select either Send Text File or Send Binary File.

When you select a send option from the Action to take list, the Select a File dialog box appears, allowing you to select the file that you want to send automatically in response to the incoming e-mail message.

6. Choose a file in the Select a File dialog box, and click on the OK button.

You return to the Edit Rule dialog box, where the full path of the file now appears below the Action to take list box.

7. Click on the OK button to accept your new automatic-reply rule.

Now the selected file will be sent automatically in response to messages that contain the specified trigger text.

Obviously, before you can select a file to be sent by this automatic-response method, you need to create this file. To do so, you need to use your word processing program and type the information that you want to deliver automatically. When you finish typing the information, save the file as text.

Pegasus is not a full e-mail information server, but it has valuable features that allow you to use your personal e-mail account more effectively. Pegasus is simple to use, and it's also a great e-mail client program.

Replying from a UNIX shell account

If you're a do-it-yourself type, you can create your own automatic-reply e-mail account by obtaining a UNIX shell account from a service provider. A UNIX shell account comes with its own e-mail address, and you can use a special UNIX utility, called the *vacation program,* to reply automatically to incoming e-mail.

To use the vacation program to reply automatically to incoming e-mail, you need a UNIX shell account from an Internet service provider. Your service provider must give you access to the vacation program, so be sure to ask ahead of time whether a vacation program is available.

To use the vacation program to reply automatically to incoming e-mail, follow these steps:

1. **Before doing anything else, verify that your UNIX shell account has access to the vacation program by logging in to your UNIX shell account.**

2. **Type the following command at a command prompt:**

   ```
   which vacation
   ```

   This command tells your UNIX shell account to search for the vacation program. If the account locates the vacation program, you see something like this:

   ```
   /usr/ucb/vacation
   ```

   If your UNIX shell account can't find the vacation program, you see something like this:

   ```
   no vacation in /usr/local/bin /usr/ucb /usr/bin
   ```

   If your UNIX shell account responds with a suggestion such as `Caribbean Cruise` or `Hawaii`, or with `which: Command not found`, it probably misunderstood your request. Ask your service provider for help.

3. **When you're sure that your UNIX shell account can locate the vacation program, type the following command at the command prompt:**

   ```
   touch .vacation.msg
   ```

   This command creates a new file called .vacation.msg. This file will contain the automatic-reply message to be used by the vacation program. Because editing a file in a UNIX shell account is easier said than done, we've decided to show you a way to create your reply message without editing a file. (This method isn't the only one — just the easiest.)

4. **Type the following command at the command prompt:**

   ```
   cat >> .vacation.msg
   ```

   After you type this command, your UNIX shell account doesn't display anything; it just sits there, waiting for you to type.

5. **Type the message that you want to send as your reply to incoming e-mail.**

Be sure to press Enter at the end of each line. To leave a space between paragraphs, simply press Enter twice. To include a subject in the e-mail reply, type the subject on the first line. The following is an example:

```
Subject: Automatic reply from Virtual Corporation
Thank you for sending e-mail to Virtual Corporation.
    Due to the volume of e-mail we receive, it will take
    a few days for a human being to read your message.
    If you need to contact us immediately, you can call
    (800) 555-1212 to reach any of the following
    departments:
Sales : ext. 216 Marketing : ext. 840
Public Relations : ext. 408 Human Resources : ext. 600
Be sure to check out our other Internet information
    resources:
WWW : http://www.virtualcorporation.com/
Gopher : gopher://gopher.virtualcorporation.com/
FTP : ftp://ftp.virtualcorporation.com/
Thank you for your interest in Virtual Corporation.
```

6. **When you finish typing your reply message, press Ctrl+D.**

This action saves your reply message to the .vacation.msg file and returns you to the command prompt.

If you make a mistake while typing your message, press Ctrl+D to save the incorrect message. Then erase the .vacation.msg file, using the following command:

```
rm .vacation.msg
```

Then repeat the preceding instructions, beginning with the command touch .vacation.msg.

If you prefer, you can create your reply message on your personal computer and then send it to your UNIX shell account. (Contact your service provider for help on sending a file to your UNIX shell account.)

1. **Repeat the preceding six steps.**

2. **After you send the text file, be sure to rename it, using the following command:**

```
mv TextFile .vacation.msg
```

3. **Replace TextFile with the name of your file.**

4. Type the following command to activate the vacation program:

```
vacation
```

After typing this command, you should see something like the following:

```
This program can be used to answer your mail automatically
when you go away on vacation.
You have a message file in .vacation.msg.
Would you like to see it?
```

If you don't see a similar response after typing the vacation command, contact your UNIX shell account service provider for assistance.

The last line asks whether you want to see your reply message.

5. Type y and press Enter to view your message.

After displaying your message, vacation asks if you'd like to edit it:

6. Unless you know how to edit a file in your UNIX shell account, you should type n and press Enter.

Next, vacation asks whether you'd like to enable the vacation feature by creating a .forward file.

7. Type y and press Enter.

Vacation creates the special .forward file to activate the vacation feature and then displays the following message:

```
Vacation feature ENABLED. Please remember to turn it off
when you get back from vacation. Bon voyage.
```

Now your vacation program is ready. Anyone who sends e-mail to your UNIX shell account will receive an automatic reply from the vacation program.

To turn off the vacation program, type the following command to remove the .forward file:

```
rm .forward
```

One last thing you should know is that the vacation program will, by default, send the reply message only once per week to a given e-mail address. If the same person sends e-mail to your UNIX shell account twice in one week, that person gets a reply only the first time. To change this situation, you must modify the .forward file. If you know how to modify files in your UNIX shell account, make the change described in the following paragraphs; otherwise, keep reading for a simpler way to modify the .forward file.

To modify the .forward file in your UNIX shell account, look at the original file. The original version of the .forward file should have a line something like this:

```
\youruserid, "|/usr/ucb/vacation youruserid"
```

The change that you need to make is small. Immediately following the word *vacation*, you need to insert this:

```
-t2s
```

Your new .forward file looks something like this:

```
\youruserid, "|/usr/ucb/vacation -t2s youruserid"
```

This change tells the vacation program to wait two seconds, instead of one week, before sending the reply message to the same e-mail address. This way, the vacation program responds to every message that it receives, even if a particular user has already received a reply within the past week.

If modifying this file in your UNIX shell account proves to be too difficult, you can erase the file and create a new one by following these steps:

1. **View the current .forward file by typing the following at the command prompt:**

   ```
   cat .forward
   ```

2. **At the command prompt, remove the current .forward file by typing the following:**

   ```
   rm .forward
   ```

3. **Now type the following command to create a new .forward file:**

   ```
   cat > .forward
   ```

   After you type this command, your UNIX shell account waits for you to type.

4. **Type the following (be sure to replace *youruserid* with your UNIX shell account login ID and to replace */path/vacation* with whatever was there before in the old .forward file):**

   ```
   \youruserid, "|/path/vacation -t2s youruserid"
   ```

5. **Press Ctrl+D to save the new .forward file.**

The vacation program is an excellent way to create your own automatic-reply e-mail account. If you already have a UNIX shell account on the Internet, using the vacation program won't cost you a penny.

Starting Your Own E-Mail Information Service

Automatic-reply e-mail accounts are great when you have only one message to send to people on the Internet. When you want to distribute many messages and files through e-mail, however, you need an *e-mail information server* — a program that reads incoming e-mail and responds to special commands within the message.

One command that most e-mail information servers respond to is the following request for help:

```
help
```

When an Internet user sends a message that contains the command help to an e-mail information server, the server replies with a message that contains instructions. Following is another command to which most e-mail information servers respond:

```
get filename
```

Sometimes, users type the send command instead of the get command, as follows:

```
send filename
```

When an e-mail information server receives a message that contains a command of this sort, it checks to see whether a file named *filename* exists in its file archive. If *filename* does exist, the server replies to the e-mail message by sending a copy of the file. If *filename* doesn't exist in the archive, the server replies with an error message.

Many e-mail information servers are smart enough to send help if the incoming message doesn't contain a valid command.

You can provide information through an e-mail information server in two ways:

⌐ Subscribe to an e-mail information service on the Internet.

⌐ Set up your own e-mail server on your personal computer.

The next few sections describe these two options.

Using an Internet e-mail information service provider

E-mail information service providers vary greatly in terms of the services that they offer and in the ways in which their services operate. The two commands mentioned in the preceding section — `help` and `get` (or `send`) — have become informal standards for e-mail information servers on the Internet. If the service offered by your provider doesn't support these commands, or at least the `help` command, your e-mail information server may be difficult for people to use. Before you subscribe to an e-mail information service on the Internet, ask for a demonstration, and make sure that the `help` command is supported.

The basic idea behind subscribing to an e-mail information service offered by a service provider is that you rent space for your files on the provider's computer. The provider gives you a new e-mail address, and anyone who wants to receive one of your files through e-mail sends a command to that e-mail address. The procedure is a bit like FTP, but instead of an FTP client program, e-mail messages are used to transfer files.

Providing files through e-mail has one major advantage over traditional FTP: Internet users can receive copies of your files through e-mail rather than directly from your FTP server. Because you don't need direct Internet access to receive e-mail, people still can have access to your files. If you use only FTP to transfer files to interested visitors to your site, you may be eliminating a large number of potential visitors who cannot access FTP.

To subscribe to an e-mail information service on the Internet, contact a service provider, and ask for a demonstration of its e-mail service. This demonstration typically involves sending an e-mail message to a demonstration server, so you need access to an e-mail account of your own. If you like the way that the provider's server responds to your message, sign up!

Your service provider will give you the following when you subscribe:

- The e-mail address of your new e-mail information server
- Instructions on adding files to your e-mail information server

One file that you should be sure to add to your server is a text file called index. The index file should contain a list of the files that are available from your e-mail information server. This file enables users of your e-mail information server to retrieve a list of available files by sending a command like this:

```
get index
```

Depending on the service provider, you also may need to create or modify the file that is mailed to users when they ask for help. After you do that, your e-mail information server is ready to respond to messages and to send files through e-mail to anyone on the Internet.

Telling others how to access your e-mail information server

To tell other people how to access your e-mail information server, give them the e-mail address of your server. You also may want to provide simple instructions, similiar to this:

```
Virtual Corporation has an e-mail information server. To
access it, send e-mail to infobot@virtualcorporation.com,
with the word "help" in the body of the message.
```

You can use a special type of hyperlink in the World Wide Web to create a link to an e-mail address. This special type of hyperlink is called a *mailto* link. Here's an example:

```
mailto:infobot@virtualcorporation.com
```

To turn a mailto link into a World Wide Web hyperlink, create an anchor, using the mailto syntax. The following HTML line creates such an anchor:

```
<A HREF="mailto:infobot@virtualcorporation.com">Send us e-mail</A>
```

An HTML anchor is used to create a hyperlink in the World Wide Web. For instructions on creating anchors and HTML documents, refer to Chapter 3.

The mailto syntax doesn't serve any purpose outside the World Wide Web. Adding a mailto link to your stationery or to your business card, for example, wouldn't make sense. Simply give people your e-mail address so that they can request more information about your site by using the get index command.

Making money with your e-mail information server

E-mail information servers are similar to FTP, World Wide Web, and Gopher servers in that anyone on the Internet can obtain information from them. You normally can't charge for *access* to your files, but you can charge for the *use* of your files.

Some e-mail information service providers offer a special type of e-mail information service that does allow you to charge for access to your files. With this service, you create user accounts and passwords for each person who accesses your e-mail information server. To retrieve a file from your e-mail information server, a user must include his or her password in the e-mail message, along with the file request. If the password is valid, the file is sent, and the user's account is billed accordingly.

Using Your Personal Computer As an E-Mail Server

If your computer has a direct connection to the Internet, you can set up your own e-mail server. An *e-mail server* is a program that receives e-mail from other computers and then routes the mail to its destination. With an e-mail server of your own, you can create both automatic-reply e-mail accounts and e-mail information servers without paying extra to your Internet service provider. As a result, you don't need to worry about breaking open the piggy bank if you need to provide many types of information through several automatic-reply e-mail accounts.

Best of all, because your computer acts as an Internet e-mail server, you can create as many normal e-mail accounts as you need at no extra charge. If you run a small- or medium-size business, this method is the best way to give your employees Internet e-mail accounts of their own.

All e-mail servers on the Internet speak the same language: *Simple Mail Transfer Protocol*, or SMTP (pronounced *ess em tee pee*). Don't confuse an e-mail server, which actually speaks SMTP, with an e-mail information server, which simply reads incoming e-mail and responds to commands within the message. Because an e-mail server speaks SMTP, it can receive e-mail directly from other e-mail servers. E-mail information servers, which can't speak SMTP, must rely on an e-mail server to function.

To run your own SMTP-based e-mail server on your personal computer, your computer must be directly connected to the Internet. You need a domain name of your own (explained in Chapter 3), and your Internet access provider must provide domain-name service for your domain to allow people on the Internet to send mail to your e-mail server.

How to set up an e-mail server without a direct Internet connection

SMTP e-mail servers on the Internet are designed to deliver mail directly to their intended recipients. These servers have a motto similar to that of their physical counterparts: "Neither line noise, nor network congestion, nor power outages shall keep an e-mail server from its appointed tasks." But if *your* e-mail server isn't available when another e-mail server wants to deliver a message, your e-mail could end up in Larry's closet in Argentina.

SMTP was meant to be used to deliver mail between e-mail servers that reside on the Internet. If your e-mail server is available on the Internet for only a few minutes each day because you don't have a dedicated Internet connection, other SMTP servers may have trouble delivering your e-mail. A few Internet access providers have special e-mail services that eliminate this problem, but this new type of SMTP e-mail service isn't common yet. It's very important that you talk with your access provider about the implications of running your own SMTP e-mail server without dedicated Internet access.

If you don't have a direct Internet connection, SMTP isn't the best way to receive e-mail from your service provider. UNIX to UNIX Copy (UUCP) — a communications protocol that exchanges files between two computers automatically — is a much better option for receiving Internet e-mail if you're going to connect to the Internet only occasionally. UUCP is designed to do what SMTP has trouble with: deliver e-mail to computers that don't have a direct connection to the Internet.

At least one UUCP software package is available for MS-DOS and Macintosh, but it's complicated, and we don't like using it. Other UUCP packages for Windows and Macintosh will be available soon; these packages will enable you to do everything described in this chapter without a direct Internet connection. More important, Internet access providers everywhere soon will offer SMTP e-mail service that is reliable even if your connection to the Internet isn't.

Besides communicating with other Internet e-mail servers through SMTP, an e-mail server provides normal e-mail accounts to individual users. When delivering e-mail to individual users, an e-mail server acts a little like an electronic post office. E-mail messages arrive at the post office and are delivered to each person's electronic mailbox. To pick up their e-mail, users must request their e-mail from the e-mail server, using the *Post Office Protocol* (*POP*).

E-mail servers that speak Post Office Protocol are known as *POP servers*. POP is an important term to remember because the people who have e-mail accounts on your server must use a program known as a *POP client* to retrieve e-mail stored in their electronic mailboxes. The most common POP client is a program called *Eudora,* although many POP clients exist for every type of computer. For the most part, there is no difference between a POP client and a normal e-mail client because most e-mail clients use the Post Office Protocol.

Are you blown away by all the acronyms — SMTPs, POPs, UUCPs? Perhaps this brief wrap-up will help:

- ✔ An e-mail server is a program that receives e-mail from other computers and then routes the mail to its destination.

- ✔ Post Office Protocol (POP) is the protocol that sorts and delivers mail on an SMTP server to the appropriate user's mailbox.

- ✔ UNIX to UNIX Copy (UUCP) is a communications protocol that exchanges files between two computers automatically.

- ✔ Simple Mail Transfer Protocol (SMTP) is the language that all e-mail servers on the Internet speak.

- ✔ An e-mail information server is a program that reads incoming e-mail and responds to special commands within the message.

- ✔ The vacation program is a UNIX utility used to reply automatically to incoming e-mail.

- ✔ An automatic-reply e-mail account is a service that you set up to provide mail to be sent when interested parties request information. You can use your Internet service provider or your own system to set up this account.

- ✔ Larry's closet is the place where your e-mail goes if the electronic post office misplaces it.

Setting up your Windows e-mail server

One of the software packages that inspired this book is WinSMTP Daemon, written by Jack De Winter. WinSMTP Daemon is a complete Windows SMTP server that supports both automatic-reply and e-mail information server e-mail accounts. The server also is a functional POP server, which you can use to set up as many e-mail accounts as you want. For all these features, you pay a one-time charge of $50 for the shareware version or $100 for the enhanced commercial version.

To run WinSMTP Daemon, you need Windows 3.1 or Windows 95 and TCP/IP access to the Internet through a Winsock-compliant communications program. Be sure to communicate extensively with your Internet access provider when you set up your e-mail service so that the provider fully understands what you're doing. This communication will help your provider configure its computers to work correctly with your WinSMTP Daemon and will keep your e-mail from getting lost.

To begin, obtain the WinSMTP software, and install it on your computer. You can find WinSMTP on the World Wide Web at `http://www.seattlelab.com/`

WinSMTP has a simple installation utility that copies the software to the directory of your choice. We installed WinSMTP in the following directory:

```
C:\WINSOCK\WINSMTP
```

Create a program icon in the Program Manager for WinSMTP, and double-click on the icon to run the program. A license notice appears, followed by the WinSMTP Daemon main window (see Figure 5-3).

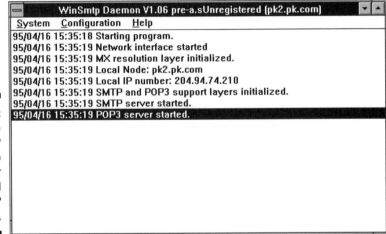

Figure 5-3:
Run the
WinSMTP
program to
start your
SMTP and
POP
servers.

When you start WinSMTP for the first time, it uses the settings in your existing Internet software to configure itself; the main window shows you some of the settings that it chooses. Even if WinSMTP gets everything right, checking the detailed configuration, just to be sure, is a good idea.

To configure WinSMTP, follow these steps:

1. Choose System from the Configuration menu.

The System Options dialog box, shown in Figure 5-4, appears. For WinSMTP to work, you must set up the four sections of the System Options dialog box correctly.

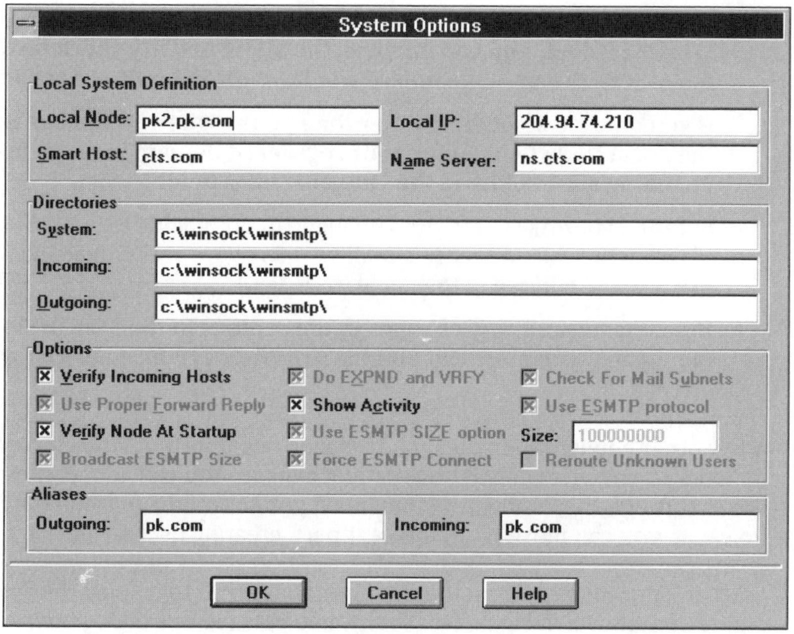

Figure 5-4:
Change the
configuration
of WinSMTP
by using the
System
Options
dialog box.

2. **In the Local Node field, enter the full name of the computer on which you're running WinSMTP.**

   In the example shown in Figure 5-4, the computer's name is pk2.pk.com. Be certain that the Local Node field contains the full domain name of your computer.

3. **Enter your computer's IP address in the Local IP field.**

4. **In the Smart Host field, enter the full name or the IP address of your Internet access provider's e-mail server.**

   This host is the computer to which outgoing e-mail will be directed if WinSMTP decides to allow another e-mail server to help deliver certain messages.

5. **Make certain that each of the directories listed in the Directories section is valid.**

   System is the directory in which you installed WinSMTP. The Incoming and Outgoing directories determine where e-mail is stored as it is processed by WinSMTP. The same directory can appear in all three fields.

   You probably won't need to change anything in the Options section unless your Internet access provider tells you to do so.

6. **If you don't want to see a play-by-play narration of everything that WinSMTP does, you can uncheck the Show Activity check box, but leave the other settings alone unless you have a good reason to change them.**

7. **If you entered something other than your registered domain name in the Local Node field, enter your registered domain name in both the Incoming alias field and the Outgoing alias field.**

   Entering your registered domain name in both fields tells WinSMTP that it's okay to send and receive mail by using your real domain name instead of the name entered in the Local Node field.

8. **If you have made any changes in the settings in the System Options dialog box, you must exit and restart WinSMTP for your changes to take effect.**

A few other configuration dialog boxes may be important if you have a complex network or an unusual mail-transfer mechanism. You can access these dialog boxes through the Configuration menu. If you're setting up a standard system, however, you can move on to the best part: creating user e-mail accounts.

You can choose Users from the Configuration menu to display the System Users dialog box, shown in Figure 5-5. Every time you see this dialog box, think about all the people in the world who pay unreasonable rates for a single e-mail account through an online service — and even then may be charged for each e-mail message that they send. This dialog box releases you from the prison of online-service e-mail by enabling you to create your own Internet e-mail accounts on your WinSMTP e-mail server.

The System Users dialog box allows you to create five types of e-mail accounts. By creating different types of accounts, you can do more with your WinSMTP server than simply receive e-mail. The five account types are:

- Alias
- User
- Responder
- Forward
- Mailing List

Alias accounts

Alias accounts, which are the simplest type, just provide other names by which particular users can receive e-mail. Figure 5-5 shows that the adm account is an alias for the user named root, which means that any e-mail sent to adm will be directed to the user named root.

You can create as many aliases as you need by following these steps from the System Users dialog box:

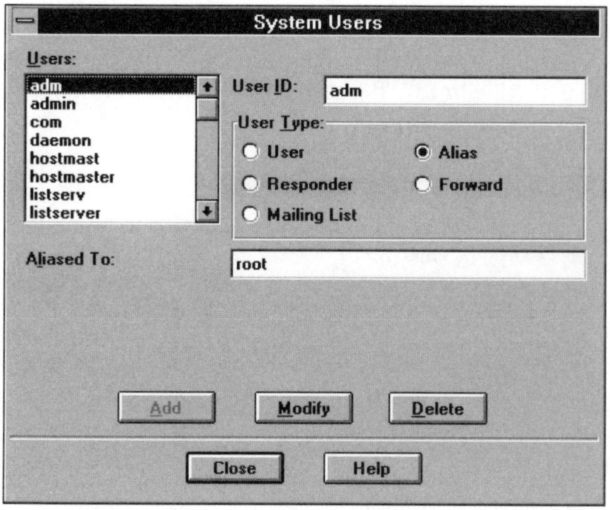

Figure 5-5:
Create
Internet
e-mail
accounts on
your
WinSMTP
server
through the
System
Users dialog
box.

1. **Type a user ID for the new alias account in the User ID field.**

   The user ID should not contain spaces.

2. **Click on the Alias radio button in the User Type box.**

3. **In the Aliased To field, type the user ID of the existing user for whom you want to create an alias.**

4. **Click on the Add button to create the new alias.**

User accounts

User accounts are the normal e-mail accounts through which people send and receive mail. Each person who has a User account on your WinSMTP server can use a POP client, such as Eudora, to access his or her mailbox.

To create a new User account, follow these steps from the System Users dialog box:

1. **Type a user ID for the new account in the User ID field.**

   The user ID should not contain spaces.

2. **Click on the User radio button in the User Type box.**

3. **Type the user's full name (or any other descriptive text) in the User Name field (see Figure 5-6).**

4. **Enter a password for the account in the Password field.**

   The user must supply this password to access his or her account on your WinSMTP server. As you type the password, each character appears as an asterisk (*), so enter the password carefully.

5. Verify that the Mailbox field contains an acceptable filename.

The mailbox file usually is given a name similar to the User ID (see Figure 5-6). This file is the file in which e-mail will be stored for this user.

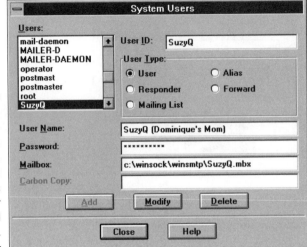

Figure 5-6:
Add User accounts to create individual mailboxes for your e-mail users.

6. Enter an e-mail address in the Carbon Copy field, if you want to send a copy of the messages received by this user to another e-mail address.

7. Click on the Add button to accept the new user.

The User ID is the name that other people will use to send e-mail to this user. The user's full e-mail address is his or her user ID, followed by @ (the *at sign*) and then by your registered domain name, as in the following example:

```
UserID@virtualcorporation.com
```

Responder accounts

Responder accounts allow you to set up an automatic-reply e-mail account or a full e-mail information server by using WinSMTP. To create a new Responder account, follow these steps from the System Users dialog box:

1. Type the User ID for the Responder account in the User ID field.

The ID used in this example is info.

2. Click on the Responder radio button in the User Type box (see Figure 5-7).

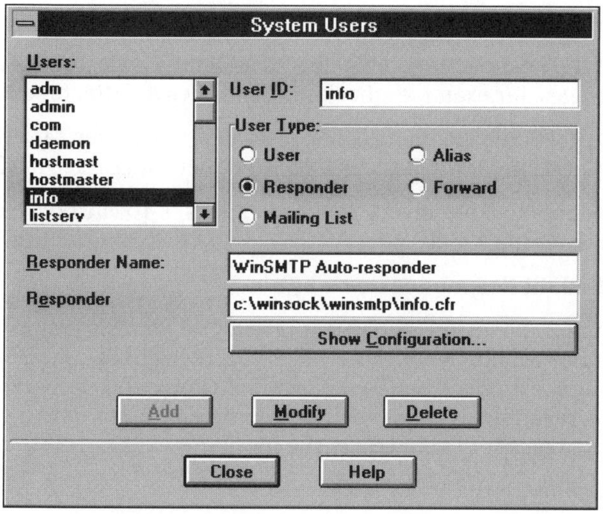

Figure 5-7:
Create a
Responder
account to
set up an
automatic-
reply
account or
an e-mail
information
server.

```
┌──────────────────── System Users ────────────────────┐
│ Users:                     User ID:  [info          ] │
│ ┌───────────────┐┌─┐      ┌─User Type:────────────┐   │
│ │ adm           ││▲│      │ ○ User      ○ Alias    │   │
│ │ admin         ││ │      │ ● Responder ○ Forward  │   │
│ │ com           ││ │      │ ○ Mailing List         │   │
│ │ daemon        ││ │      └────────────────────────┘   │
│ │ hostmast      ││ │                                    │
│ │ hostmaster    ││ │  Responder Name:                   │
│ │ info          ││ │  [WinSMTP Auto-responder        ]  │
│ │ listserv      ││▼│  Responder                         │
│ └───────────────┘└─┘  [c:\winsock\winsmtp\info.cfr   ]  │
│                          ┌────Show Configuration...───┐ │
│                          └────────────────────────────┘ │
│         ┌───Add───┐  ┌──Modify──┐  ┌──Delete──┐          │
│         └─────────┘  └──────────┘  └──────────┘          │
│              ┌───Close───┐   ┌──Help──┐                  │
│              └───────────┘   └────────┘                  │
└─────────────────────────────────────────────────────────┘
```

3. **Enter a descriptive name for the responder in the Responder Name field.**

   The Responder Name is just for decoration, so use any name you want.

4. **Verify that the filename listed in the Responder field is okay; then click on the Show Configuration button to open the Configure Auto-responder dialog box, shown in Figure 5-8.**

   The Responder file is the file in which you want to store the configuration information for this Responder account.

Figure 5-8:
Configure
your auto-
responder
so that it
can reply to
incoming
e-mail
properly.

```
┌──────────────── Configure Autoresponder... ─────────────────┐
│ ☒ Send Files Only On User's Request  ☐ Send Files As Attatchments │
│ ☐ Copy User With Messages         [                        ]     │
│ ☒ Log Responses To File           [response.log           ]     │
│         ┌──────Browse Response File...──────┐                    │
│         └───────────────────────────────────┘                    │
│         ┌──────Edit Responder Items...──────┐                    │
│         └───────────────────────────────────┘                    │
│      ┌───OK───┐   ┌──Cancel──┐   ┌──Help──┐                      │
│      └────────┘   └──────────┘   └────────┘                      │
└─────────────────────────────────────────────────────────────────┘
```

5. **To use this Responder account as an e-mail information server, check the Send Files Only On User's Request check box.**

   This option tells the Responder account not to respond with a file unless the incoming e-mail contains a valid file request. Otherwise, uncheck this box so that the Responder will reply to any incoming e-mail by sending the file or files that you specify.

6. Change the other settings to meet your needs.

If you want the Responder to send files as attachments instead of as normal e-mail messages, for example, check the Send Files As Attachments box.

To send a copy of the incoming e-mail messages to another e-mail address, check the Copy User With Messages box and then enter the e-mail address.

To log responses to a file, check the Log Responses To File box and then enter a name for the log file.

7. Click on the Edit Responder Items button.

The dialog box shown in Figure 5-9 appears. You use this dialog box to tell the Responder which files it can send. If you checked the Send Files Only On User's Request check box in the last dialog box, the Responder sends a file only if it receives an e-mail message containing a command such as the following, in which *filename* is in the file list:

```
send filename
```

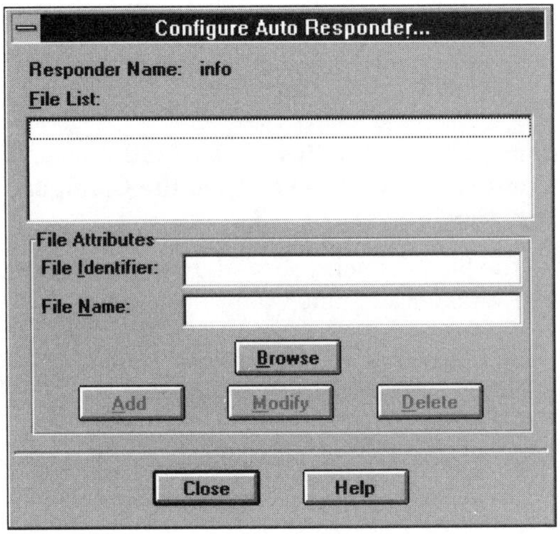

Figure 5-9: Configure your auto-responder by adding to the file list.

8. To add an item to the file list, enter a file identifier and a filename; then click on the Add button.

If you don't know the name of the file, click on the Browse button to select one from the Open dialog box.

9. When you finish adding to the file list, click on the Close button.

Figure 5-10 shows the file list for a simple Responder account.

10. Click on the OK button in the Configure Autoresponder dialog box to accept your changes and return to the System Users dialog box.

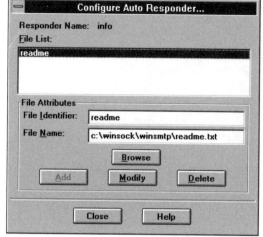

Figure 5-10:
Add as
many files
as you want
to your
Responder
account's
file list.

Forward accounts

Sometimes, you have to forward mail for a particular user to a new e-mail
address. If an employee named John leaves your company and goes to work for
another, for example, you may want to forward his mail to his new e-mail
address (depending, of course, on how much you like John and what his reason
was for leaving your company).

To forward mail to another e-mail address, you create a *Forward account*. If you
want to create a Forward account with the same name as an old User account
(as in the case of your ex-employee, John) you first must delete the old User
account. Select the User account from the list in the System Users dialog box,
click on the Delete button, and then follow these steps to add a new Forward
account:

1. **Type a User ID for the new Forward account.**

   If you're replacing an old user account, the user ID should be the same as
   the old User account.

2. **Click on the Forward radio button.**

3. **In the Forwarded To field, enter the new address to which e-mail should
   be forwarded (see Figure 5-11).**

4. **Click on the Add button to accept the new account.**

5. **When you finish adding users, click on the Close button.**

Chapter 6 presents the Mailing List account type in detail.

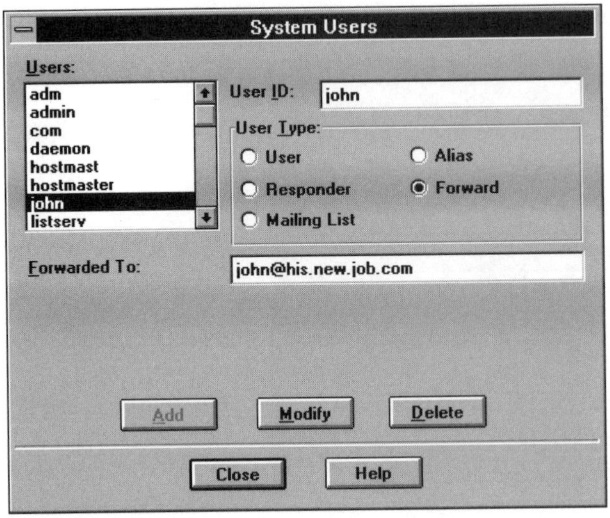

Figure 5-11:
Using a
Forward
account to
forward
e-mail
automatically.

Using WinSMTP if you have only dial-up TCP/IP Internet access

WinSMTP is an ideal Internet e-mail server for Windows if you have a direct, dedicated, TCP/IP Internet connection. WinSMTP also is designed to work if you have only *dial-up* TCP/IP access to the Internet, meaning that you are connected only while sitting in front of your computer using the Internet, and can't keep your connection up all day every day. To enable dial-up mode, follow these steps:

1. Choose Mode from the Configuration menu.

The System Mode dialog box appears, giving you two options:

  ✔ Network Always Present

  ✔ Dialup To Network

2. Click on the Dialup To Network radio button to enable dial-up mode.

3. Select a time interval from the Force Connection drop-down list.

This selection tells WinSMTP how often to connect to the Internet to send and receive e-mail — which is where dial-up mode becomes a little confusing.

Because SMTP wasn't designed to operate in dial-up mode, Jack De Winter added a feature that gives WinSMTP the capability to force your Internet access provider to send any mail that's waiting to be delivered to your computer. This way, WinSMTP can connect to the Internet, receive any incoming mail that's waiting to be delivered, and then disconnect.

If your Internet access provider doesn't support this feature, you have to remain connected to the Internet until your access provider's computer decides to try delivering your mail again. This process can take several hours, which means that you must connect to the Internet for several hours each day to receive your new mail. Ask your Internet access provider if it supports this WinSMTP feature; if not, ask for that support.

Setting up an e-mail server on a Macintosh

A great e-mail server package called MailShare is available free for the Macintosh. MailShare, written by Glenn Anderson, is a full Simple Mail Transfer Protocol and Post Office Protocol server program that makes your Macintosh a complete Internet e-mail server. To set up automatic-reply, e-mail information server, and Mailing List accounts, use an add-on product called AutoShare. To find more documentation on AutoShare and a link to download MailShare on the Web, go to the following URL:

```
http://www.science.org/internetsite/
```

To run MailShare and AutoShare, you need a Macintosh that runs System 7 or later. You also must have MacTCP 1.1.1 or later, and you need TCP/IP access to the Internet. Be sure to communicate extensively with your Internet access provider when you start using MailShare so that the provider knows what you're doing and can better meet your needs.

Installing Mailshare

To configure Mailshare, follow these steps:

1. **Obtain the MailShare software, and install it on your computer.**

2. **Double-click on the MailShare icon to start the program.**

   The program starts and displays a Debug window (shown in Figure 5-12) that tells you more about your MacTCP configuration.

3. **If any of this information seems to be incorrect, check the configuration of MacTCP, using the MacTCP Control Panel.**

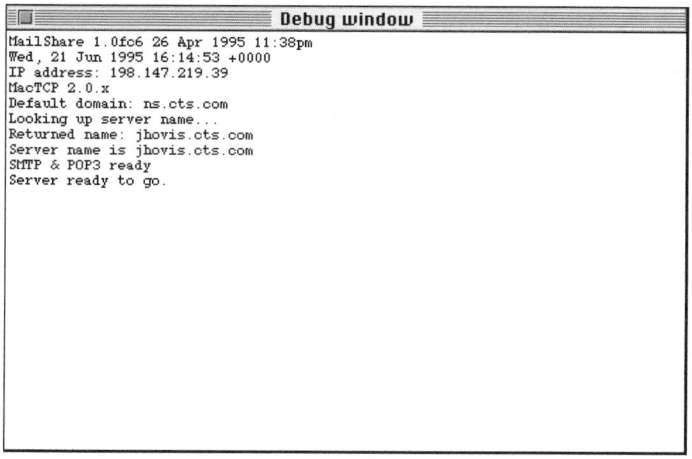

Figure 5-12:
Verify your
MailShare
setup by
reading the
Debug
window.

```
▁▁▁▁▁▁▁▁▁▁▁▁▁▁▁▁ Debug window ▁▁▁▁▁▁▁▁▁▁▁▁▁▁▁▁
MailShare 1.0fc6 26 Apr 1995 11:38pm
Wed , 21 Jun 1995 16:14:53 +0000
IP address: 198.147.219.39
MacTCP 2.0.x
Default domain: ns.cts.com
Looking up server name...
Returned name: jhovis.cts.com
Server name is jhovis.cts.com
SMTP & POP3 ready
Server ready to go.
```

The Debug window also gives you important messages when MailShare is running, particularly if something goes wrong. Check this window often to make sure that your e-mail server is functioning correctly.

4. **Choose Account Information from the Server menu to set up user accounts on your e-mail server.**

   The Account Information dialog box, shown in Figure 5-13, appears.

Figure 5-13:
Add, edit, or
remove user
accounts
with the
Account
Information
dialog box.

5. **Click on the Add button to add a new user.**

6. **Enter a name in the User name field.**

   This name should not contain spaces because it will be part of the address to which other Internet users send e-mail.

7. **Type a Password for this user account.**

   The user must specify this password to access his or her e-mail with a POP client.

8. **Enter the user's full name in the Full name field.**

9. **Check the Account enabled check box.**

10. **Check the Login enabled check box.**

11. **Click on the Save button to save the new user.**

12. **Choose Preferences from the Server menu.**

    This command displays the MailShare Preferences window, shown in Figure 5-14.

13. **Verify that the settings shown in the dialog box — especially the default server name — are acceptable.**

    The default server name should match the name of your computer.

14. **If everything is okay, click on the close box in the upper-left corner of the window.**

15. **Restart MailShare if you change the settings in this window.**

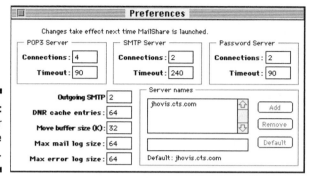

Figure 5-14:
Verify your
MailShare
Preferences.

Installing AutoShare

Next, you should obtain the AutoShare software and install it on your computer.
Figure 5-15 shows the AutoShare 1.0 folder, which contains two other folders.
The main AutoShare software is located in the AutoShare folder; the Samples
folder contains important files that you will use to configure AutoShare. The
first step in configuring AutoShare is checking the Map Control Panel.

Figure 5-15:
Install
AutoShare
and open
the
AutoShare
1.0 folder.

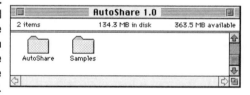

To check the panel and then install AutoShare, follow these steps:

1. **Choose Map from the Control Panel in your Apple menu.**

   AutoShare uses the Map Control Panel (see Figure 5-16) to determine the
   time and date in your area of the world.

2. **Click on the map or click on the Find button to choose a city near you.**

3. **Open the Samples folder, and click on the Auto folder.**

4. **Choose Duplicate from the File menu.**

   Figure 5-17 shows the Samples folder with the new copy of the Auto folder.

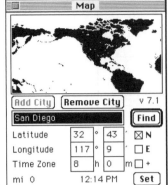

Figure 5-16:
Choose the
city in which
you live.

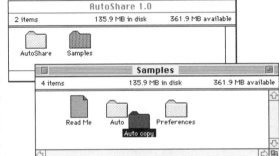

Figure 5-17:
Duplicate
the sample
Auto folder.

5. **Move the Auto copy folder to the root folder of your hard drive.**

   You can change the name of the folder to something other than Auto copy,
   if you want, but doing so is not necessary. Inside the Auto copy folder, you
   will find several folders that AutoShare requires. (For simplicity, we're
   assuming that you have not renamed the Auto copy folder.)

6. **Close the Samples folder, and open the AutoShare folder.**

   Figure 5-18 shows the AutoShare folder.

7. **Double-click on the AutoShare icon to start the AutoShare program.**

   When AutoShare starts, a blank window titled Status appears. A warning
   message is likely to appear at the bottom of this window, instructing you to
   reconfigure AutoShare (see Figure 5-19). Because you haven't yet configured AutoShare in the first place, this warning is not surprising.

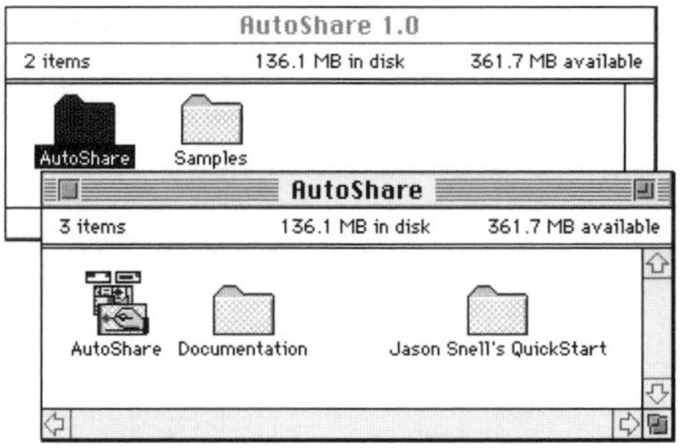

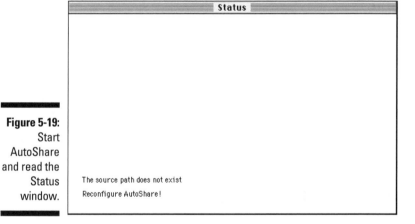

Figure 5-18:
Double-click
on the
AutoShare
icon to start
AutoShare.

Figure 5-19:
Start
AutoShare
and read the
Status
window.

Now that you've started AutoShare, the first thing that you need to do is tell AutoShare where to find the AutoShare folders. The AutoShare folders are the ones inside the Auto copy folder. Follow these steps:

1. **Choose Folders from the Preferences menu to access the AutoShare folders configuration screen, shown in Figure 5-20.**

2. **Click on the Select button (next to the Filed Mail folder field), and choose the Filed Mail folder inside the Auto copy folder (see Figure 5-21).**

   This action tells AutoShare which folder to use for incoming e-mail.

3. **Then click on the Select Filed Mail button to select the folder.**

4. **Select the Incoming Mail folder inside a MailShare folder named Mail Folder, located in your System Folder.**

5. **Click on the Select button next to the Incoming Mail folder field, and choose the Incoming Mail folder inside the Mail Folder. (Look in your System Folder for these folders.)**

6. **Click on the Select Incoming Mail button to select the Incoming Mail folder (see Figure 5-22).**

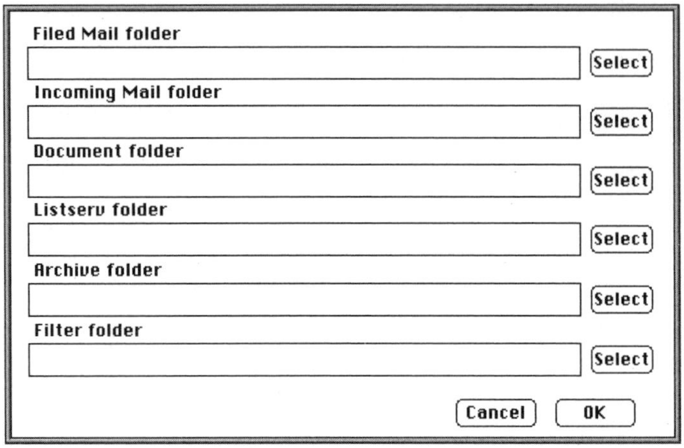

Figure 5-20:
Tell
AutoShare
where to
find its
folders.

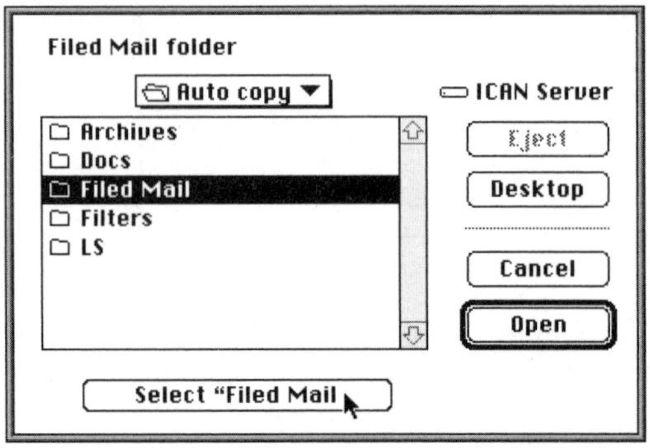

Filed Mail folder
[   ] [Select]
Incoming Mail folder
[   ] [Select]
Document folder
[   ] [Select]
Listserv folder
[   ] [Select]
Archive folder
[   ] [Select]
Filter folder
[   ] [Select]

[Cancel] [OK]

Figure 5-21:
Select
AutoShare's
Filed Mail
folder.

Filed Mail folder
[📁 Auto copy ▼]   ▭ ICAN Server
📁 Archives   [Eject]
📁 Docs
📁 **Filed Mail**   [Desktop]
📁 Filters
📁 LS   [Cancel]
                                       [Open]
[Select "Filed Mail"]

Figure 5-22:
Select the
Incoming
Mail folder,
located
inside the
System
Folder.

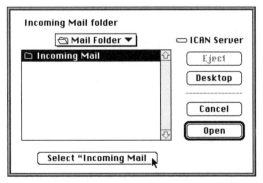

Incoming Mail folder
[📁 Mail Folder ▼]   ▭ ICAN Server
📁 **Incoming Mail**   [Eject]
                                       [Desktop]
                                       [Cancel]
                                       [Open]
[Select "Incoming Mail"]

7. **Choose Docs, LS, Archives, and Filters to set up the remaining four folders that you need. They are located inside the Auto copy folder.**

Now your screen should look something like Figure 5-23, with all the folder fields filled.

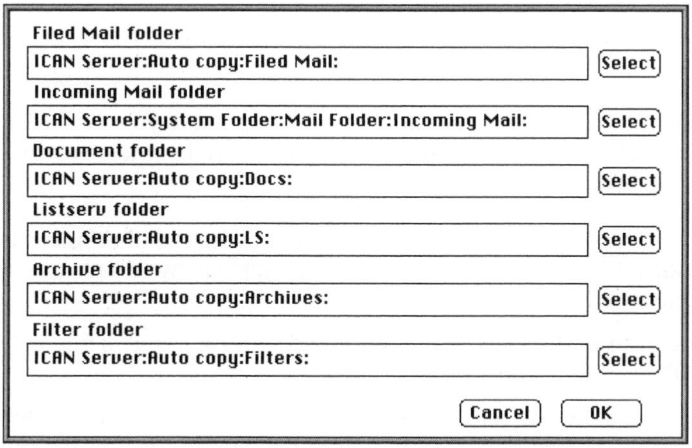

Figure 5-23:
Choose a folder for each of the folder fields.

Filed Mail folder
ICAN Server:Auto copy:Filed Mail: [Select]
Incoming Mail folder
ICAN Server:System Folder:Mail Folder:Incoming Mail: [Select]
Document folder
ICAN Server:Auto copy:Docs: [Select]
Listserv folder
ICAN Server:Auto copy:LS: [Select]
Archive folder
ICAN Server:Auto copy:Archives: [Select]
Filter folder
ICAN Server:Auto copy:Filters: [Select]

                                              [Cancel] [OK]

8. **Click on the OK button to accept these folders.**

The Status window reappears, no longer displaying the reconfigure warning.

9. **Choose Miscellaneous from the Preferences menu to access the AutoShare Preferences window, shown in Figure 5-24.**

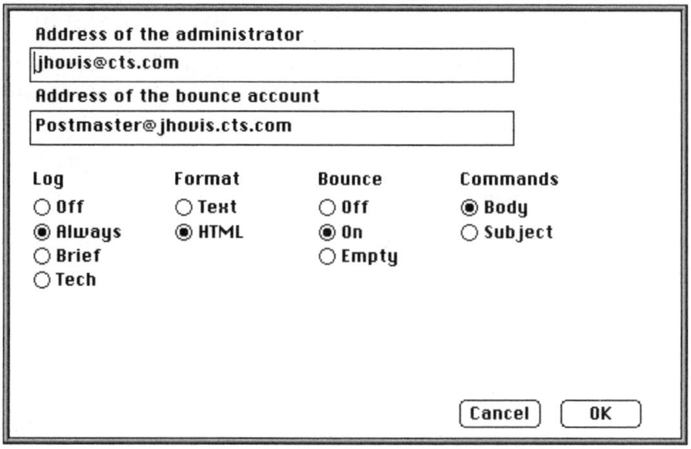

Figure 5-24:
Configure miscellaneous AutoShare preferences.

Address of the administrator
jhovis@cts.com
Address of the bounce account
Postmaster@jhovis.cts.com

Log   Format   Bounce   Commands
○ Off   ○ Text   ○ Off   ⦿ Body
⦿ Always   ⦿ HTML   ⦿ On   ○ Subject
○ Brief   ○ Empty
○ Tech

                                              [Cancel] [OK]

10. **Change the address of the Bounce Account to Postmaster@*host.domain* (*host.domain* is the full domain name of your computer, as displayed in the MailShare Debug window).**

    In our example, the computer's domain name is `jhovis.cts.com`. Be sure that the address of the administrator contains your correct e-mail address; otherwise, important AutoShare messages will not reach you.

    The remaining preferences most likely are acceptable as they appear by default.

Now that AutoShare is fully configured, you can create your first automatic-reply account. The following instructions show you how to create an automatic-reply account named info.

1. **To create an info account in MailShare, switch to MailShare, and choose Account Information from the Server menu to bring up the Account Information dialog box.**

2. **Type info in the User Name field, and enter a password in the Password field.**

3. **Type a Full name, such as Auto-reply info acct, and make sure that the Account enabled check box is checked.**

4. **Uncheck the Login enabled check box because this automatic-reply account will not be accessed with a POP mail client.**

Login enabled needs to be checked only for e-mail accounts that a human being will use to receive e-mail. When Login is enabled, a person can retrieve his or her e-mail from your server by using a POP client such as Eudora.

5. **Select Save as files from the Forwarding drop-down list.**

    This selection tells MailShare that all incoming e-mail for the info account should be saved as individual files in the location that you specify.

6. **In the field below the Forwarding list box, type the name of your Filed Mail folder, just as it appears in Folder Preferences within AutoShare (refer to Figure 5-23).**

    Be sure to leave off the trailing colon; MailShare doesn't like folder names that end with a colon.

    Figure 5-25 shows how your Account Information window should appear at this point. (Remember to use your own Filed Folder line instead of the one that appears in this figure.)

7. **Switch to the Finder, and open the Auto copy folder on your hard drive.**

Figure 5-25:
Create an
info account
in
MailShare.

8. **Open the Docs folder within Auto copy, and create a new folder by choosing New Folder from the file menu.**

9. **Change the name of the new folder to info.**

10. **In the info folder, create a new file named Default (see Figure 5-26).**

    AutoShare will send the contents of the Default file automatically in reply to any e-mail message sent to the info account.

This procedure is all there is to setting up an automatic-reply e-mail account with AutoShare and MailShare. To set up an e-mail information server account — one that provides many files and sends only the ones that users request — simply create an automatic-reply e-mail account and add files to the account's AutoShare folder.

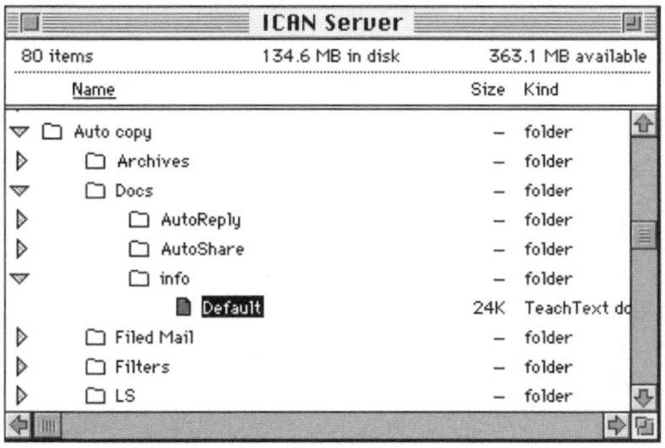

Figure 5-26:
Create a
new file
named
Default
within the
info folder.

To request a file, an Internet user need only send to your automatic-reply account an e-mail message that contains the name of the file. AutoShare looks in the automatic-reply account's folder within the Docs folder, and if it locates the requested file, it sends a copy to the requester. The special file named Default is sent automatically in reply to any e-mail message that doesn't contain a valid file request.

What to Do with Your E-Mail Information Server

Immediately upon setting up an e-mail information server, you can begin doing several creative things. Whether or not you do the things described in this section, you should at least incorporate your e-mail information resource into your World Wide Web page by using a `mailto` link. Adding an e-mail information server to your home page makes your Internet presence more interactive — and also sets your company apart from those that seem to believe that the World Wide Web is the only thing on the Internet that matters.

Send binary files through e-mail

To send binary files through e-mail, you first must encode the file using a utility like *BinHex* or *UUEncode*. When you *encode* a binary file, it is converted to text-only format. This text-only file then can be sent through e-mail, and all the recipient needs to do is *decode* the message to end up with a binary file again. Many e-mail readers decode the message automatically, making it even easier for people to receive and use your binary files.

Several programs available on the Internet allow you to UUEncode and UUDecode files. You can obtain more information about UUEncode and UUDecode online. The *Setting Up an Internet Site* home page can also help you. You can reach this page at the following URL:

```
http://www.science.org/internetsite/
```

The entire process of sending a binary file with e-mail sometimes confuses the receiver. With so many people just coming on to the Internet, one more step in receiving and sending files may be too much for many people to handle.

For documents that do not rely on specific formatting and for those documents that don't include graphics, consider sending them in text format. This procedure eliminates the need for you to UUEncode or BinHex encode the file — and, more important, relieves the recipient of the responsibility for knowing how to deal with this strange-looking file that you sent.

Provide World Wide Web documents

One of the neatest things that you can do with your e-mail information server is provide World Wide Web documents. When Internet users retrieve one of your documents through e-mail, they can save that document to a file on their personal computers and then view it with their Web browsers. If the users have TCP/IP connections to the Internet, they can click on any hyperlink in your document; their Web browser will respond exactly the way that it (the Web browser) would if the user had contacted your HTTP server to view the document. This method is a creative way to provide World Wide Web documents without running an HTTP server or paying a publishing service for the use of its server.

An e-mail information server is just as important to your Internet site as a World Wide Web home page. There's no better way to distribute information than e-mail because it allows you to reach more people cheaper and faster than other methods. Also, e-mail allows you to find out exactly who contacts you. E-mail is true two-way communication — something that any psychologist or business professional knows is an essential part of any relationship (even an electronic one).

Chapter 6

Setting Up an Automated Electronic Mailing List

● ●

In This Chapter

▶ Creating a mailing list for your Internet site

▶ Using an Internet service provider to run a mailing list

▶ Turning your mailing list into an interactive information resource

● ●

*S*ince the days of jungle drums and smoke signals, man has looked for ways to broadcast information to groups of people. Automated-mailing-list software is this century's answer to that age-old challenge. Send e-mail to an automated mailing list, and the mail is distributed automatically to everyone who subscribes to that list.

An *electronic mailing list* is exactly what it sounds like: a list of e-mail addresses. Like traditional mailing lists, you can use electronic mailing lists to send the same message to many people at the same time.

Anyone can create an electronic mailing list simply by compiling a list of e-mail addresses. Many e-mail programs allow you to create such a list. Some of the programs even allow you to define special groups — family members, corporate departments, work groups, and any other type of group.

This type of electronic mailing list is so straightforward that we're not covering it in this chapter. If you want to create this type of electronic mailing list, start collecting e-mail addresses of people to whom you want to send e-mail; then ask your e-mail service provider for help if you need a few tips on sending e-mail to those people.

 You can't prevent people from adding your e-mail address to their mailing lists. The fact that e-mail is very inexpensive to send (free, in most cases) makes electronic junk mail (unwanted e-mail) a fact of life that isn't going to change any time soon.

This chapter covers a type of electronic mailing list that is more useful: automated electronic mailing lists. An *automated electronic mailing list* is a list of e-mail addresses, with a few twists:

- ✔ Anyone can add his or her e-mail address to an automated mailing list by sending a special subscribe request via e-mail.

- ✔ Anyone can remove his or her e-mail address from an automated mailing list by sending a special unsubscribe request by e-mail.

- ✔ The mailing list makes it possible for anyone to send a message to everyone on the mailing list without compromising the privacy of the mailing-list subscribers.

People choose to be part of an automated mailing list. When they no longer want to receive e-mail through the mailing list, they remove their e-mail addresses from the list. This sense of freedom makes people much more comfortable with the idea of subscribing in the first place. There have been some cases in which users have had difficulty getting their names removed from a list, but when they send a complaint to everyone on the list, they find that the problem is solved quickly.

If you want to create your own electronic mailing list, make it an automated mailing list. An automated mailing list is a valuable information resource for its members, and because people decide to join the mailing list, you stand less chance of sending e-mail that your recipients consider to be junk. Some automated electronic mailing lists have tens of thousands of subscribers. These mailing lists are a very effective way of delivering excellent Internet content.

Mail-bomb headaches

If you've been on the Internet for a while, you've probably received several pieces of electronic junk mail. You may even have been affected by one of the infamous electronic mail bombs that continue to grab media attention. Electronic mail bombs sound really sinister, but you really have no reason to be scared; they sound worse than they really are. A mail bomb can cause some electronic headaches but won't cause physical harm to you or your computer.

An *electronic mail bombing* occurs when somebody sends thousands and thousands of e-mail messages, all at the same time, to a list of e-mail addresses with the intention of causing havoc.

This massive flood of e-mail often causes a computer's hard drive to fill up, preventing the system from functioning correctly until the e-mail is deleted. Sometimes, this situation causes valid e-mail to get lost because the computer's e-mail server is disabled temporarily.

Unfortunately, the e-mail sent in an electronic mail bombing usually is vicious, vulgar, hateful, and threatening. And that's just the replies sent to the mail bomber by the people who are affected by the bombing; the original message in the e-mail bomb often is even worse. Electronic mail bombs are examples of radical abuse of electronic mailing lists.

Creating Automated Mailing Lists for the Listless

You can set up an automated mailing list in two ways:

✔ Establish mailing-list service with a service provider on the Internet.

✔ Set up an automated mailing list server on your personal computer.

Either way, the setup process is straightforward when you know the anatomy of an automated mailing list. One of the mailing list's vital organs is its e-mail address, which is known as the *mailing-list address*. This address is where people send e-mail if they want that mail to go to the entire mailing list. A mailing-list address can be something like the following:

```
mailinglist@virtualcorporation.com
```

The mailing-list address is connected to the *list-request address* — the address to which people send `subscribe` and `unsubscribe` requests for the mailing list. Remember that all the messages sent to a mailing list end up in all subscribers' electronic mailboxes. No one wants a mailbox full of "please add me to the mailing list" requests, so commands of this sort are sent to the list-request address instead. The list-request address usually is the name of the mailing list, followed by `-request`, as in the following example:

```
mailinglist-request@virtualcorporation.com
```

The list-request address is connected to a *mailing-list server* — the program that makes the mailing list possible. The server maintains the list of e-mail addresses for the mailing list and responds to commands sent to the list-request address. If you have subscribed to mailing lists on the Internet, you may have encountered two common mailing-list server programs: MajorDomo and Listproc.

The mailing-list server is connected to the mailing-list manager's (or administrator's) e-mail address. The mailing-list manager is the person who oversees the operation of the mailing list server. The mailing-list server (the listserver software that reports errors) and the members of the mailing list, need to know who the mailing-list manager is so that they can send messages to a human being if problems occur.

If the mailing list is moderated, the mailing-list moderator's e-mail address is connected to the mailing-list server. A *mailing-list moderator* is a person who reads each message submitted to the mailing list and then approves or declines it. If the moderator approves a message, it is sent to everyone on the mailing list; if the moderator declines a message, members of the mailing list never see it.

Mailing-list moderators can be very valuable if they do their jobs. By reviewing all the mail that comes to a list before it gets posted to everyone, a moderator can screen posts that don't need to be read by the entire list. The moderator may choose to eliminate duplicate posts on a subject, posts that have nothing to do with the list, and solicitation posts (product sales, announcements, and so on) that the moderator deems will waste the reader's time. The work of a good list moderator can save the members of the list a great deal of time, because members don't have to weed through the additional messages that these types of lists can generate.

Keep these important points in mind:

- ✔ Electronic mailing lists are lists of e-mail addresses.

- ✔ Automated electronic mailing lists are interactive lists of e-mail addresses to which Internet users can subscribe and unsubscribe at will. The term *mailing list* is used on the Internet to refer to an automated electronic mailing list.

- ✔ A mailing-list address is the address to which a mailing-list subscriber sends e-mail so that it will be distributed to the other mailing-list subscribers.

- ✔ The list-request address is the e-mail address to which subscription requests are sent to an automated electronic mailing list.

- ✔ A mailing-list server is a software program that makes an automated electronic mailing list possible.

- ✔ A mailing-list manager is the person who oversees the operation of an automated electronic mailing list.

- ✔ A moderated mailing list is a mailing list in which each message sent to the list is approved or rejected by a mailing-list moderator.

- ✔ A mailing-list moderator is a person who approves or rejects messages that are sent to a moderated mailing list.

Using an Internet automated-mailing-list service

Many Internet service providers offer automated-mailing-list services. One of our favorite service providers — Web Communications in Santa Cruz, California — offers a unique World Wide Web interface to its mailing-list server. To set up a new mailing list through Web Communications, you simply fill out a form (see Figure 6-1). Users still interact with your mailing list by using e-mail.

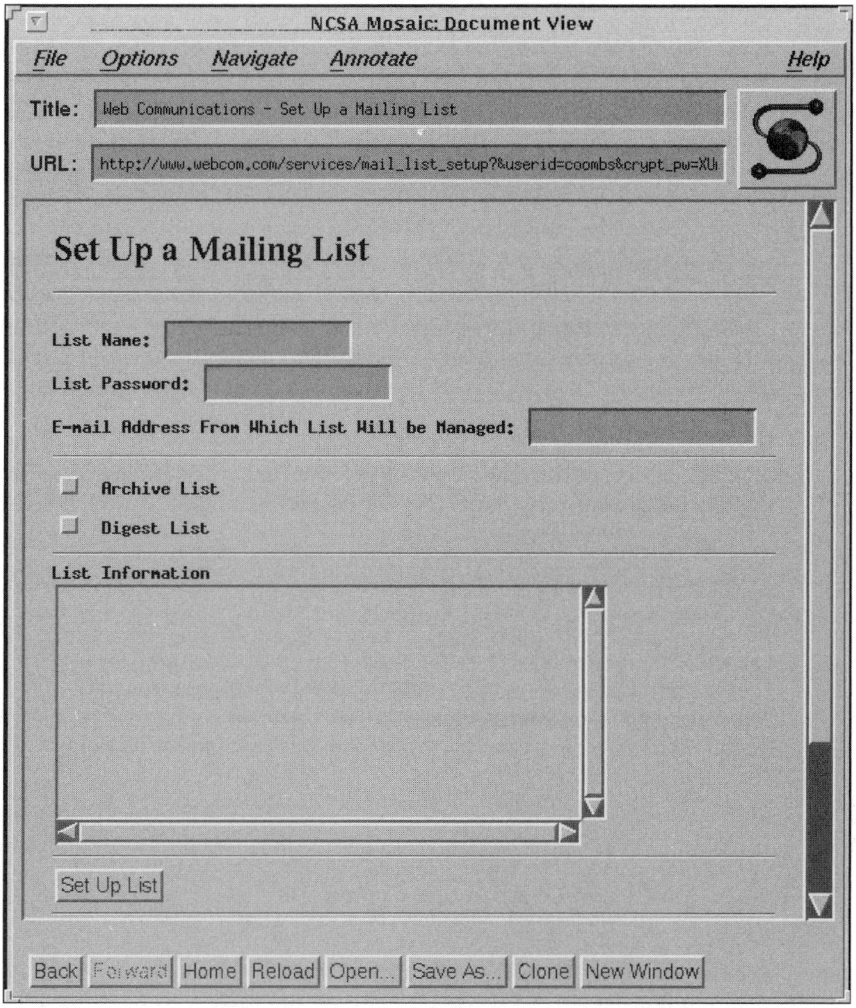

Figure 6-1:
Setting up a new mailing list is easy with a Web interface.

Other service providers' mailing-list services may not be as easy to use, but you shouldn't have too much trouble as long as the provider that you choose gives you reasonable instructions. Unfortunately, all the services provide different listservers; otherwise, we'd tell you exactly how to use them. Just remember these key elements:

- ✔ Your mailing list needs a name and a mailing-list address.
- ✔ Your mailing list needs a list-request address.
- ✔ You must provide the mailing-list manager's e-mail address at some point.
- ✔ You need to decide whether to set up a moderated or an unmoderated mailing list.

You'll probably want your mailing list address to use your registered domain name. Using your registered domain name is something you need to work out with your service provider. Typically you need to send the provider a monthly fee in exchange for using the provider as your domain-name server. Your domain-name service will apply to other services that your provider may offer, such as FTP and Web service.

Subscribing to your automated mailing list

Mailing lists can be public (you advertise your list) or private (for family members or internal company communications, for example). Chapter 13 provides tips on how to advertise your mailing list to the public.

Whether your mailing list is public or private, Internet users need to join your mailing list before they can send or receive mailing-list messages. To join your mailing list, a user must send to your list-request address an e-mail message that contains the following command:

```
subscribe ListName
```

ListName is the name of the mailing list to which the user wants to subscribe. Giving instructions to people on how to subscribe to your mailing list is simple. The following text provides instructions on accessing a mailing list called mailinglist:

```
To join Virtual Corporation's automated mailing list, send
e-mail to mailinglist-request@virtualcorporation.com,
including the following command in the body of the message:
subscribe mailinglist
```

Another option is to tell people how to obtain help on using your mailing list. Your mailing-list software can respond automatically by sending a help file so that people can find out more about the mailing list before subscribing. Here is an example of instructions you can give people so that they can get help from your listserver:

```
For instructions on using Virtual Corporation's automated
mailing list, send e-mail to
mailinglist-
request@virtualcorporation.com,
including the following
command in the body of the message:
help
```

After a person subscribes to your mailing list, he or she can send a message to the subscribers on the list by sending e-mail to the mailing-list address.

Creating an Automated Mailing List on Your PC

An automated-mailing-list-server program is a cross between an automatic-reply e-mail system and a simple electronic mailing list. Instead of responding to file requests, however, the automatic-reply component of a mailing-list server accepts subscription and cancellation requests from Internet users.

Setting up an automated-mailing-list software package involves two steps:

1. **Configuring the automatic-reply account**

2. **Creating a mailing list**

The following sections show you how to perform these steps with Windows and Macintosh mailing-list software.

Using your Windows e-mail server to run a mailing list

The same software that allows you to run a full Internet e-mail server on your Windows-based PC, WinSMTP, allows you to set up automated mailing lists. (For instructions on setting up WinSMTP, see Chapter 5.) This section describes using WinSMTP to set up a mailing list called setupshop — a mailing list for discussions about setting up shop on the Internet. Follow these steps:

1. **Run WinSMTP and then choose Users from the Configuration menu.**

   The System Users dialog box appears.

2. **In the User ID field, type the user ID for the new mailing list (in this case,** setupshop**).**

3. **In the User Type section, select Mailing List.**

4. **In the Mailing List Name field, type a descriptive name for the mailing list.**

   Be sure to verify that the Mailing List field contains a valid path and filename.

5. **Click on the Add button to add your new mailing list.**

   Figure 6-2 shows a sample setting.

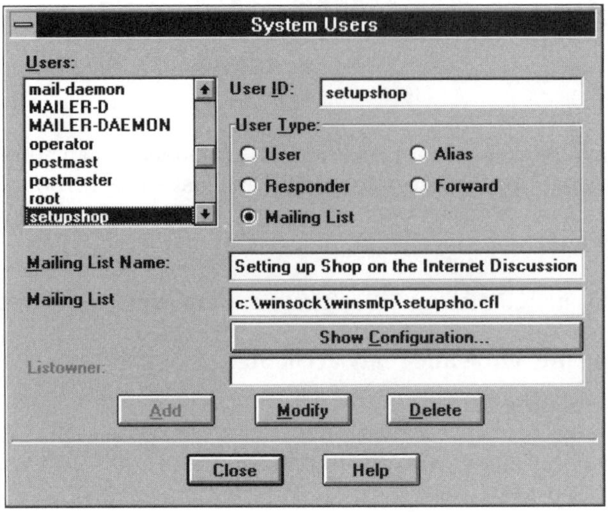

Figure 6-2:
Add a new
mailing-list
user to
create an
automated
mailing list.

Now follow these steps to configure your new mailing list:

1. **Click on the Show Configuration button in the System Users dialog box.**

   The Configure Mailing List dialog box appears (see Figure 6-3).

2. **Check or uncheck configuration items to set up your mailing list.**

Figure 6-3:
Configure
your mailing
list so that it
operates the
way you
want it to.

The settings shown in Figure 6-3 are good for a typical mailing list. Be sure to check the Send Welcome and Send Footer check boxes; then select a file to send for each. Then your software will automatically add a welcome message and footer information to each message it sends.

3. Click on the OK button.

Your mailing list is ready. To manage the mailing list, choose Mailing List Maintenance from the System menu. The dialog box shown in Figure 6-4 appears, displaying a few statistics and allowing you to edit the member list manually. (Remember that list members usually add their names to your list.)

Figure 6-4:
Manage
your mailing
lists by
using the
Mailing Lists
dialog box.

To edit the member list for one of your mailing lists manually, select the mailing list from the Mailing Lists box and then click on the Edit Members button. The List Members dialog box appears (see Figure 6-5). This dialog box displays the member list and allows you to add, modify, and delete members.

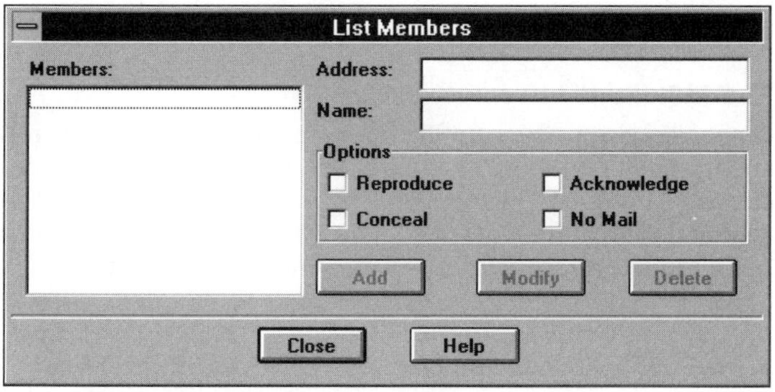

Figure 6-5:
Add, modify,
or delete
members
manually
by using
the List
Members
dialog box.

To add a new mailing-list member manually, follow these steps:

1. **Type the new member's e-mail address in the Address field.**

   If the Address field is already filled in, just type over its contents.

2. **Type the member's full name in the Name field.**

3. **Set any options you want for this new user by making selections in the Options section.**

4. **Click on the Add button to add the new member.**

Deleting members is easy; just click on the member's e-mail address in the Members box and then click on the Delete button. To modify a member's entry, select the member in the Members box; make your changes; and then click on the Modify button.

Using your Macintosh to run a mailing list

Two good Macintosh mailing-list software packages are available on the Internet. AutoShare (which you learned about in the preceding chapter) and Macjordomo (discussed in this chapter) are complete automated-mailing-list servers.

Macjordomo uses a different approach to receiving incoming e-mail. AutoShare relies on MailShare to put new e-mail in the Filed Mail folder. Macjordomo, on the other hand, uses POP to retrieve new e-mail from an e-mail server. You can use Macjordomo with any e-mail server that supports POP, not just MailShare.

AutoShare is ideal if you also use MailShare and want to run a mailing list. If you don't use MailShare, Macjordomo is a good alternative. The following sections show how to use these software packages to create and run an automated mailing list on your Macintosh.

Creating a mailing list in AutoShare

AutoShare mailing lists, like AutoShare automatic-reply accounts, rely on MailShare accounts that store incoming e-mail in the Filed Mail folder. To use AutoShare as an automated-mailing-list server, you first must create a MailShare account named AutoShare. This account serves as the subscription and cancellation request address for all the mailing lists that you create in AutoShare.

To create the AutoShare account in MailShare, follow these steps:

1. **Switch to MailShare and choose Account Information from the Server menu.**

2. **Click on the Add button to add a new account.**

3. **Type** AutoShare **in the User name field.**

4. **Enter a password (any password).**

5. **Type** AutoShare Listserver **in the Full name field.**

6. **Check the Account enabled check box.**

7. **Uncheck the Login enabled check box.**

8. **Choose Save as files from the Forwarding drop-down list.**

9. **In the entry field below the Forwarding list box, type the Filed Mail folder name.**

   This name should match the *Filed Mail folder* selection when you configured AutoShare (see Figure 6-6). Be sure to leave off the trailing colon.

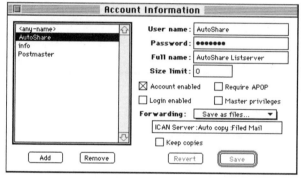

Figure 6-6:
Create a
MailShare
user
account
named
AutoShare.

10. **Click on the Save button to save the AutoShare account.**

Like an automatic-reply account in AutoShare, the special account that you just created in MailShare needs a corresponding folder in the Docs directory. The difference is that this account is a special AutoShare account that needs more than a few simple files in its folder; it needs a lot of special script files with specific names. Luckily, the AutoShare user-account folder and its required script files are already installed in your Docs folder (see Figure 6-7). This AutoShare folder was provided for you when you copied the Auto folder from AutoShare 1.0 Samples.

The Default file in the AutoShare user-account folder contains helpful instructions, including a full list of commands that the AutoShare mailing-list server recognizes. This file is sent in reply to messages that don't contain a valid command. Edit the contents of the Default file to customize it for your setup. Double-click on the Default file to open it and then follow these steps:

1. **Replace the domain name in the e-mail address** (autoshare@domain) **with your computer's full domain name.**

ICAN Server			
101 items	134.3 MB in disk		363.5 MB available
Name	Size	Kind	Last Modified
▽ 🗀 Auto copy	—	folder	Thu, Jun 22, 1995, 3:32 PM
▷ 🗀 Archives	—	folder	Sun, May 14, 1995, 3:33 PM
▽ 🗀 Docs	—	folder	Thu, Jun 22, 1995, 2:51 PM
▷ 🗀 AutoReply	—	folder	Thu, Jun 22, 1995, 3:13 PM
▽ 🗀 AutoShare	—	folder	Mon, May 29, 1995, 2:55 PM
📄 Default	16K	TeachText document	Mon, May 29, 1995, 2:59 AM
📄 Get	16K	TeachText document	Sun, Feb 26, 1995, 7:01 PM
📄 Help	16K	TeachText document	Tue, May 23, 1995, 12:00 AM
📄 Index	16K	TeachText document	Sun, Feb 26, 1995, 5:13 PM
📄 List	8K	TeachText document	Sun, Dec 4, 1994, 8:56 AM
📄 Query	8K	TeachText document	Sun, May 14, 1995, 3:05 PM
📄 Release	16K	TeachText document	Sun, Feb 26, 1995, 8:22 PM
📄 Review	8K	TeachText document	Thu, Jan 12, 1995, 7:47 PM
📄 Set	16K	TeachText document	Thu, Jan 12, 1995, 9:09 AM
📄 Sub	16K	TeachText document	Thu, Jan 12, 1995, 8:38 AM
📄 Sub.fun-1	16K	TeachText document	Sun, May 14, 1995, 3:06 PM
📄 Unsub	16K	TeachText document	Thu, Jan 12, 1995, 8:20 PM
📄 Which	16K	TeachText document	Sun, Feb 26, 1995, 8:02 PM
▷ 🗀 info	—	folder	Thu, Jun 22, 1995, 3:50 PM
▽ 🗀 Filed Mail	—	folder	Thu, Jun 22, 1995, 3:55 PM
▷ 🗀 Filters	—	folder	Sat, Apr 1, 1995, 9:55 AM
▷ 🗀 LS	—	folder	Sun, May 14, 1995, 3:54 PM

Figure 6-7:
The
AutoShare
user-
account
folder must
contain
scripts for
mailing-list
operation.

2. **Replace listmaster@domain with your full e-mail address.**

3. **Notice the address <list>@domain; you need to replace this address with the address of your mailing list.**

   If you don't know the address of your mailing list yet, remember to come back to this step later.

4. **Add a few pleasantries to make the message friendlier.**

5. **Save the file.**

Another file, named Help, exists in the AutoShare user-account folder. Unfortunately, the Help file isn't as helpful as the Default file. Delete the Help file so that the Default file will be sent in reply to messages that contain the help command.

With the AutoShare account set up in MailShare and the AutoShare folder present within the Docs folder, you are ready to create a mailing list. Creating a mailing list is very easy. The following exercise shows you how to create a sample mailing list named fun-l.

First, you must create three MailShare accounts for the mailing list. Follow these steps:

1. **Switch to MailShare and choose Account Information from the Server menu.**

2. **Type fun-l in the User name field.**

3. **Give the account a password.**

4. **Type something in the Full name field.**

5. **Uncheck the Login enabled check box.**

6. **Make sure that the Account enabled check box is checked.**

7. **Choose Save as files from the Forwarding drop-down list.**

8. **In the box below the Forwarding list box, type the full name of the Filed Mail folder (see Figure 6-8).**

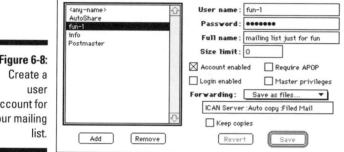

Figure 6-8:
Create a
user
account for
your mailing
list.

9. **Click on the Save button.**

The fun-l user account is the e-mail account for the fun-l mailing list. This account needs two support accounts, named fun-l.m and fun-l.d. Every AutoShare mailing list needs three MailShare accounts, as in this example. The names of the mailing-list support accounts must contain .m and .d extensions, as in this example.

To create the two support accounts for the fun-l mailing list, follow these steps:

1. **Choose Account Information from the Server menu.**

2. **Enter** fun-l.m **in the User name field.**

3. **Enter a password.**

4. **Enter a name in the Full name field.**

5. **Choose Mailing list from the Forwarding drop-down list.**

6. **In the box below the Forwarding list box, type the following:**

   RootFolderName:Auto copy:LS:fun-l.m

   RootFolderName is the name of the root folder on your hard drive (see Figure 6-9).

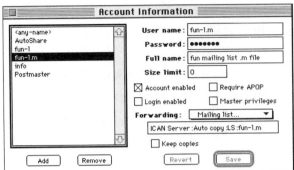

Figure 6-9:
Create a *.m*
support
account.

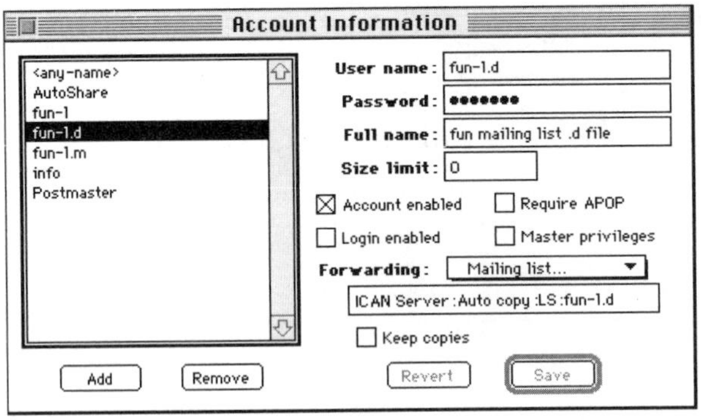

Figure 6-10:
Create a *.d*
support
account.

7. Click on the Save button.

Repeat the preceding steps to create a fun-l.d account. Figure 6-10 shows the fun-l.d account in MailShare.

Next, open the LS folder in Auto Copy and create a file named fun-l (see Figure 6-11). This file stores the list of subscribers to the mailing list. The LS folder may already contain a fun-l file. If so, double-click on the file to edit its contents. Remove the sample e-mail addresses and save the empty file.

Now the fun-l mailing list is ready to use. To subscribe to the mailing list, Internet users need to send a message to AutoShare@*your.domain.name* (the AutoShare e-mail address uses your computer's domain name instead of *your.domain.name*), including the following command:

```
SUBSCRIBE fun-l FirstName LastName
```

FirstName and *LastName* are the user's first and last names. To get help on using your AutoShare mailing-list server, a user can send a message that contains the help command — or no command at all — to the AutoShare e-mail address.

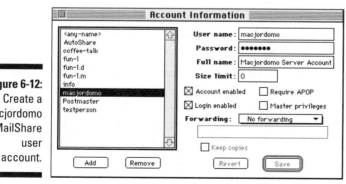

Figure 6-11:
Create a
fun-l file to
store the
list of
subscribers.

Serving a delicious mailing list with Macjordomo

Using Macjordomo with MailShare to run a mailing list is easy. The first step is creating a Macjordomo user account in MailShare. The Macjordomo user account serves the same purpose as the AutoShare user account described in the preceding section; it acts as the automatic-reply account for the mailing-list server, enabling Internet users to subscribe to and unsubscribe from your Macjordomo mailing lists.

1. **Switch to MailShare and choose Account Information from the Server menu.**

2. **Create a new user account named macjordomo.**

3. **Check both the Account enabled and Login enabled check boxes and leave Forwarding set to No forwarding (see Figure 6-12).**

Remember the password that you give this user account; you need this password to configure Macjordomo.

Figure 6-12:
Create a
Macjordomo
MailShare
user
account.

You're ready to configure Macjordomo for your subscription list. Follow these steps:

1. **Start Macjordomo and choose Subscription List from the Lists menu.**

   A Macjordomo configuration dialog box appears (see Figure 6-13). This dialog box is the most important configuration dialog box in Macjordomo. In it, you specify the Macjordomo account name and password, the name of your SMTP server for outgoing mail, and an e-mail address to which users can send messages if a problem occurs.

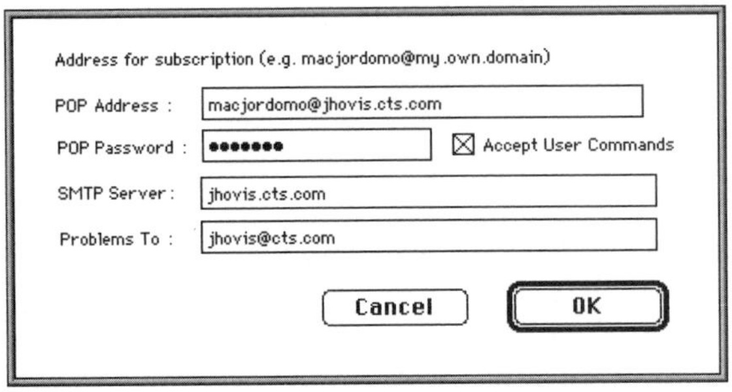

Figure 6-13: Configure Macjordomo by entering values in this dialog box.

Address for subscription (e.g. macjordomo@my.own.domain)

POP Address : macjordomo@jhovis.cts.com

POP Password : ●●●●●●●   ☒ Accept User Commands

SMTP Server : jhovis.cts.com

Problems To : jhovis@cts.com

Cancel   OK

2. **In the POP Address field, type the full e-mail address of the Macjordomo MailShare account that you created earlier.**

   In the example in the figures, the e-mail address is the name of the MailShare account (Macjordomo), followed by the @ sign and the full domain name of our computer:

   `macjordomo@jhovis.cts.com`

3. **In the POP Password field, type the password that you assigned to the Macjordomo MailShare account.**

   Each character in the password appears as a dot as you type, so be careful to enter the password exactly as you entered it when you set up the Macjordomo account.

4. **Check the Accept User Commands check box to enable command processing in Macjordomo.**

5. **In the SMTP Server field, enter the full domain name of your computer.**

   For this example, we entered `jhovis.cts.com` — the name of the computer on which we run MailShare. Remember that MailShare is your SMTP server as well as your POP server, so nothing is wrong with using the same domain name in both the POP Address and SMTP Server fields.

6. **Enter a valid e-mail address to which problem reports should be sent.**

7. Click on the OK button when you finish entering values in each field.

Next, you create a new user account in MailShare. Follow these steps:

1. Switch back to MailShare and create a new user account for your mailing list.

In the example shown in Figure 6-14, we named our mailing list coffee-talk. (All we need now is a digital picture of Mike Myers wearing a wig, and we'll have a head start on the Internet edition of "Saturday Night Live.")

Figure 6-14:
The account
is named
coffee-talk.

2. When you select a password for the mailing-list account, be sure to remember it; you need this password later.

3. Make sure that you have a check in the Login enabled check box.

4. Click on the Save button to save the new MailShare account.

Now you're ready to create a Macjordomo mailing list. Follow these steps:

1. Switch back to Macjordomo, and choose New List from the Lists menu.

The new list window appears (see Figure 6-15). Use this window to configure your new mailing list.

2. Enter the name of your mailing list in the List Name field.

In our example, the list name is coffee-talk.

3. Type the e-mail address of the mailing list in the List Address field.

4. In the POP Password field, enter the password that you assigned to the mailing-list user account.

5. In the SMTP Server and Problems To fields, enter the same values that you entered when you configured Macjordomo.

In Figure 6-15, the SMTP Server name is jhovis.cts.com, and the Problems To e-mail address is jhovis@cts.com.

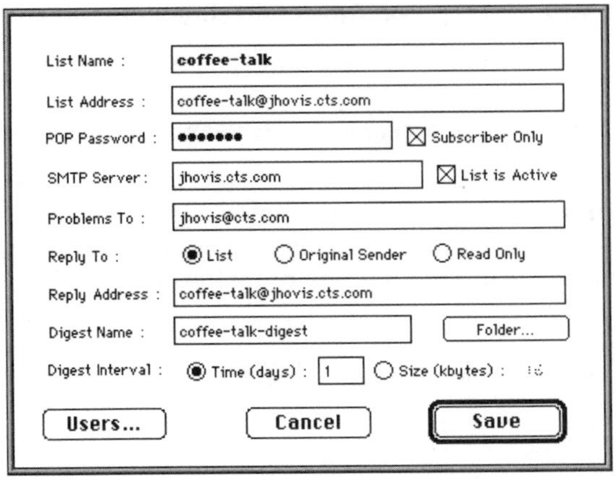

List Name :	**coffee-talk**
List Address :	coffee-talk@jhovis.cts.com
POP Password :	●●●●●●● ☒ Subscriber Only
SMTP Server :	jhovis.cts.com ☒ List is Active
Problems To :	jhovis@cts.com
Reply To :	⦿ List ○ Original Sender ○ Read Only
Reply Address :	coffee-talk@jhovis.cts.com
Digest Name :	coffee-talk-digest ⌷ Folder... ⌷
Digest Interval :	⦿ Time (days) : 1 ○ Size (kbytes) : 1⌇
	⌷ Users... ⌷ ⌷ Cancel ⌷ ⌷ Save ⌷

Figure 6-15:
Configure your Macjordomo mailing list.

6. **Check both the Subscriber Only and List is Active check boxes.**

   To create a mailing list to which anyone can send e-mail messages, leave the Subscriber Only check box unchecked. By checking this box, you tell Macjordomo to reject any e-mail message sent by a nonsubscriber.

7. **Click on the List radio button and enter the e-mail address of your mailing list again in the Reply Address field.**

   This address is the address to which subscribers will reply when they respond to a mailing-list message.

8. **Type a digest name in the Digest Name field.**

   A *digest* is like a summary file that collects mailing-list messages during the specified Digest Interval and sends the summary file to any mailing-list subscriber who instructed Macjordomo to send digests. You can set the default digest interval by changing the value in the Digest Interval field. Many users prefer digests, because they receive a single large e-mail message periodically instead of many e-mail messages continually.

9. **Click on the Save button to save these mailing-list settings.**

10. **To customize the Macjordomo response messages, choose Edit Generic Messages from the Special menu.**

    You see the Edit Generic Response dialog box, shown in Figure 6-16.

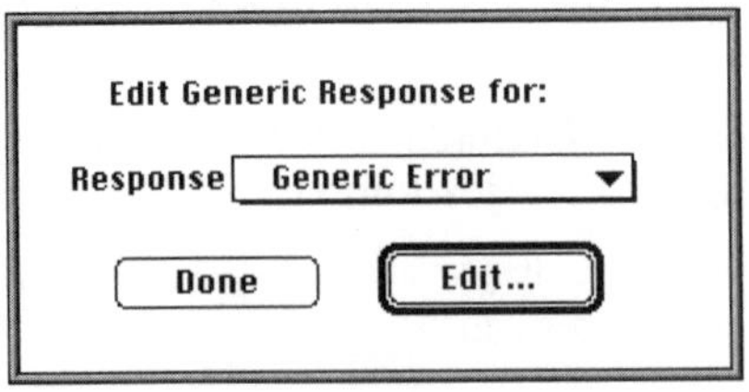

Figure 6-16:
Edit the Macjordomo response messages to customize your server.

Edit Generic Response for:
Response ⌷ Generic Error ▼ ⌷
⌷ Done ⌷ ⌷ Edit... ⌷

11. **In the Edit Generic Response dialog box, select the response message that you want to edit and then click on the Edit button.**

Figure 6-17 shows the generic Help message displayed in the edit window.

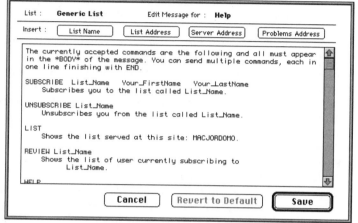

Figure 6-17: Edit the Help response message to provide your own helpful insights.

Each mailing list can have its own version of each response message.

12. **To edit the mailing-list-specific versions of these response messages, choose Edit List Messages from the Special menu and add a custom message for each type of response.**

This feature allows you to use some of your creative writing talent.

Using Your Automated Mailing List

Automated mailing lists are excellent interactive tools, and running a list of your own presents several interesting possibilities. Two possibilities that we're excited about (and that we describe in the following sections) are using your mailing list to serve World Wide Web pages and to distribute files.

Send World Wide Web documents to the mailing list

One of the best aspects of a mailing list is the fact that you can send World Wide Web documents to all the subscribers. Any World Wide Web HTML document can be sent to any mailing list without requiring additional configuration or any special type of mailing-list service. The HTML documents simply end up in the electronic mailboxes of the list's subscribers.

Why would you want to send Web documents via a mailing list? The answer is access. Remember that the World Wide Web is not available to all people on the Internet. The graphics used in Web pages place a heavy load on the connections that people have to the Internet. Dial-up connections to the Internet over older, slower modems make surfing the Web a painfully slow and annoying process. In many cases, surfing the Web is not even a viable option because of the time that downloading a graphically rich page takes.

If your objective is to distribute information, an automated mailing list may be a more efficient and more widely accessible means of delivery. The connection demands of e-mail file distribution can be insignificant compared with those of delivering the same information via the Web. The Web may be more glamorous, but e-mail can be more effective in delivering information to a larger user base of Net surfers.

To view a World Wide Web document, a subscriber simply saves the e-mail message to a file and opens that file with his or her World Wide Web browser. Any hyperlinks within the HTML document will be accessible, provided that the subscriber is connected to the Internet. If you have subscribers who don't have Internet access, they can still view your basic World Wide Web document if they have browsers; they just can't access any of the links to other Internet sites.

A mailing list becomes even more like a magazine when you send World Wide Web documents to your subscribers. Using a mailing list in this way gives you a great deal of flexibility in content, format, and advertising and opens new possibilities for interactive publishing.

Distributing files with a mailing list

Another great use for a mailing list is distribution of *binary files* (such as word-processing documents). To send a binary file through e-mail, you first must convert it to text-only format; e-mail can handle only text. The most common way to perform this conversion from binary to text is to use a program called UUEncode. After a binary file is UUEncoded (turned into text), you can send it to your mailing list, and the file will end up in the electronic mailboxes of the list's subscribers. Users must UUDecode the file to return it to its original binary form. More information on UUEncode and on sending files via e-mail is available on the Setting Up an Internet Site page on the World Wide Web. The address is:

```
http://www.science.org/internetsite/
```

Making Money with Your Automated Mailing List

An automated mailing list is similar to a traditional magazine publication. A mailing list has subscribers, each message sent to the mailing list is like a magazine article, and a successful mailing list can attract advertisers. If your mailing list is especially useful, you may be able to charge for subscriptions to the list.

You can charge for subscriptions in several ways. One popular means of charging for information is the voluntary approach. Put the information out there and indicate that if the information is useful, the user may elect to pay a specified fee. You can collect the money via traditional "snail mail" (you know, the mail delivered by the guy in the uniform walking down the street with the dogs at his heels) or through some type of online commerce system.

The voluntary approach is a low-pressure means of generating revenue from your mailing list. A more aggressive method involves requiring a subscription fee before you distribute information. In this method, you structure your mail-delivery system to provide information on how to subscribe to your list as part of the auto-response system. When a person subscribes, you add that person's name to the list, and then he or she can begin receiving your information. How you decide to collect fees for your information depends on the information that you have to deliver and on the methods that you use to attract interested users to your site.

Other money-making opportunities exist with an automated mailing list, depending on how your list is configured. If the list is moderated, you can charge to distribute messages to the mailing list. If you distribute World Wide Web documents through the mailing list, you can charge users a fee for including hyperlinks to their Internet resources in your documents. If you're going to charge, of course, you should have a loyal subscriber base and your mailing list should have enough value to support fees or advertising.

Mailing lists have a great deal to offer, both to potential subscribers and to your Internet site. An automated electronic mailing list is, in some ways, better than the World Wide Web. You can reach anyone who has an e-mail account, and you know exactly who subscribes to your list — capabilities that the World Wide Web doesn't offer yet.

A mailing list is more interactive than most World Wide Web sites, and it has a greater chance of becoming a regular tool for its users because it relies on the one resource that all users have in common: e-mail. To extend the capabilities of your mailing list and make it even more useful, you can distribute World Wide Web documents to the subscribers, thus combining the benefits of a mailing list along with the power of the World Wide Web.

The 5th Wave By Rich Tennant

"FOR ADDITIONAL BBS SUPPORT, DIAL 9, #, THE EXTENSION NUMBER DIVIDED BY YOUR ACCOUNT NUMBER, HIT THE ENTER KEY, BLOW INTO THE RECEIVER TWICE, PUNCH IN YOUR HAT SIZE, . . .

Chapter 7

Setting Up an Internet BBS

● ●

In This Chapter

▶ Deciding whether to run a BBS on the Internet

▶ Configuring Internet BBS software

▶ Providing simple access to your Internet BBS

● ●

A BBS, or *bulletin-board system* is an electronic online service accessible via computer and modem, typically at very little or no cost. BBSs are available around the world, and each one provides a unique electronic community, special-interest focus, or particular company's customer support. Anyone can run a BBS simply by connecting a computer and modem to a phone line and running special BBS software. Even the U.S. government has several BBSs — which proves that anyone can run a BBS.

A BBS differs from the Internet in one very important way — the manner in which you access the site. To contact a BBS, you must dial a specific phone number provided by the administrator of the site. To go to your favorite BBS dealing with movie reviews, for example, you must make a modem connection using a phone number for that site. When you're finished with the movie site and want to go to your favorite game BBS, you must disconnect from the movie site and then make another modem connection using another phone number. Jumping from one BBS to another really gives your modem a workout.

An Internet BBS is much simpler to use. An *Internet BBS* is an electronic online service accessible via the Internet that enables users to access BBS-style services such as discussion groups, file exchange areas, and user-to-user e-mail.

Nobody calls them BBSs anymore, though. Now they're known by a variety of names depending on the type of service they offer. For example, HotWired (`http://www.hotwired.com/`) is a superb interactive electronic magazine that resembles a traditional BBS. Even CompuServe and other commercial online services now seem like huge Internet BBSs that just happen to provide Internet access around the globe, too. The term *Internet BBS* fits as well as anything else, so it's the one we use in this chapter. In the following sections, you'll find everything you need to know to set up your own Internet BBS using a software package called FirstClass by SoftArc, Inc.

Software that enables people to work together on a computer network is often known, in the corporate world, as *groupware*. Very little technical difference exists between groupware and a BBS package.

The primary difference is that BBS software must provide a more robust set of capabilities to handle new user login, daily usage limits, more sophisticated security mechanisms, and so on. Groupware also implies features not available in traditional BBS software such as document management, workflow tracking, and other business-oriented productivity tools. SoftArc's FirstClass software is both groupware and BBS software — just one of the reasons that it is widely used in the corporate workgroup software market.

Why Set Up an Internet BBS?

The $10,000.00 question is why set up an Internet BBS? If you already have a World Wide Web site, distribute files through an anonymous FTP server, run an interactive mailing list for customer support, and have an e-mail information server and a Gopher site just to make sure that everyone in the world can access information from you on the Internet, why should you bother with an Internet BBS?

We can offer several good answers to this question. First, setting up and maintaining an Internet BBS is simple compared to setting up even the most trivial World Wide Web site. The FirstClass system touts the fact that installing the entire server portion of the program requires only two disks and takes only a few minutes to get it on your machine. Configuring the system to your liking is a simple process of pointing and clicking on icons. On the other hand, installing an Internet server package is a project that often can test the patience of a saint. A lot of effort has gone into making the FirstClass installation and configuration as seamless as possible.

Consider also the sophisticated set of interactive tools made available through these types of systems. The typical BBS software provides many of the same communication and information-sharing resources that you can find on the Internet. Items such as newsgroup-style conferencing, real-time private chat, complete e-mail support including person-to-person file exchange, and powerful database query interfaces are a few of the resources a BBS system like FirstClass offers. Even the most technical Internet expert would run and hide at the mere thought of having to provide all these features using the World Wide Web and other Internet utilities.

If this information weren't enough, consider the fact that with a BBS you control everything. You aren't at the mercy of the often aggravating Internet Anarchy. If a user of your BBS becomes inappropriate, you delete him or her by removing his or her access to your system. If you don't like the content of a certain conference or chat area, simply deny access to this part of your system. The BBS package gives you control over content, access, and privileges, features that are sometimes very elusive, if not downright impossible, to create on the Web.

The enhanced control and sophisticated communication features of a BBS open the doors to revenue-generating possibilities. Because you control everything, you can charge for access to your BBS and to any or all the resources you provide through it. Having your own BBS is like having your very own Internet kingdom, and you're the ruler.

One of the most compelling reasons for setting up a BBS on the Internet is the cost savings of using the Internet's communications backbone. Installing phone lines to enable people to access your system is expensive and requires a great deal of overhead to support your site. Remember that, as a dial-up system, the older BBS needs a phone line and modem for every person who wants to access the site at the same time. Therefore, if you have 25 people online at once checking out your site, your system requires 25 phone lines and 25 modems. If you make your BBS available via the Internet, you do not require cumbersome and expensive duplicate phone lines and modems. The Internet becomes your own private network connecting those people interested in your site to the BBS you have made available on the Net.

And to top it all off, the BBS package covered in this chapter, FirstClass, will soon provide Internet server programs including World Wide Web and built-in FTP servers. Internet users will be able to access your Internet BBS through the easy-to-use FirstClass client program or through a World Wide Web browser. Other Internet BBS and groupware programs are heading in the same direction. Lotus Notes will probably be Internet-capable soon. For people who use Lotus Notes at work, this one development represents the elimination of the last great barrier to practical telecommuting.

Pretty cool stuff, right? Makes you think that setting up a BBS on the Internet is a great idea. And it may be for the right application.

Real-world Internet BBS examples

The Internet offers a growing list of BBS applications accessible through a normal Internet connection. Many of the systems are freely accessible, but some require you to pay a fee to gain access.

Most of the BBSs using FirstClass software fall into three categories: business, education, and user groups. Some of the applications cross over into more than one of the categories. In all cases, the administrators have found a definite advantage to making their BBSs available via the Internet.

The business BBS

Many companies already have adopted some type of groupware as part of their internal communications strategy. Employees on a company local area network (LAN) can exchange e-mail, transfer files, and participate in online, live discussions through conference chats (depending on the system the corporation has chosen).

The FirstClass package has become very popular in the business market due to its simple setup and maintenance requirements. Many business network administrators familiar with the FirstClass system are seeing the benefits of going on the Net. Why? The simple reason is that with little effort, they can turn their LAN into a wide area network, or WAN.

Think about this concept for a moment. Wouldn't it be great if you had a way to connect employees, customers, and other key personnel on whom your business depends to the information they need to keep your business moving 24 hours a day, seven days a week, no matter where they are in the world?

Creating such a system is possible without the Internet if your business is willing to accept the high cost of telephone communications from remote sites around the world. With the Internet, telephone costs begin to evaporate.

In today's world of Internet communications, local Internet access is available in the majority of business centers around the world. Local access means low- or no-cost phone calls that ultimately and instantly connect your field personnel to the information they need back at the home office. The reliable security features available with BBS packages make using them both an economical and a secure business solution.

Some businesses see the Internet as a way to extend their networking capabilities dramatically without drastically increasing their networking costs. Network administrators accustomed to the FirstClass system like the fact that porting the existing package to the Internet doesn't require them to become Internet gurus to convert their LAN to a WAN quickly. Using the Internet this way brings to mind the old adage "having your cake and eating it, too!"

Customer service applications appear to be an attractive business enhancement on the Internet. Consider designing and administering a full-service customer support Internet site using the FirstClass system. This site could offer a wide array of online documentation, technical support, and customer-to-customer interface without a great deal of additional manpower for the business itself.

The manufacturer of the FirstClass system is SoftArc. You can visit its Web site by going to `http://www.softarc.com/`. Here, you will find more information about FirstClass and instructions on how to connect to its BBS via the Internet.

You also may want to look at the Canadian Jobs Exchange. This online classified section provides an easy-to-use, low-cost service for companies to announce job openings and for prospective employees to consider applying for these positions. You can visit the Web site of this BBS by going to `http://www.inforamp.net/~jelliott/`.

Just like the SoftArc site, the Canadian Jobs Exchange Web presence is nothing more than a place where administrators announce access to the BBS site for those individuals who have the FirstClass client package. Also, as with the SoftArc site, you can download a free copy of the FirstClass client so that you can find a job in Canada.

These Internet BBSs and their associated Web pages are good examples of the appropriate use of Internet technology. The companies that run these Internet BBSs use their Web sites simply to direct Internet users to their BBS resources. These companies don't spend lots of time updating their Web page or redesigning it whenever Netscape announces enhancements to the HTML language. This chapter and this entire book have a simple message: don't get stuck in the Web; look for better solutions and keep an open mind to new Internet technology.

The education BBS

FirstClass seems to have a strong market with the educational community. And why not? The graphical nature of the package, its ability to connect Macintosh and Windows-based machines, and the ease of maintenance and operation make it an ideal package for the education market.

This concept seems to be expanding to the Internet as well. School systems, colleges, and other teaching institutions are finding that they can expand their reach, or "create schools without walls," by widening the ability to access the important information and knowledgeable people within those systems.

We suggest that you investigate two sites in the education arena. First, you should examine School District #38, Richmond, British Columbia. This educational system is made up of 22,000 students in kindergarten through grade 12. Stewart Lynch, Director of Technology and Information Services in the district, believes the FirstClass system is ideal for schools to consider for instituting an e-mail and online conferencing system. You can see more about the project by visiting

```
http://137.82.136.19/Stew_L./Stew_Lynch.html
```

You also should visit Heritage On-line. Heritage On-line uses the FirstClass system to support on-line dialog and student-to-instructor classes through FirstClass. These classes are offered for university credit as continuing education for K – 12 teachers. You can visit the Heritage On-line Web site at

```
http://www.seattleantioch.edu/Heritage/FirstClass.html
```

Colleges and universities are always looking for ways to expand their enrollment base; however, restrictions in faculty size and the inability of the campus to house more students greatly restrict the ability for schools to expand. Using the "schools without walls" concept, one business approach may be to help a school set up a correspondence curriculum using the FirstClass BBS on the Internet as the delivery mechanism.

The user group BBS

One of the largest groups of users of the FirstClass system is interest groups who want to connect their members via the computer. Therefore, it is no surprise that user groups make up the largest number of Web presences announcing access to their BBS via the Internet.

One of the user groups you may want to visit is MotoBoard. Their Web site is located at

```
http://loonlink.com/motobo~1/motobrd.html
```

MotoBoard is a bulletin-board system for motorsports enthusiasts. This system offers information relating to motorcycles, snowmobiles, and automobiles. Members of various auto clubs and associations make up the subscriber base to this BBS. Conferences, e-mail, and other FirstClass communication resources are available to members of MotoBoard.

Next, consider the Chicago Area Macintosh User Group. This online service for Macintosh users provides file updates, configuration assistance, Macintosh classifieds, and a host of other services that Mac users may find useful. This user group is one of the many Macintosh user groups you can find on the Internet that uses the FirstClass system as its BBS package. You can visit their Web site at

```
http://www.macchicago.com/
```

You also should visit Designlink in San Francisco. As their Web site points out, "Designlink is a San Francisco based FirstClass Bulletin Board system for creative professionals, providing networking and E-Mail services to the design and photo communities as well as online resources including reference archives, shareware software, and complete portfolios of artwork from photographers, designers, illustrators and other artists." You can access the Designlink Web site at

```
http://www.designlink.com/DLPages/aboutDL.html
```

One group that is not represented as a BBS on the Internet consists of local governments and government organizations. A number of other government agencies and public service-related entities already utilize the SoftArc's FirstClass system. Adding access to their sites via the Internet could create some interesting advantages for the entities. Consider approaching local public service bodies, such as the Chamber of Commerce, City Council, Human Services, and so on, and providing assistance with establishing an Internet presence for their FirstClass BBS.

Setting Up a FirstClass Internet BBS

If you have some interest in actually setting up a BBS on the Internet using the FirstClass system, don't panic. You haven't just committed to something that will take a lifetime to complete. Setting up a FirstClass Internet BBS is not as difficult as you may think.

First, you need to have these network elements:

- ✔ A server. It can be either a Windows-based machine or a Macintosh.

- ✔ The FirstClass BBS package, Version 2.6 or higher for Macintosh servers, Version 3.0 or higher for Windows NT servers. This package provides the necessary TCP/IP support that will enable access to your BBS via the Internet.

- ✔ The TCP/IP protocol module available through SoftArc. This module enables people to enter your FirstClass BBS via the Internet.

Granted, this description of what you need to get started is pretty vague. You may be wondering how much RAM is required on the server? How big of a hard drive should you get? Which type of license structure should you consider from SoftArc? All these great questions are answered as you define how your site will be used.

The actual configuration of the machine and the number of licenses you need from SoftArc depends on the volume of traffic you expect to handle with the BBS. SoftArc representatives can help you determine how to configure your BBS hardware and software requirements to ensure optimal performance.

To operate the FirstClass server on a Macintosh machine, you need System 7. Although the server package can operate with only 4MB of RAM, additional memory is needed to handle the number of potential simultaneous users accessing the system. SoftArc recommends that you consider adding 100K of RAM for every simultaneous user that will visit the site. If you expect to have 100 simultaneous users (the maximum allowed by the software), you will need a minimum of 14MB to operate the system.

To run the FirstClass Internet BBS on a Windows-based machine, you need a server using the Windows NT operating system. The server system will not run under Windows 3.1 or Windows 95. Small BBSs (with light data and download requirements) can run on a 486-66 machine with 20MB of RAM. BBSs that require larger data and download capabilities may need faster processors and additional RAM. SoftArc recommends a minimum of 41MB of RAM to operate a Windows NT server with 100 simultaneous users.

If you decide to use FirstClass in setting up your BBS, you will find that the instructions provided by SoftArc are extremely comprehensive. For this reason, we will not go into the fine details of setting up the system. Instead, we will focus on the general tasks required to get a BBS operating on the Internet. You may also notice that most of the screen shots provided in this chapter are from a Windows machine. The screens for the Windows NT package have been designed to look identical to the Macintosh version (in most cases).

Setting up the server software

If you have the computer and the FirstClass software, you can now bring the BBS to life. You start by installing the server software. With the FirstClass system, setting up the server is only a two-disk operation. This critical step takes about five minutes.

In the server setup process, you will go through the following steps. Again, because the FirstClass documentation provided with the product is so complete, we will provide a high-level overview of the process itself.

1. **License the server.**

   The first step in the installation is entering the license information. You must know your license information and enter it when prompted.

2. **Configure the server name.**

   You must identify your server. The name you give to your server will be used to access your FirstClass BBS over the Internet.

3. **Set up the modem session.**

   If you anticipate people accessing the BBS via modem connections (the traditional BBS setup), you will need to follow the steps in setting up modem sessions.

4. **Set up the network session.**

   Set up this portion of the server if you will have people coming into the system via a computer network. You need to set up this portion of the server package so that people can access the BBS via the Internet.

5. **Back up the server.**

Regular backups are critical in maintaining a BBS on the Internet. Start your backup protocol with a clean server setup.

Now you are ready to actually start the server system. To launch the server, first make sure that the FirstClass tools system is not active. If it is operating, shut it down before attempting to launch the server. After you have disabled the tools package, launch the server system. Double-click on the FirstClass icon in the folder or window where it is located.

When the system is launched, you will see a window like the one shown in Figure 7-1.

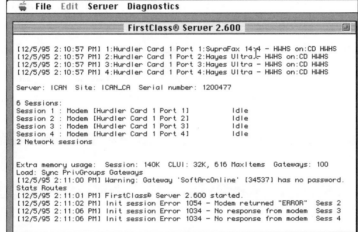

Figure 7-1:
Read the FirstClass server screen after starting the application.

This screen, containing a great deal of information about what is happening with your FirstClass system, remains active as long as you are operating the server. You can review who is accessing the system, when that person came online, and what method of connection (modem or network) he or she used to gain access. A comprehensive archive system built into the FirstClass product stores this information.

FirstClass installs a folder or subdirectory, called FirstClass Post Office, on your system. In it, you will find all the data relating to messages, files, and other important FirstClass information. Maintaining this folder as installed is very important. Do not move, rename, change, or delete it. Doing so could cause serious damage to your BBS, resulting in lost data.

When you first install your server, the system is empty. No users, conferences, or information files can be accessed. You must add to the FirstClass system the details that will bring your BBS to life.

Administering the system

After you install the software, you need to configure the server to handle information and accounts the way you want. Again, this process is simple after you get used to the look and feel of the FirstClass system.

To administer the FirstClass server, you must log into the system as the Administrator. To do so, double-click on the icon or folder labeled FirstClass Administrator. A screen similar to the one shown in Figure 7-2 then appears.

Almost all the functions you, as the administrator, need to perform are available through this window. You can access this window remotely by using the FirstClass client setup to log in as Administrator. You will need to set up the client with the user ID and password for the Administrator. After you do so, you can monitor the system and make changes from anywhere, as long as you can connect to the server.

Accessing the system remotely is a powerful feature of FirstClass. Remote access enables you to be away from the system and perform most duties needed to keep your system up and running. It also brings up a potential security problem.

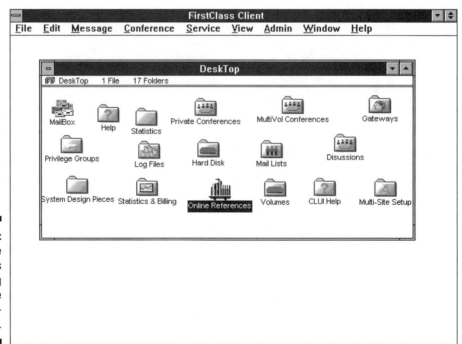

Figure 7-2:
Use the FirstClass client to log in as the Administrator.

Make sure that you carefully protect the Administrator's account information. If someone gains access to your server with the Administrator's privileges, he or she can change everything about your system — not a pretty prospect for those BBSs that have elaborate structures. Just like any site on the Internet, the FirstClass BBS requires that a carefully planned security strategy be implemented and maintained.

On the Administrator's desktop are a number of icons. Each of these icons provides access to the inner workings of the FirstClass system. Table 7-1 describes the icons you can use to manage the FirstClass BBS:

Table 7-1   Icons Used to Manage the FirstClass BBS

Icon	Name	Description
MailBox	MailBox	This icon opens the mailbox for the Administrator. Here, you can find all incoming and outgoing mail sent to or generated by the Administrator.
FirstClass News	FirstClass News	This icon opens a folder containing general news and system information. You may access this icon when you first launch the system, and you rarely use the icon after the system is in full operation.
Private Conferences	Private Conferences	In this folder, you store information regarding FirstClass conferences. A powerful feature of FirstClass, the Private Conferences allows information to be delivered to a carefully controlled base of BBS users. After you set up the private conference, people who want to gain access need to know the password to enter. You control the access and the information that may be shared within the conference.
Help	Help	FirstClass comes with a fairly detailed online Help screen, which provides information on how to operate the various features of the BBS. By double-clicking on this icon, you can search the various available help files. You can customize and add to the help files to create your own online help screens for your BBS users.

(continued)

Table 7-1 *(continued)*

Icon	Name	Description
Log Files	Log Files	This icon opens a directory for the log files kept by the FirstClass system. In this directory, you find information listing who uses your BBS each day. The log files are named by the date they were created. The size of the Log Files folder grows each day you operate the system because FirstClass creates a new log file each day. To save disk space, you may need to erase files from this directory periodically.
Hard Disk	Hard Disk	This folder gives you access to any storage device available to the FirstClass server system. These devices include the hard drive on your computer as well as CD-ROMs and other storage devices that may be connected to the system. This folder is useful in enabling visitors to your system to access files stored in various locations on your server.
Privilege Groups	Privilege Group	This icon gives you access to a part of FirstClass that enables you to carefully construct access to information on the system. As the administrator, you want to ensure that all your users have access to information on your system and prevent them from doing things they shouldn't.
Statistics & Billing	Statistics & Billing	This icon gives the administrator access to the section of FirstClass that collects statistics. FirstClass monitors what each visitor to the site does when he or she comes into the FirstClass system. Using the Statistics folder, you can generate detailed reports about what people do at your site and create bills for information that people access via your system. How you use this folder depends on how you use the FirstClass BBS to present your information. Because so many options are available for using the Statistics folder, we will not go into any more detail about this section here. Your FirstClass documentation provides comprehensive instructions on how to access and manipulate data in the Statistics folder.

Icon	Name	Description
Mail Lists	Mail Lists	This folder is a place where you can store information about the public mailing lists on your FirstClass system. Mailing lists are great tools that enable users of your system to send mail to specific groups of people on the server. Say that you have a group of horseshoe manufacturers on your BBS. A user of your system may want to announce a new horseshoe convention to your subscriber base. Instead of sending individual mail to 1,000 manufacturers' accounts, the user can call up the mailing list and send one piece of mail to all 1,000 users. This capability is similar to an automated Internet mailing list described in Chapter 6.

Also included on the Administrator's desktop are icons for gateways, address books, and other features of the FirstClass system that we will not examine in this book. Rest assured, the documentation that comes with the FirstClass product provides details on how you can use these items to augment your FirstClass BBS.

Managing users on the system

When you first launch the FirstClass server, no users are registered on the system. You must either manually register each user or set up the server so that users can automatically register new accounts. Due to the potential traffic of users who may access your system via the Internet, manual registration is not a viable option. Manual registration is more acceptable for those BBSs in which you want to greatly restrict who gains access to the information you provide.

Auto-registration gives new visitors to your site a screen that they can use to set up their own user IDs and passwords. It also forces the users to complete detailed information about themselves. To use the auto-registration feature, follow these steps:

1. **Choose Admin⇨System Profile from the Administrator's desktop menu bar.**

   The window shown in Figure 7-3 then appears.

2. **Check the Network auto-registration box found under the Options listing.**

When users connect to your BBS for the first time, they see the screen shown in Figure 7-4.

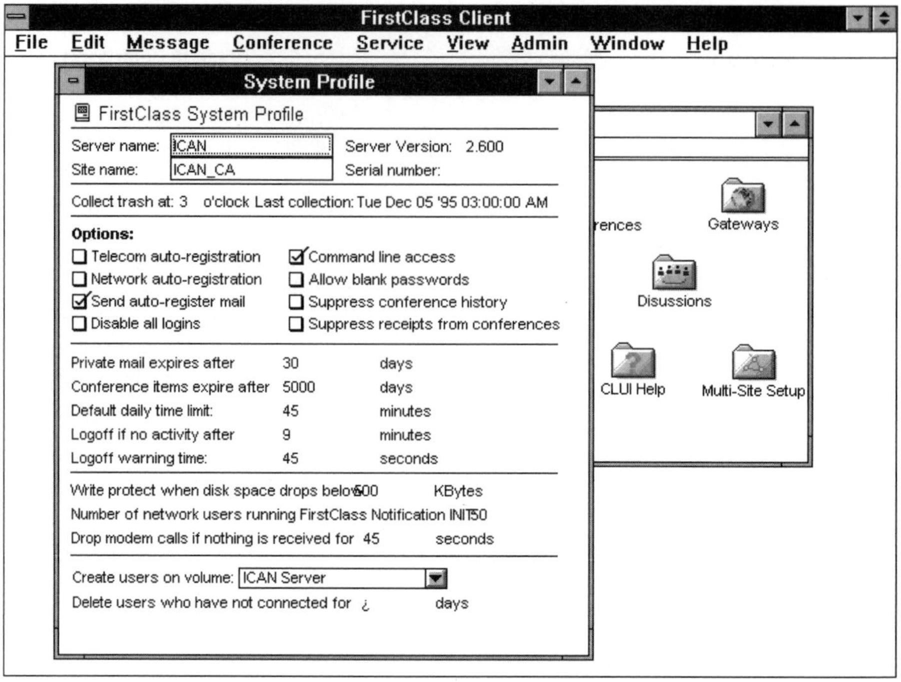

Figure 7-3:
Configure
your
FirstClass
system
using the
System
Profile
window.

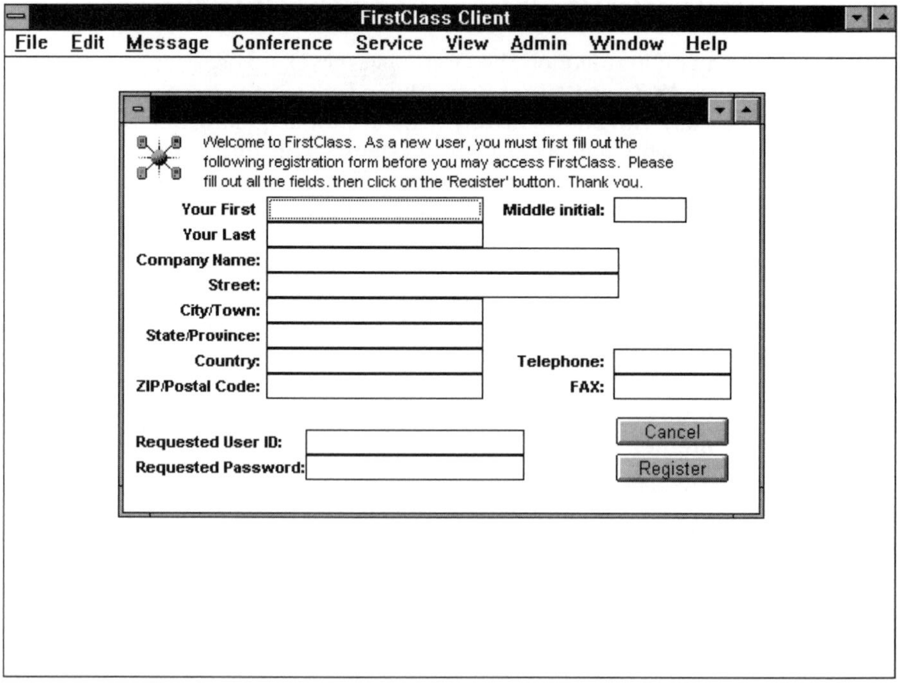

Figure 7-4:
New users
see this
screen if
auto-
registration
is enabled.

After the users complete the information screen and click the Register button, a confirmation screen displays their user ID and a password they have selected. If the information is okay, the users close the window and are ready to log into your FirstClass system.

The information the users enter in the auto-registration screen is placed in the appropriate sections of the User Listing. You can view the list of users registered to your site by choosing Admin⇨List Users from the menu bar of the Administrator's desktop.

You can have the server notify you when a person auto-registers a new account. If you choose the Send auto-register mail option in the System Profile window, you find mail highlighting who requested a new account at your site. Be aware that choosing this option could create a great deal of mail activity if your site is visited by many new visitors who decide to auto-register.

You can easily view user information on the FirstClass system. You can open specific user information by double-clicking on the user's name in any of the following places: the List Users window (under the Admin menu option); the from, to, or cc list of a message; a directory list; a history list; the system monitor; a Who's Online list; the participate list of a chat; a chat invite; a Permission list; or a list of subscribers. Just about anywhere you see a user's name, you can double-click on it and get the information shown in Figure 7-5.

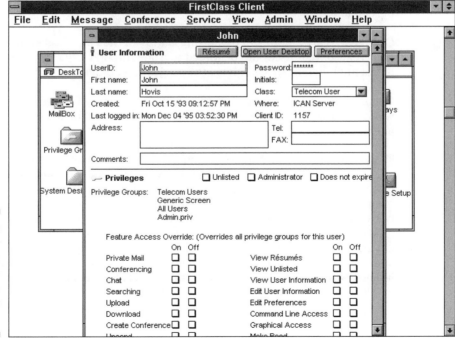

Figure 7-5:
View User
Information
by double-
clicking on
the user's
name.

With the User Information screen open, you can view and change the users' account information. You can also view the users' desktop and see how they have customized it to better utilize your site. You can also access the users' résumés to view customized information the users have entered about themselves.

At the User Information screen, you also can view the features to which you want the users to have access. You can change the feature list to modify the functionality each user has with your FirstClass BBS. For example, you may want to limit their chat, conferencing, download features, or a host of other features available to all FirstClass BBS users. The items you check here override the default items you select for all users who come on the system.

FirstClass gives you as much control as you could possibly want over how users access your site and what they can do while they are there. Having this ability built into the BBS package makes administering a site on the Internet much easier than what is normally required using more conventional protocols to set up a site on the Internet.

Setting up FirstClass conferences

You may be saying, "I know what a conference is in the real world, but what are you talking about with a BBS conference?" In FirstClass terms, a *conference* is nothing more than a shared mailbox or bulletin board that stores messages on a particular topic.

Conferences are a powerful organizing feature of the FirstClass system. Without conferences, visitors would be forced to wade through large volumes of information to find specific items (messages) that pique their interest.

Conferences are much like newsgroups on the Internet. They represent a place where visitors to your site can go to view and comment on specific topics of interest.

To make the FirstClass conferences more like newsgroups, SoftArc provides an add-on product that enables conferences you initiate to be connected directly to newsgroups on the Internet. This way, visitors to your site can access posts from people all over the Net to newsgroups on specific topics by opening a conference folder on your system. This newsgroup gateway product also makes it possible for visitors to respond to posts to specific newsgroups without having to have a newsgroup reader client. Just by having the FirstClass client and access to your site, people can enjoy greater connectivity to areas of interest without having to configure additional software and figure out how to connect to different sites hosting different topics.

Now look at the specifics of setting up conferences on FirstClass. When you first launch the FirstClass system, only one conference, the News Conference, appears on the system. By default, this conference appears on every user's desktop. You can change this default by deleting it using the Sample Desktop option in the Privilege group setup.

As a FirstClass administrator, you are responsible for everything about conferences. You must plan their structure, create the conferences themselves, and define their access by the general public. You must configure the conference options, organize the data that will be stored there, and determine how the data will be managed once it is in the conference.

Setting up and maintaining a conference requires a lot of work. But don't worry; it's all made easy with the FirstClass system. To create a conference, you must first determine whether you want the conference to be public or private. You can make a public conference to be viewed by all users of the system. Or you can set up a private conference to be viewed by specific groups of people given permission to view this information.

To set up a public conference, simply choose Conference⇨New Conference from the desktop menu bar. Choosing this option places a New Conference icon on the Administrator's desktop. If you are going to be creating a number of public conferences, create a folder (Conferences⇨New Folder) and drag and drop the public conferences into that folder. This way, you can keep the desktop organized and give the visitor to your site an easier path to navigate.

To set up a private conference, follow these steps:

1. **Open the Private Conferences folder on the Administrator's desktop.**

2. **Choose Conference⇨New Conference from the menu bar on the Administrator's desktop.**

   An icon for the conference then appears in the Private Conferences folder (see Figure 7-6).

3. **You can give the conference a name by either highlighting the conference name beneath the conference icon and typing the new name or by choosing File⇨Get Info and then typing the name in the dialog box that appears.**

   Give the conference a descriptive name that will help the visitors to your site quickly find topics of interest.

After you create and name conferences (both public and private), you may want to protect them from accidental deletion by the Administrator. To do so, highlight each conference, choose File⇨Get Info from the desktop menu bar, and check the Protected box in the resulting dialog box. You need to uncheck the Protected box to make changes to this conference in the future.

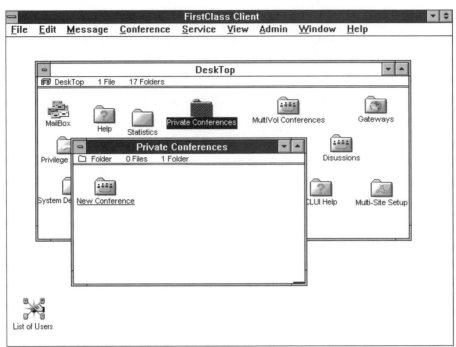

Figure 7-6:
Create a
new private
conference.

Many conferences require specific access control. To add or change the access to a specific conference, highlight that conference (by clicking on it once) and choose Conference⇨Permissions from the menu bar on the Administrator's desktop. The screen shown in Figure 7-7 then appears.

From this screen, you can control who has access to the conference, what information they can view, what they can do with the information in the conference, and who can make changes to the conference itself. When you're creating private conferences, you use the screen shown in Figure 7-7 to specify who can enter the conference itself. By listing the subscribers, you ensure that only those people identified will have access to the information presented in the conference.

How you use those conferences at your site will depend on what your objectives are and how you want to control the information flow to and from your visitors. When you actually set up conferences, you will find many more interesting and powerful capabilities made available by the FirstClass BBS than we can present here.

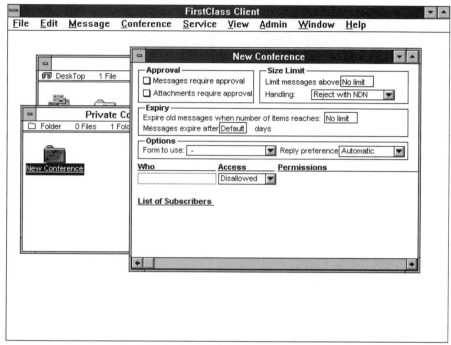

Figure 7-7:
Configure
conference
permissions
to control
access
to the
conference.

Establishing privilege groups

FirstClass is not making a social judgment when it uses the term *privilege*.
That's not what privilege groups are all about. Instead, this powerful tool is
simply another way for you, the administrator, to organize the desktops of
visitors to your site. It is another control-granting device that will help you
structure your Internet BBS site to help achieve your objectives.

In the FirstClass system, a *privilege group* is a group of subscribers who are
given specific abilities on the system. Several privilege groups are created
automatically when you install the FirstClass server. Users are automatically
assigned to these groups when you add them. If you want to control access to
commands and conferences for groups of users, you can use privilege groups as
the tool in FirstClass.

The privilege groups that are automatically included with the FirstClass
installation are All Users, Network Users, Telecom Users, Other Sites, Command
Line Users, Macintosh Users, Windows Users, and Auto-Registered Users. Each
of these groups gives the visitors to your site specific control over their stay.
You can control what they can and cannot do by making changes to the privileges defined in these groups and by adding other privilege groups as well.

By changing a Group Privilege form for a particular group, you change the privileges that group has. To open a Group Privilege form, first open the Privilege Group folder on the Administrator's desktop and then double-click on the icon for the particular group of interest (see Figure 7-8).

On this screen, you can control up to 27 aspects of what visitors to your site can do. This simple interface provided by the FirstClass system is much simpler than the control mechanisms that you use if you attempted to create an Internet site using other server/client systems.

With the Group Privilege form open, turn on or off those items that help you structure access to your BBS site. You can also view the desktop of a typical member of this privilege group by clicking on the Model Desktop button at the top of the Group Privilege form. The model desktop shows you what members of this group will see when they log in, and it enables you to customize the look of their desktops by adding and/or deleting icons from this view.

To add privilege groups, follow these steps:

1. **Open the Privilege Folder on the Administrator's desktop.**

2. **Pull down the Admin menu item and choose Privilege Group from the Add submenu.**

   A new Group Privilege form automatically opens. This form looks like Figure 7-8 without any of the Feature Access boxes checked.

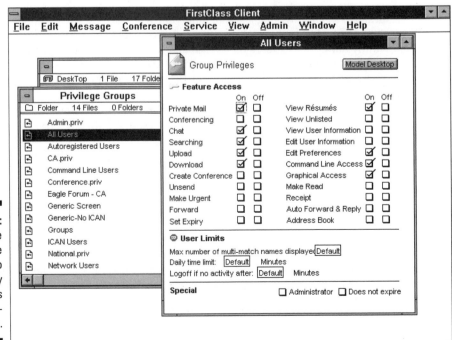

Figure 7-8: Use privilege groups to simplify FirstClass administration.

3. **Change the name of the new Group Privilege form by choosing File⇨Get Info from the menu bar.**

4. **Fill in the Group Privilege form to meet your requirements.**

5. **Close the form.**

The new privilege group is added to the list in the Privilege Folder on the Administrator's desktop. Before the privileges can take effect, you must specify users that will be restricted to or granted the privileges specified in the new group.

To add users to privilege groups, you need to go back to the User Information Form (see Figure 7-5) discussed in the section "Managing users on the system."

Follow these steps to add users to new privilege groups:

1. **Open the user's User Information form.**

   You can open this form in a number of ways. Refer to the section "Managing users on the system" for more information on opening this form.

2. **Scroll down the form to the section titled Privileges.**

3. **Enter the name of the group you want included in the privilege list.**

   You can enter as many privilege group names that completely define the functions this particular subscriber will have access to on the BBS.

4. **Close the form after you add the privilege groups.**

Now when that subscriber accesses your site, he or she will be limited to the set of features you defined in the privilege group listing on his or her User Information Form. You must repeat this process for every person who is to be assigned to different privilege groups on your BBS site.

Assigning privileges to subscribers can be a time-consuming and tedious proposition if you have thousands of people who visit on a regular basis. To reduce potential administration duties required, carefully consider how you want a new subscriber to access your site. Then think of the paths you may want to make available to more valuable visitors. As you distinguish the casual visitor from the power user, you can then add privileges to those users you want to give more access. By planning a privilege-gaining strategy, you can greatly reduce the amount of administration time you must dedicate to hosting an Internet BBS site.

Privilege groups provide a powerful means of controlling what people can do at your site. This feature will be particularly important to those site developers who want to make available some information for no charge while giving more detailed data for a fee. FirstClass makes having an access plan easier to implement than most client/server packages available on the Internet.

Creating a mailing list

Public mailing lists on the FirstClass server make it easy for users on your server to send mail to a specified group of people who visit your site.

To set up a mailing list, follow these steps:

1. **Open the Mail List folder from the Administrator's desktop.**

2. **Choose Admin⇨Add-Mail List.**

   A new empty mailing list is created.

3. **Choose File⇨Get Info.**

4. **Enter the names in the mailing list just as you would if you were mailing a note to the person you want on the list.**

   Figure 7-9 shows the mailing list screen.

5. **After you are finished adding the names, close the mailing list.**

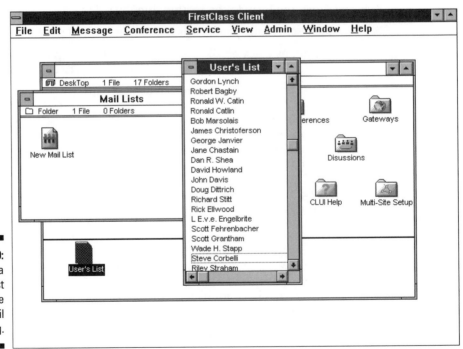

Figure 7-9:
Create a mailing list to enable group e-mail messaging.

You can create as many mailing lists as you need to suit your needs and those of your subscribers. You may want to consider carefully the use of these lists and communicate what is appropriate to be sent to the people on the list. A large subscriber base creates potential for e-mail abuse by overzealous marketers at your site. By developing a list-use policy and making it available to everyone on the system, you can better handle those people who will abuse this powerful privilege.

Connecting to the Internet

To connect your FirstClass BBS to the Internet, you need the TCP/IP Protocol Option from SoftArc. This product provides the software mechanisms that enable a Macintosh and/or Windows-based client to access your BBS over the Internet.

To install the TCP/IP protocol license from SoftArc, follow these steps:

1. **Shut down the FirstClass server.**

2. **Launch FirstClass Tools by double-clicking on the tools icon or folder.**

3. **On a Windows NT machine, choose Configure⇨Add License.**

   or

   On a Macintosh, choose Configure⇨License Limits from the menu bar.

4. **On a Windows NT server, insert the TCP/IP Network Option license disks and choose Upgrade.**

   or

   On the Macintosh, the upgrade is completed immediately, and the disk is ejected.

5. **Click on the OK button.**

6. **Quit FirstClass Tools.**

Now you must specify the TCP/IP ports that will give Internet access to your BBS. To do so, follow the steps outlined for each server type in the following paragraphs.

For the Windows NT server, you need to change the NETINFO file located in the FCPO/SERVER subdirectory. To modify the file, use a text editor such as Notepad or your word processing program. You change the NETINFO file to specify the port from which the Internet visitor will access your site. The specific port and syntax of the command you enter depends on the access method you will be utilizing. The FirstClass instruction manual clearly outlines the specific command to enter depending on your situation.

For the Macintosh server, you also need to modify the NETINFO file to call the specific port to which Internet connections will be made. Use Teachtext or Simpletext to create the NETINFO file. After you create it, save the file in the folder where the FirstClass Post Office is located. As with the Windows NT NETINFO file, the specific port you call on the Macintosh depends on what type of connection you will use with the Internet. Follow the FirstClass documentation to make the appropriate port specifications.

You are now ready to go on the Net. Before you launch your BBS, you may want to check and change your network configuration to accommodate more simultaneous visitors at your site. The FirstClass system comes set up to allow two LAN visitors at any one time. Two is probably not enough for an Internet site.

Before you raise the number of simultaneous users to the maximum FirstClass allows (100), take into account that additional RAM may be required to fulfill this request. Ideally, you should raise the number of simultaneous visitors to the maximum you anticipate at your peak operational times. You may need to tweak this number with some trial-and-error settings before compromising on a figure that meets your needs.

To change the number of network sessions, you must go back into the FirstClass Tools program. Then follow these steps:

1. **From the FirstClass Tools menu, choose Configure⇨Network Sessions.**

2. **Enter the number of network sessions to be supported.**

3. **On a Windows NT server, click on the OK button.**

    or

    On a Macintosh server, click on the Configure button.

4. **Exit FirstClass Tools and restart the server.**

With the network configured and the TCP/IP option installed, your FirstClass BBS is "Net-ready."

Distributing the FirstClass Client

To get people to access your Internet BBS site, you have to get the FirstClass client onto their computers. One of the best ways to accomplish this goal is to create a Web page with instructions on how to download the FirstClass client and instructions for the new user to follow to access your Internet BBS site.

By setting up your server to allow for automatic registration, anyone who has the client package can log on to your site and create an account for access. The process can be very simple and doesn't have to take a lot of time for your users to complete.

If you took the time to visit some of the sites described in the section "Real-world Internet BBS examples," you saw this Web/BBS strategy in action. For example, at the SoftArc Web site (`http://www.softarc.com/`), you can find a link to download the client software package based on the type of computer you use.

The SoftArc Web site also gives the IP address and port number that must be entered in the FirstClass client in order to contact the SoftArc Internet BBS. It's important to provide this information on your Web site so that new users can contact your BBS without difficulty.

Adding on Goodies

Leave it to all those creative software developers, who have nothing better to do than improve existing products, to come up with some great goodies to add to your FirstClass Internet BBS! Because the FirstClass system has developed quite a following in the BBS community, all kinds of add-on products are now available to help you expand and manage a BBS using the FirstClass client/server package.

FCCustodian is a pager system that interfaces with your FirstClass server. If the server goes down for some reason, you are sent a page alerting you to the fact that a problem exists. This capability gives the administrator running a "one-man show" a chance to have a life while administering the BBS. You can learn more about this product on the Web by accessing

```
http://fccustodian.mmcs.com/
```

Also new are game add-ons that turn your BBS into an interactive playhouse. Access the Tempest Chess site at

```
http://www.hk.super.net/~johnb/tchess.html
```

The FirstConnect add-on product is the leading database extension for the FirstClass system. This add-on can display photographs, graphics, and full text files; it adds and deletes database records; and it also retrieves sounds and even enables you to download files. You can check out this useful add-on product for the serious Internet BBS site developer at

```
http://www.together.com/products/fcn/
```

For a general listing of available add-on tools on the Internet, check out the FirstClass Administrator's Tools & Apps. site at

```
http://www.versa.com/fcadmin/index.html
```

Here you can find links to products for file utilities, games, miscellaneous information on administering a FirstClass site, and other useful utilities.

Setting up an Internet site is a challenge, no matter how you look at it. A lot of information must be gathered in one place just to make the connection between a client machine and a server take place. Using a comprehensive package such as the FirstClass system simplifies the entire process and makes it easy to add new features to your Internet site later.

All in all, the FirstClass BBS Internet offers a simple strategy for getting a site on the Net — much simpler than trying to set up an individual mail server, file transfer server, automated mailing list server, Internet news server, and so on. FirstClass gives the Internet site developer the option of being on the Net quickly with minimal time requirements and a one-time investment in hardware and software.

Part III
Setting Up Other Useful Internet Resources

The 5th Wave **By Rich Tennant**

AFTER SPENDING 9 DAYS WITH 12 DIFFERENT VENDORS AND READING 26 BROCHURES, DAVE HAD AN ACUTE ATTACK OF TOXIC OPTION SYNDROME.

In this part . . .

The best thing about the Internet is that it's an unlimited communications resource. Software designed to work on the Internet can be made to do just about anything that you can imagine a computer doing. This part introduces several more Internet software packages that will add functionality and appeal to your Internet site.

As with any Internet resource, the average user must be able to access these services easily. Until something better comes along, this means simple integration into the existing World Wide Web. Real-time communications software is rapidly emerging. Two other resources featured in this part, Gopher and Usenet news, already offer seamless integration into the Web.

Chapter 8

Real-Time Communications on the Internet

*F*rom early jungle drumming on hollow tree trunks, to the smoke signals of the North American plains, to the international satellite videoconferencing systems used in large corporate offices, humankind has gone to extraordinary lengths to communicate. As a species, we rely on and rejoice in our ability to share information. We've even spent millions of dollars sending a spacecraft off on an endless voyage through space, blaring our greetings to anyone who will listen.

The Internet is a communications tool that has no boundaries and no borders. For the first time in the history of this planet, people all over the world are freely exchanging ideas. Last month alone, people from over 47 countries logged in to a U.S. Web server at www.science.org to find out what our science-and-technology research think tank had to say. More importantly, they sent e-mail, chatted with each other using a variety of interactive tools, and spoke to each other using something known as the Internet Phone.

The World Wide Web is great, and we have no intention of understating its importance. But when it comes to developing a lasting relationship with Internet users, *real-time* communications has no equal. Real-time is different from receiving e-mail and responding to it later. The level of interactivity possible when you're communicating with someone "live" is so much greater and more exciting. We recently had a remarkable experience that demonstrates this point. The Planetary Coral Reef Foundation, or PCRF, (http://pcrf.org/pcrf/) was in need of docking space and supplies for its very large research vessel, the *Heraclitus*, while making a stop in Florida. (Does Florida have coral reefs?)

We used Internet Phone to establish a PCRF presence on the primary Internet Phone server, and within minutes, we were contacted by an interested fellow from Miami. The president of PCRF described the global coral-reef research that is being conducted aboard *Heraclitus* and asked if the organization could arrange docking space and supplies for the stay in Florida. The gentleman knew exactly who to call at several local universities, and soon, the arrangements were made.

This spontaneous business meeting in cyberspace probably wouldn't have occurred if not for the effective use of real-time communications. This chapter shows you how to create a presence for your organization through the use of real-time communications software.

Making Phone Calls over the Internet

The future is here. As you read this book, international phone conversations are being held for the price of an Internet connection, thanks to several new software products.

Internet Phone for Windows

Everyone's favorite form of communication is the gift of gab. You can't deny the facts: People like to talk. Some people even talk to themselves. Fulfill your greatest dream; free international phone calling with the most popular voice communications program for Windows, Internet Phone (see Figure 8-1), is now available via the Internet.

Vocaltec, the company that created the Internet Phone is an Israeli company. This example shows how global business is possible using the Internet. Taking a great idea and introducing it to the world is easy using the Internet. We present the challenge — think of something people all over the world will want, and then sell it over the Internet.

If you haven't already watched someone use Internet Phone or tried using it yourself, take a moment to experiment with the software. You can evaluate the Internet Phone for free. The demo version of the software allows you to talk for 60 seconds before you have to exit and restart the software. The 60-second limit applies to talk time only; you can listen to other people talk indefinitely.

To use Internet Phone, you need a PC running Windows 3.1 or later, a WinSock-compliant TCP/IP-based Internet connection, a sound card (such as SoundBlaster, from Creative Labs), a microphone connected to the sound card, and PC speakers.

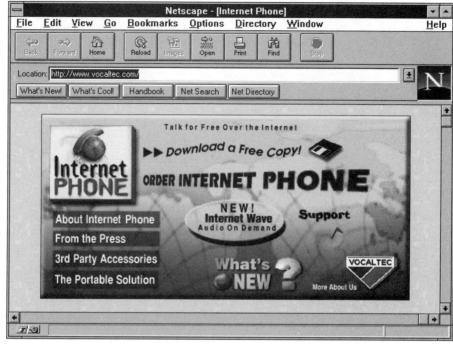

Figure 8-1:
Download a copy of the Internet Phone from Vocaltec.

So how can you use Internet Phone to establish an Internet presence for your organization? Four options are available to you (listed in order of complexity):

✔ Type your organization's name and contact information in the User Info options window.

✔ Create a new topic of conversation for your organization.

✔ Broadcast something continually, using your Internet Phone.

✔ Set up your own Internet Phone server.

When you configure your Internet Phone software, be sure to choose User Info from the Options menu. This command brings up the window shown in Figure 8-2, allowing you to enter your name and contact information. By typing the name of your organization, you create an Internet Phone presence any time you use the program.

If you have a dedicated Internet connection, consider leaving your Internet Phone software connected all the time, so that people can always see your name in the list of users. Even if they can't reach you, people will see your contact information (such as your Web home page and phone number), and they'll think about contacting you again the next time they use Internet Phone.

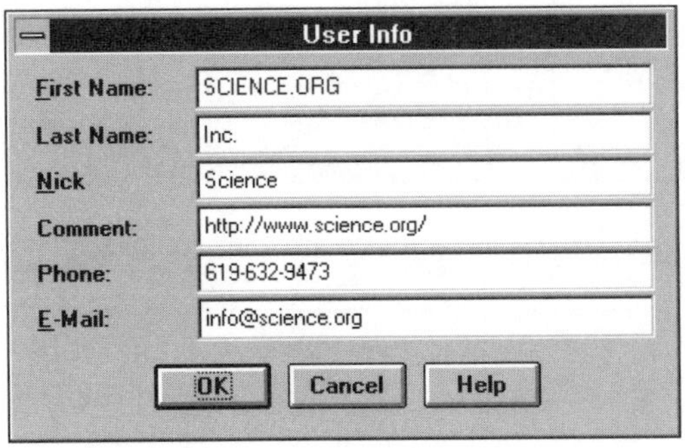

Figure 8-2:
Type your
organization's
name and
contact
information
in User Info.

The next thing that you want to do is create one or more new topics that fit with your organization's purpose. A *topic* is an area of conversation that is given a particular name on an Internet Phone server. Users can join topics that they find interesting and talk with others who share these interests.

To create a new topic, follow these steps:

1. Choose Phone➪Call.

2. When the Call dialog box appears, click on the Topics button.

The Join Topic window, shown in Figure 8-3, appears. This window displays existing topics, such as those topics that you previously joined.

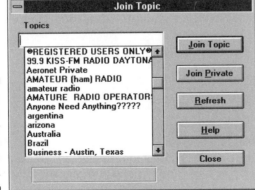

Figure 8-3:
Create a
new topic by
using the
Join Topic
window.

3. Type the name of the topic that you want to create.

4. Click on Join Topic.

The new topic is created, and you are the first user to join.

5. Wait for other users to see your topic in the Join Topic window and join as well.

After you use Internet Phone for a while, you'll notice that several radio stations maintain a permanent presence on Vocaltec's Internet Phone server. Some of these stations broadcast continually to anyone who will listen. Setting up a continual Internet Phone broadcast actually is very easy: simply keep talking! Any sound picked up by your microphone is transmitted to the caller. This method is an excellent way to provide an automated information line that repeats a recorded message. We're looking forward to the day when our local theater broadcasts its movie schedule over Internet Phone.

Setting up your own Internet Phone server is much more involved than the other three options. The first obstacle is the availability of the server software for your computer. Currently, you must use a UNIX workstation to run one of these servers. This situation may change, however, especially now that Netscape offers a server product that works with the Netscape Chat software. (See "Chatting with Netscape" later in this chapter.) Netscape Chat uses the same type of server as Internet Phone, so the Netscape Chat server program works with both.

Read the Frequently Asked Questions (FAQ) document that is dedicated to using the Internet as a telephone. The document is available at the following URL:

```
http://www.northcoast.com/savetz/voice-faq.html
```

NetPhone for Macintosh

NetPhone, from Electric Magic, was the very first Macintosh Internet telephone software. If your Macintosh has hardware that supports *full duplex operation* (the capability to send and receive sound simultaneously), you can have two-way conversations with anyone who is using the same software.

NetPhone is fully integrated with the World Wide Web, allowing you to click on a Web link to place a call. You also can use NetPhone to visit *NetPubs.* Like Internet Phone servers, NetPubs are places for users to gather and find someone to chat with. Electric Magic maintains a NetPub for people who are looking for a place to hang out and chat.

NetPhone uses the same technology as the European digital cellular-phone system to give you very high audio quality. You can yack to your heart's content on any Macintosh, ranging from a Mac IIsi to faster models.

To use NetPhone, you need a 20 MHz Mac II or later with System 7, MacTCP, and a TCP/IP-based Internet connection. You also need a microphone and speakers. For versions of System 7 before version 7.5, the use of software called Sound Manager is recommended. If you need the Sound Manager software, you can get it from Apple Computer's FTP site:

```
ftp://ftp.info.apple.com/Apple.Support.Area/↩
Developer_Services
```

You can download an evaluation copy of the NetPhone software from the following Web site:

```
http://www.emagic.com/
```

The registered version of NetPhone also allows you to receive a call even when you're not running NetPhone. Then you can start the software and begin talking. This arrangement makes establishing a presence with NetPhone much easier than with Internet Phone, because you don't need to connect to a NetPhone server to receive calls.

Talking without Moving Your Lips

Some linguists believe that before humans developed spoken language, they used sign language to communicate. Writing is an extension of that idea; written characters are signs that we have been taught to understand. Extending this early form of communication to the Internet, two-way chat programs allow you to converse over the Internet by typing back and forth with others in real-time.

Chatting with Netscape

When you hear the name *Netscape,* you probably think of the World Wide Web. Netscape Communications, which is well known for its Web browser, has released a new chat program called *Netscape Chat.* This communications program allows you to have text conversations with other users around the world. Netscape Chat is designed to work with the familiar Netscape Navigator so that while you use the chat program to chat with your friends, you also can send and receive URLs with the capability to then access them automatically in your browser.

Download the Netscape Chat program from the Netscape Web site:

```
http://www.netscape.com/
```

Netscape Chat comes in both 16-bit form (for Windows 3.*x*) and 32-bit form (Windows 95 or Windows NT).

Chat programs are a wonderful way to communicate directly with people on the Internet. From the early days of bulletin boards, real-time chat has been one of the most popular online activities; it lends a personal touch that comes as close to talking on the phone as you can get without using technology like Internet Phone.

The advantage of chat technology is that no one with whom you want to chat needs to have any special hardware. All anyone needs is the Netscape Chat program and someone to chat with. Finding someone to chat with is easy; thousands of people are online just waiting to meet someone new.

Figure 8-4 shows a sample chat session with Netscape Chat.

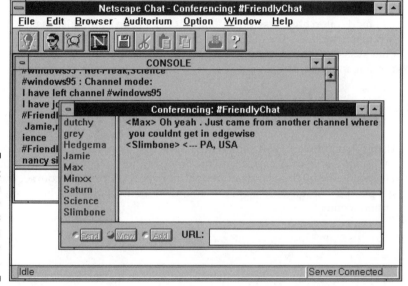

Figure 8-4:
Carry on interactive conversations by using Netscape Chat.

With Netscape Chat, you can send the URL of your home page (or any of your other Internet resources) and invite people to take a look. The process is a little like standing in the grocery store and handing out tasty samples. You can add your URL to a special place in the Chat software that will send it to others you happen to be chatting with. Everyone who receives the URL you've sent can then choose to view the information your URL points to. Get immediate feedback from the group, start discussions, and share the Internet surfing experience with others. This feature is also a useful tool for researchers chatting about information presented over the Internet. You can throw your own online conferences.

Holding a meeting

Netscape Chat allows you to carry on a moderated chat session. The Auditorium menu selections allow you to select a moderator, give permission for someone to chat (called *giving them the microphone*), or take chat privileges away.

Don't let the Auditorium menu selections fool you. You may think that the reference to the microphone means that Netscape Chat permits voice communication, like Internet Phone. But Netscape Chat is text-only. The menu selections were named to correspond to the way that you might run a meeting in an auditorium.

In a moderated chat session, the moderator controls the discussion. This arrangement keeps the discussion clear and focused on a topic. Unmoderated chat sessions tend to include several simultaneous conversations about nothing in particular.

Running your own discussion group

Using chat software, you can create online discussions similar to the ones held on CompuServe or America OnLine. Some of these discussions are attended electronically by thousands of people all over the world. Of course, the way to get people to come is to send out announcements. Following is a sample announcement:

```
Discussion: Do spotted owls live in new-growth forests?
Server: iapp.netscape.com
Group: #spotted_owls
Time: 12:00 PM +0800 GMT
Date: 09 November 1996
```

If you're trying to figure out how or where to send these announcements, here are some starter ideas:

- Send e-mail to friends and associates.
- Send the announcement to newsgroups.
- Make use of electronic mailing lists.
- Don't forget the old "end-up-in-the-mail-slot-for-your-dog-to-chew" type of mail.

These electronic get-togethers can be informal gatherings to chat about fun things, or they can be controlled, moderated, directed conversations about serious topics. For instance, kids can chat about their favorite Web sites, or communities can have town meetings electronically. The uses for these group communications are limited only to your imagination.

Allowing people to communicate in real-time is an exciting enhancement to your Internet site. More people will visit and feel as though they are getting the attention they need. These communication technologies are very new; many of them are not even fully developed yet. Real-time communications is one of the most exciting, fastest-growing areas of the Internet. Make sure that you log in regularly to www.science.org/internetsite,our Setting Up An Internet Site page on the World Wide Web, to see what we think is hot for your Internet site.

"I DON'T THINK OUR NEWEST INTERNET CONNECTION IS GOING TO WORK. ALL OF THE FILES WE'RE DOWNLOADING SEEM TO BE COMING IN OVER MY ELECTRIC PENCIL SHARPENER."

Chapter 9

Citellus How to Gopher

*W*ho would have thought that a small furry animal of the genus *Citellus* would become synonymous with the new global information infrastructure? Gophers are more than just cute and cuddly rodents; they also represent one of the first information systems on the Internet. Like the FTP, Gopher allows you to provide files to other Internet users.

Like its namesake, Gopher relies on a brute force approach to getting things done. Unlike the World Wide Web, Gopher is not fancy. If you know how to work with files on your computer, you know how to provide files through Gopher. Providing information through Gopher is easy because you don't need to learn a special language like you do with the World Wide Web.

Providing files through Gopher may be easier than providing files through the World Wide Web, but the fact remains that Gopher is now relatively unused compared with the World Wide Web. Although Gopher is not the accepted mainstream method for providing files, it does have some key advantages that may make it suitable for your particular Internet strategy.

When you provide information through the World Wide Web, the server program requires at least one file that has a special name. In addition, you need to know the HyperText Markup Language (HTML) to create Web pages. Neither of these restrictions applies to Gopher; you just run a Gopher server program, and instantly, the files that you want to share are available to other people on the Internet. Gopher is a little like a simple, anonymous FTP interface.

When you add files to your existing Gopher resource, they're automatically available to Gopher users. Conversely, on the World Wide Web, you usually need to update your HTML documents with new links when you add files. Providing information through Gopher requires very little administrative overhead compared with the World Wide Web. And Gopher servers can be accessed through World Wide Web browsers just like FTP servers, so you don't sacrifice a user-friendly interface.

If you want to get fancy with Gopher, you can even create links to other Internet resources. Used alone or in conjunction with the World Wide Web, a Gopher resource is a potentially valuable and simple way to provide information on the Internet.

Expanding Gopherspace

The vast network of interconnected Gopher resources is called *Gopherspace*. To provide information in Gopherspace, you need a Gopher server. A *Gopher server* is a program that communicates with Gopher clients, using the Gopher protocol. *Gopher clients* are programs that are used to communicate a request to a Gopher server.

Understanding how Gopher works is easier if you know a little about the protocol. Four basic ideas are behind Gopher:

- ✔ Just about every computer in the world uses files to store information. The creators of Gopher decided that providing information on the Internet should be a simple matter of making existing files available to Internet users.

- ✔ Instead of merely publishing a list of filenames in a file system, as FTP requires, the creators of Gopher wanted software that would automatically give users a visual cue to file types.

- ✔ Gopher was designed to make creating links between Gopher servers around the world easy.

- ✔ The *Gopher protocol* — the behind-the-scenes communication between a Gopher server and a Gopher client — is English based and is meant to be easily read.

The basic Gopher protocol defines two things:

- ✔ A method for Gopher client programs to obtain a list of files that are available from a Gopher server

- ✔ A way for Gopher client programs to request specific files from a Gopher server

To obtain a list of files on a Gopher server, a Gopher client simply contacts the server and sends a blank line, followed by a carriage return. The Gopher server responds with a list of the available files, formatted according to the Gopher protocol. The Gopher client then displays the list, allowing the user to select a file.

When the user selects an item from the list, the Gopher client sends a file request to the appropriate Gopher server. The Gopher server sends the file and then waits for another request.

Using an Internet Gopher Publishing Service

If you want a permanent, high-speed Gopher site through which to publish information, using somebody else's Gopher server is a down-to-earth approach. Many service providers offer Gopher publishing services, which usually are very easy to use. Typically, your Gopher service provider tells you three things when you sign up:

- ✔ How to log in with your user ID and password
- ✔ The name of your Gopher directory (and how to find it)
- ✔ How to send files to your Gopher directory

Using the UNIX telnet program to experiment with Gopher

If you want to watch the interaction between a Gopher client and server, you can use a program called telnet to establish a text-based communication link with any Gopher server. Telnet to the Gopher server at the University of Minnesota, for example, using a telnet command like the following, in a UNIX shell account:

```
telnet umn.edu 70
```

This command establishes a telnet session with the host umn.edu on port 70 (the Gopher port). When a connection is established, press Enter. The Gopher server sends a list of available items and then rudely hangs up on you. The list looks something like this:

```
7Search U of MN Directory?
x500.tc.umn.edu 70
```

```
OUniversity of Minnesota, US.
x500.tc.umn.edu 70

1 Academic Retirees ou=Academic
Retirees/ x500.tc.umn.edu 70

1 Alumni Association ou=Alumni
Association/ x500.tc.umn.edu 70

1 Application Services
ou=Application Services/
x500.tc.umn.edu 70

1 Duluth Campus Gopher Server
ua.d.umn.edu 70

1 Twin Cities Campus Gopher
Server gopher.tc.umn.edu 70

.
```

You will most likely use FTP to send files to your Gopher directory. Files are published as soon as they're placed in your directory; no additional work is necessary. Suppose that you sent the following files to your Gopher directory:

```
README
BROCHURE
HLPWANTD
PRODUCTS
SUPPORT
```

When a Gopher user accesses your Gopher site, he or she sees a menu like the one shown in Figure 9-1. Most Gopher servers alphabetize the file listing automatically, so the order in which you send the files isn't important.

As you can see in Figure 9-1, informative filenames help create meaningful Gopher menus. Even people who are new to Gopher can understand that the file 2CONTACT.US contains information such as contact names, phone numbers, and other ways to reach people in your organization. Likewise, the BROCHURE file clearly contains an electronic brochure for your company.

Sometimes, informative filenames just aren't good enough. In such cases, you can create *aliases* (other, even more descriptive names) for the files in your Gopher directory.

Figure 9-1:
A Gopher directory illustrates that informative filenames create an under-standable Gopher menu.

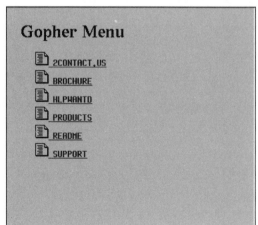

Using aliases to create user-friendly Gopher menus

Using file aliases, you can display informative titles for your files, instead of just the filenames. The following is a possible alias for the BROCHURE file:

```
Virtual Internet Corporation's Online Brochure & Price List
```

To define a file alias for the BROCHURE file, you need to create a special text file on your own PC. You can call the file whatever you want because you'll need to rename the file to something strange after sending it to your Gopher directory. The text file should contain the following two lines:

```
Path=./BROCHURE
Name=Virtual Internet Corporation's Online Brochure & Price List
```

The Path= line tells your Gopher server which file to alias. The ./ path means that this file is located in the root Gopher directory. If the file were in a subdirectory, you would include the subdirectory name in the path. The Name= line is the alias itself. You can continue adding paths and names to this file so that every file in your directory has an alias. Simply add a Path and Name definition for each file for which you want to create an alias.

After you create this text file, you need to send it to the Gopher directory that contains the BROCHURE file that you want to alias and give the text file a special name. Follow these steps:

1. **Save the text file on your PC.**

   The name you give the file isn't important right now.

2. **Send the text file to your Gopher directory.**

   Be sure to send the file to the directory that contains the files you're renaming. In this case, the text file should be in the same directory as BROCHURE.

3. **Rename the text file something like** .names **or** .aliases.

   The name must begin with a period. Files that begin with a period are special to the Gopher server. These files contain instructions for the server, such as aliases to display in file lists. The following command renames the file if you're using the standard UNIX FTP client (replace *TextFileName* with the name of your text file):

   ```
   RENAME TextFileName .aliases
   ```

Now the BROCHURE file appears with the more informative title when a user connects to your Gopher site. If you want to have aliases for more than one file in a Gopher directory, simply separate the aliases in your special text file with blank lines, like this:

```
Path=./BROCHURE
Name=Virtual Internet Corporation's On-line Brochure & Price List

Path=./2CONTACT.US
Name=How to contact Virtual Internet Corporation
```

You also can use this special text file to override the alphabetical sorting that your Gopher server does. You can tell the Gopher server the order in which it should display filenames and aliases. To tell the Gopher server that the BRO-CHURE and 2CONTACT.US aliases should appear first and second in the menu, add a Numb= line to each alias entry, as follows:

```
Path=./BROCHURE
Name=Virtual Internet Corporation's Online Brochure & Price List
Numb=1

Path=./2CONTACT.US
Name=How to contact Virtual Internet Corporation
Numb=2
```

Now the aliases for these two files will always be first and second in your Gopher menu, regardless of what files you add or remove in the future.

Instead of giving an alias for each file (a process that can become time-consuming if you publish many files), create a table-of-contents file, and update it each time you add new files. Give the table-of-contents file a meaningful alias, and make it one of the first files in your Gopher menu. Then the user sees both the table of contents and the files listed by filename. The following alias and position entry work for a filenamed TOC:

```
Path=./TOC
Name=Table of Contents for this Gopher site
Numb=1
```

Telling others how to access your Gopher site

The best way to tell others how to access your Gopher site is to give them a Gopher URL. A Gopher URL looks like this:

```
gopher://servername/directoryname
```

For example, the following Gopher URL refers to the SCIENCE.ORG Gopher server:

```
gopher://gopher.science.org/
```

Your Gopher URL begins with `gopher://`, followed by the name of your Gopher server and Gopher directory (if any), separated by slashes. Your Gopher service provider will tell you the URL for your Gopher directory. If you add directories to organize your files better, you can direct someone straight to the directory that contains the file in which he or she is interested by adding the directory name to the end of the URL.

Serving Gopher Links

Gopher links, eggs, and demi-litre du lait — the perfect meal for an exhausted Internet navigator. Gopher links are used like anchors in the World Wide Web: They provide links to other resources on the Internet. To create a link to an item on another Gopher server, you need three pieces of information:

  ✔ The host name or IP address of the Gopher server

  ✔ The full path of the item on the Gopher server

  ✔ The *type code* for the item (see Table 9-1)

Type codes are unfortunate aspects of a Gopher link, because having to remember which code to use is inconvenient. These codes are single-character identifiers that tell Gopher more about a particular item. The type code 1, for example, tells Gopher that an item is a Gopher directory. You must know the type code for an item to create a link to it. Table 9-1 shows the most common type codes in Gopher.

Table 9-1	Common Item Types in Gopher
Type Code	*Type*
0	Text file
1	Gopher directory
7	Searchable Gopher index
9	Binary file
h	HTML document
I	Image file

When you have the necessary pieces of information handy, create a text file that contains the following lines:

```
Name=LinkName
Type=TypeCode
Port=70
Path=ItemPath
Host=ServerName
```

Each of the lines in this file is important to the proper functioning of the Gopher link. Descriptions of each line follow:

- ✔ *Name.* LinkName is the name to give to your new link. The name is similar to the alias created earlier in this chapter in the section "Using aliases to create user-friendly Gopher menus" and appears along with the other aliases and filenames when a user views your Gopher menu.

- ✔ *Type.* TypeCode is the code for the type of the item.

- ✔ *Port.* This line is very important; it tells a user's Gopher client or Web browser how to contact the other Gopher server.

- ✔ *Path.* ItemPath is the full path to the item. A Gopher client sends this text to the Gopher server to retrieve the item.

- ✔ *Host.* ServerName is the host name or the IP address of the computer on the Internet that runs the Gopher server.

A good way to test the ItemPath in your Gopher link is to telnet to ServerName on port 70 and then type ItemPath exactly as it appears in your link file. If ItemPath is correct, the Gopher server at ServerName sends the item that you request; if ItemPath is incorrect, the server responds with an error message.

Now send this text file to your Gopher directory, and rename it .links (or some other name that begins with a period). Remember, files that begin with a period are special to the Gopher server.

The following text file creates a Gopher link to Gopher Central, a Gopher directory at the University of Minnesota:

```
Name=Gopher Central
Type=1
Port=70
Path=/
Host=gopher.tc.umn.edu
```

This text file creates a Gopher link to the list of Frequently Asked Questions about Gopher:

```
Name=Frequently Asked Questions about Gopher
Type=0
Port=70
Path=/Gopher.FAQ
Host=mudhoney.micro.umn.edu
```

Some Gopher servers require a `TypeCode` as part of `ItemPath`. If, for example, the `ItemPath` for a text file is `/help.txt`, but the server complains that the file doesn't exist, try using `0/help.txt` for `ItemPath` instead. The extra `TypeCode` in the beginning of the `ItemPath` may help the server find the right item.

You may wonder why Gopher doesn't use URL syntax to create links, the way the World Wide Web does. Using that syntax certainly would make sense and would be much simpler to understand. URL syntax isn't used simply because Gophers don't understand URLs.

Gopher and the World Wide Web evolved at the same time. The creators of the World Wide Web simply had a better idea. Future versions of Gopher may indeed use URL syntax to create links; we can only hope. If, like us, you're too impatient to wait, you *can* be creative and use URL syntax to create links. See "Being Creative with Your Gopher Server" at the end of this chapter for more information.

Making Money with a Gopher

A Gopher server is similar to an FTP server. Because you can't control who has access to your Gopher directory, you can't charge people for access to your Gopher resource, but you *can* attempt to charge for the use of your files.

If you set up a Gopher resource, you have one more option that you don't have with FTP: You can sell advertising on your Gopher server, provided that your Gopher site is popular enough. Offer your advertisers one or two lines of text, a couple of files, or an entire Gopher directory for their brochures and other information, and offer to create a link to their Gopher server if they have one.

To create the advertisement text, add aliases to files on your Gopher site. If you create a link to an advertiser's Gopher server, give the link an informative name to make it part of the ad.

Installing Your Own Gopher Server

Even if you subscribe to a Gopher publishing service on the Internet, you'll want a Gopher server on your personal computer. Having a Gopher server in addition to World Wide Web and FTP servers on your personal computer ensures that you can share files directly with anyone on the Internet.

Running a Gopher server on your PC, rather than using a Gopher publishing service, eliminates ongoing Gopher publishing fees and allows you to share files directly from your PC so that you don't need to send them to your Gopher publishing service before other Internet users can access them.

Setting up a Macintosh Gopher server

The Macintosh FTP server software, *FTPd,* also is a good Gopher server. Setting up a Gopher server is a breeze after you have the FTPd software installed.

To use FTPd, your Macintosh must have System 7 or later, MacTCP version 1.1 or later, and File Sharing enabled. To allow Internet users to access your Gopher server, you need some kind of TCP/IP Internet access, such as PPP or a direct network connection. You can find the FTPd software from these sites on the Internet:

```
http://science.org/internetsite/
ftp://ftp.share.com/peterlewis/
```

Copy FTPd to your hard drive and unStufflt, if necessary. Before doing anything else, establish security for your Gopher server. Gopher-server security is controlled by Macintosh File Sharing, just like security for the FTP server. Internet users can access any file, folder, or volume that is shared with the Guest user. See "The Macintosh FTPd server" in Chapter 4 for instructions on setting up FTPd, establishing security through File Sharing, and running the Internet Config program.

After you install FTPd and set up your security, double-click the FTPd Setup icon to access the FTPd Setup window shown in Figure 9-2. The FTPd Setup window allows you to configure your Gopher server.

Figure 9-2:
The FTPd
Setup
window.

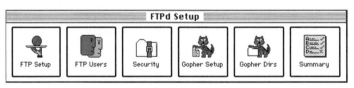

The FTPd Setup program has two Gopher configuration windows:

  ✔ Gopher Setup
  ✔ Gopher Dirs

Click on the Gopher Setup box to display the Gopher Setup window (shown in Figure 9-3), and mark the Gopher Enabled check box to tell FTPd to act as a Gopher server.

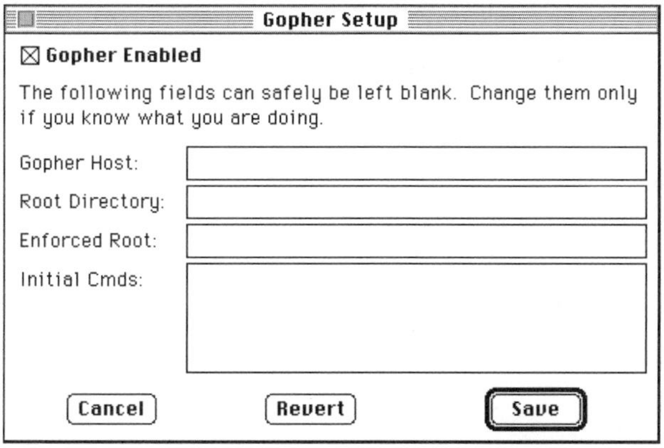

Figure 9-3:
Check the
Gopher
Enabled
check box
to tell FTPd
to be your
Gopher.

```
▤▦▦▦▦▦▦▦▦▦▦▦ Gopher Setup ▦▦▦▦▦▦▦▦▦▦▦▦
  ⊠ Gopher Enabled
  The following fields can safely be left blank.  Change them only
  if you know what you are doing.

  Gopher Host:    [                                        ]

  Root Directory: [                                        ]

  Enforced Root:  [                                        ]

  Initial Cmds:   [                                        ]
                  [                                        ]
                  [                                        ]
                  [                                        ]

  ( Cancel )         ( Revert )              ( Save )
```

Creating a special folder for the files that you're going to provide through your Gopher server is a good idea. You can use the same folder that your FTP server uses. The Gopher files don't interfere with your FTP server, so this approach has no drawbacks.

Whether you create a separate Gopher folder or share a folder with FTP, you should enter the path to the folder in the Root Directory field in the Gopher Setup window. This information tells the Gopher server which folder to display when a Gopher user connects to your server. If your folder is named FTPandGopher on the volume SharedVol, the directory path is:

`/SharedVol/FTPandGopher`

Both the volume SharedVol and the folder FTPandGopher must be shared with the Guest user so that anonymous FTP and Gopher users can access them.

Click on the Save button to save your changes to Gopher Setup. Then click on the Gopher Dirs box to finish setting up your Gopher server. The window shown in Figure 9-4 appears, allowing you to choose a Gopher folder. Choose your Gopher folder and then click on the Select button at the bottom of the window.

A window resembling Figure 9-5 then appears. This window lists the contents of your Gopher folder and allows you to add links to other Gopher servers on the Internet.

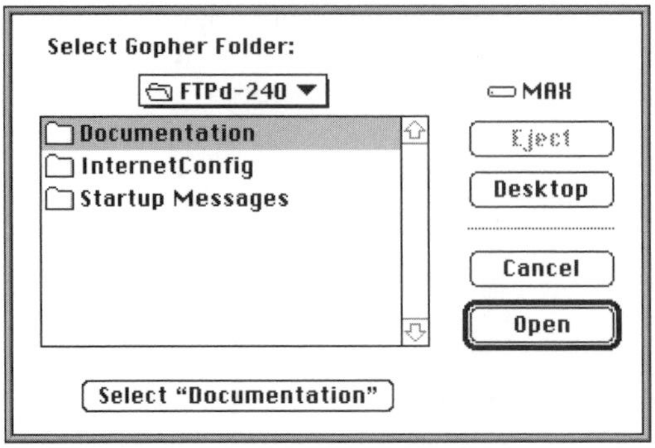

Figure 9-4:
Select your Gopher folder with the Gopher Dirs window.

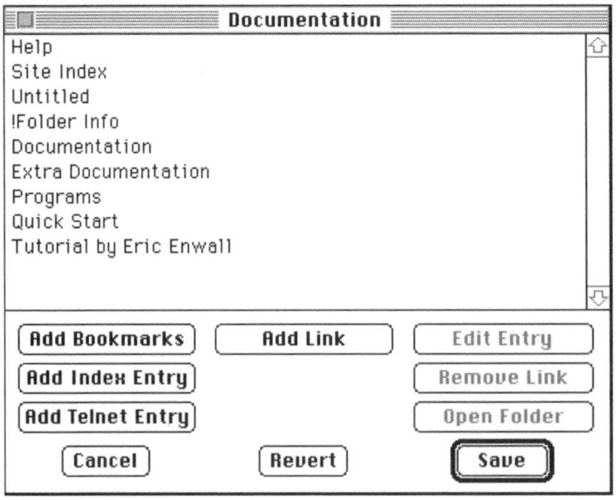

```
Select Gopher Folder:

    📁 FTPd-240 ▼              ⬜ MAX

  📁 Documentation      ⬆    [  Eject  ]
  📁 InternetConfig
  📁 Startup Messages        [ Desktop ]

                              [ Cancel  ]
                        ⬇    [  Open   ]

  [ Select "Documentation" ]
```

Figure 9-5:
The Gopher window for adding a Gopher link to other servers.

```
▤          Documentation          ▤
Help                              ⬆
Site Index
Untitled
!Folder Info
Documentation
Extra Documentation
Programs
Quick Start
Tutorial by Eric Enwall
                                  ⬇

[ Add Bookmarks  ] [  Add Link  ] [  Edit Entry  ]
[ Add Index Entry ]               [ Remove Link  ]
[ Add Telnet Entry ]              [ Open Folder  ]
[ Cancel ]        [ Revert ]      [   Save    ]
```

To add a link to another Internet resource, click on the Add Link button. The pop-up window shown in Figure 9-6 appears.

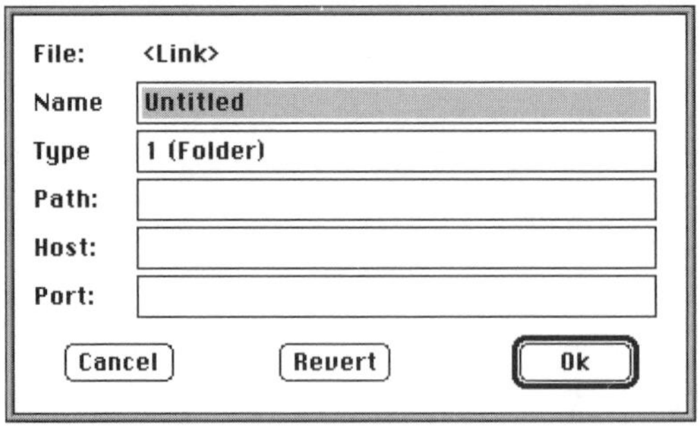

Figure 9-6:
Add a Gopher link by filling in this window.

```
File:    <Link>
Name    Untitled
Type    1 (Folder)
Path:   [                    ]
Host:   [                    ]
Port:   [                    ]
[ Cancel ]     [ Revert ]     [  Ok  ]
```

Fill in the following five fields to create the link:

- ✔ *Name:* The name of this link. Users of your Gopher site see this name when they access the Gopher directory.

- ✔ *Type:* Type code for the item to which you're creating a link. By default, the type code is 1, meaning that the item to which you're linking is another Gopher directory. Refer to "Serving Gopher Links" earlier in this chapter for more information.

- ✔ *Path:* The path to the item. If you simply want a link to another Gopher server, you can leave the Path field blank; otherwise, you must fill in the exact path to the item. Without a Path entry, the link doesn't specify a particular item on the other Gopher server. When a user chooses a link that doesn't have a Path entry, the Gopher server specified in the link is asked to display its default Gopher menu.

- ✔ *Host:* The name or the IP address of the Internet host to contact.

- ✔ *Port:* The port number to contact on the host. The Port field normally should be 70, which is the Gopher port.

Click on the OK button when you finish defining the link. Be sure to check the Summary window by clicking on Summary in the FTPd Setup window. If you have any problems, the Summary window tells you so (see Figure 9-7).

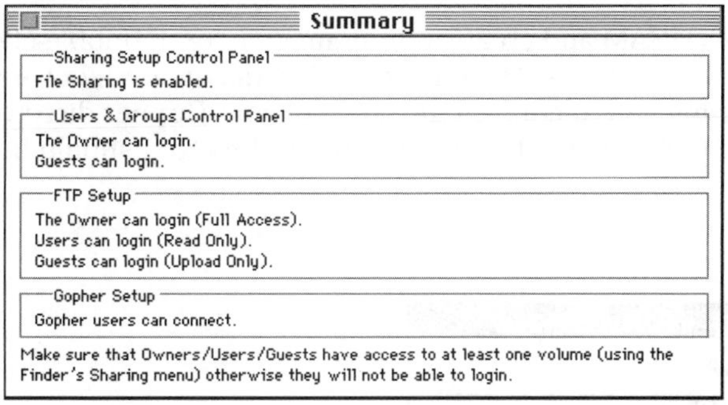

Figure 9-7:
The FTPd
Summary
window
indicates
whether
your Gopher
server is
ready.

```
┌──────────────────── Summary ────────────────────┐
│ ┌─Sharing Setup Control Panel──────────────────┐ │
│ │ File Sharing is enabled.                      │ │
│ └───────────────────────────────────────────────┘ │
│ ┌─Users & Groups Control Panel─────────────────┐ │
│ │ The Owner can login.                          │ │
│ │ Guests can login.                             │ │
│ └───────────────────────────────────────────────┘ │
│ ┌─FTP Setup────────────────────────────────────┐ │
│ │ The Owner can login (Full Access).            │ │
│ │ Users can login (Read Only).                  │ │
│ │ Guests can login (Upload Only).               │ │
│ └───────────────────────────────────────────────┘ │
│ ┌─Gopher Setup─────────────────────────────────┐ │
│ │ Gopher users can connect.                     │ │
│ └───────────────────────────────────────────────┘ │
│ Make sure that Owners/Users/Guests have access to at least one volume (using the │
│ Finder's Sharing menu) otherwise they will not be able to login. │
└──────────────────────────────────────────────────┘
```

To quit FTPd, start FTPd Setup and then quit FTPd Setup while holding down the Option key. This way, you close both FTPd Setup and the active FTPd program. This method also shuts down your Gopher server.

Setting up a Windows Gopher server

One of the pioneers of Gopher server software for Windows is Gunter Hille, who wrote GO4HAM. GO4HAM is a functional Gopher server for Windows that has one major drawback: You must update an index file each time you add files to your Gopher directory. This extra step makes the Gopher server less useful, but it does work, so if you want to run a Gopher server in Windows, that's how to do it.

To run GO4HAM, you need Windows version 3.1 or Windows 95 with a TCP/IP communications program that is compatible with WinSock version 1.1 or greater. To allow Internet users to access your Gopher server, you need some kind of TCP/IP Internet connection. You can obtain the GO4HAM from the following site on the Internet:

```
gopher://boombox.micro.umn.edu/11/gopher/PC_server/hamburg/
```

Begin by copying the software to your hard drive. GO4HAM usually comes in PKZIP format, so you need to create a new directory and then unzip the software into that directory. We put all our WinSock programs in C:\WINSOCK, so we use the following directory:

```
C:\WINSOCK\GO4HAM
```

After you install GO4HAM and create a program item for it, double-click the Server icon to start the GO4HAM application. The dialog box, shown in Figure 9-8 appears, allowing you to confirm the name of your Gopher directory. Click on the OK button to continue; the default Gopher directory should be just fine.

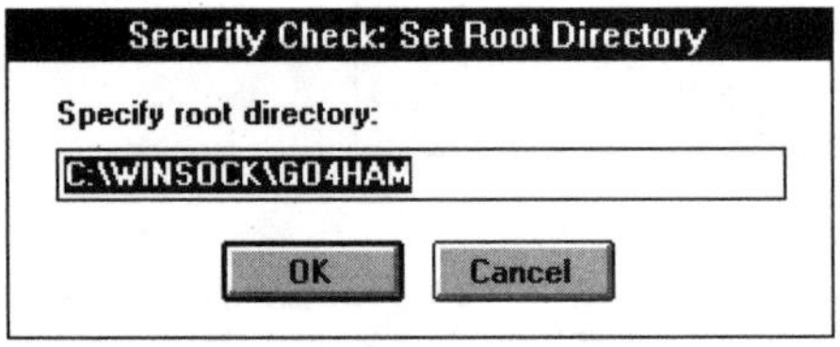

Figure 9-8:
The Security
Check: Set
Root Gopher
Directory
dialog box.

Security Check: Set Root Directory

Specify root directory:

`C:\WINSOCK\GO4HAM`

| OK | Cancel |

Now you see the GO4HAM application itself (see Figure 9-9). Choose File⇨Start Server to start the Gopher server. To stop the server, choose File⇨Exit.

After you start the GO4HAM Gopher server, you're ready to accept Gopher connections from users on the Internet. This situation is good. What isn't so good is that the files that they'll see aren't yours; they're Gunter Hille's! To change to your own files, you must follow these steps:

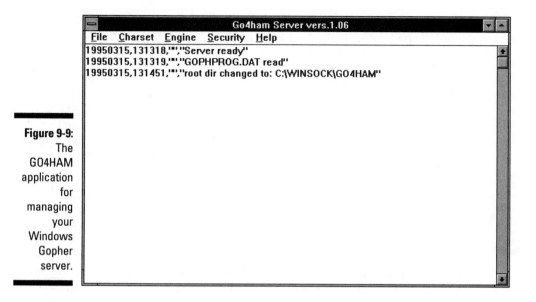

Figure 9-9:
The
GO4HAM
application
for
managing
your
Windows
Gopher
server.

1. **Delete the files 000ROOT.GOP and 00GOPHER.GOP in your Gopher directory, using the following DOS command (replace C:\WINSOCK\ GO4HAM with the name of your GO4HAM directory):**

```
DEL C:\WINSOCK\GO4HAM\*.GOP
```

2. **Create a new file called GOPHER.GOP in your GO4HAM directory.**

   Use any text editor you want. Keep reading to find out what to put in this new file.

The content of the GOPHER.GOP file determines what items the users of your Gopher server see. You also use GOPHER.GOP to create links to other Gopher servers on the Internet. Each line in the GOPHER.GOP file defines a single item. The following line defines a file named INDEX:

```
0 Index File for This Server        0INDEX     0.0.0.0    70
```

Begin the line with the type code for the item. In the preceding example, the type code is 0, because INDEX is a text file (see Table 9-1). After the type code, type a space, followed by the alias for this item. In this case, the alias is Index File for This Server. The alias is the text displayed in your Gopher menu when a user contacts your Gopher server.

Follow the alias with a tab (the tab is very important) and then type the path to the item. The path is the text that is sent to the Gopher server to retrieve an item. GO4HAM needs a type code before the path, so 0INDEX tells GO4HAM to retrieve the INDEX file in the main Gopher directory. When you're in doubt about the path for an item, you can attempt to access the item from its Gopher server. If the Gopher server returns an error message, the path that you specified is incorrect.

After the item path, enter another tab (again, the tab is very important) and then type the IP address of the Gopher server. (In the example, we used a fake IP address of 0.0.0.0). Follow the IP address with another tab and then type the port number to contact, which almost always is 70. To make this sample entry work for your Gopher server, replace the IP address 0.0.0.0 with your real IP address.

The INDEX file must exist in your Gopher directory for this entry to work. GO4HAM doesn't check to make sure that the items in your GOPHER.GOP file are actually there; it just displays the contents of GOPHER.GOP to users of your Gopher server.

Following are a few more examples. This line in GOPHER.GOP creates a link to Gopher Central at the University of Minnesota:

```
1 Gopher Central /                     gopher.tc.umn.edu    70
```

The 1 means that this item is a Gopher directory. The name Gopher Central is the alias that appears in your Gopher menu. The / is the path to the directory on the Gopher server. The Gopher server is named gopher.tc.umn.edu, and the port is 70.

This example adds an entry for another Gopher directory on your computer:

```
1 2nd Gopher Directory              1GOPHER2\ 0.0.0.0    70
```

For this entry to work, you must create the GOPHER2 directory in your main Gopher directory and change 0.0.0.0 to your real IP address. You also need to create another GOPHER.GOP file in the GOPHER2 directory if you want users to see a list of items when they access the directory.

Here's an example of a text file named TEXTFILE.TXT in the GOPHER2 directory:

```
0 Text File in 2nd Dir    0GOPHER2\TEXTFILE.TXT 0.0.0.0    70
```

The 0 indicates a text file, Text File in 2nd Dir is the alias for this item, 0GOPHER2\TEXTFILE.TXT is the path, 0.0.0.0 is the IP address, and 70 is the port.

Be sure to start your Gopher server by choosing File⇨Start Server in GO4HAM. Just running the GO4HAM program isn't enough to turn on the Gopher server. Always test your Gopher server with a Gopher client program or through your World Wide Web browser. The following URL should work (just replace 0.0.0.0 with your IP address):

```
gopher://0.0.0.0/
```

Being Creative with Your Gopher Server

Gopher combines the file-transfer capabilities of anonymous FTP with the linking capabilities of the World Wide Web to provide a useful information resource. With a little creativity, you can make your Gopher server even more effective by integrating the best aspects of the World Wide Web: HTML and URL based hyperlinks.

Using Gopher to serve Web documents

Many users may use a Web browser to access your Gopher server. If you provide World Wide Web documents through your Gopher server, these users can view your Web pages by selecting them from a Gopher menu.

Dropping a Gopher anchor

Gopher links aren't much fun; they're difficult, cryptic, and basically unpleasant. (They even smell bad.) Don't use these links any more than you have to. Instead, use HTML in your Gopher aliases to provide a World Wide Web document *within* your Gopher menu.

The following Gopher alias creates a hyperlink to the Setting Up An Internet Site home page:

```
Path=./somefile
Name=<A HREF="http://pk.com/internetsite/">Set up Internet Site</A>
```

The HTML formatting causes World Wide Web browsers to display the Gopher alias as a hypertext link. Figure 9-10 shows how this item is displayed as an http://hyperlink in Netscape.

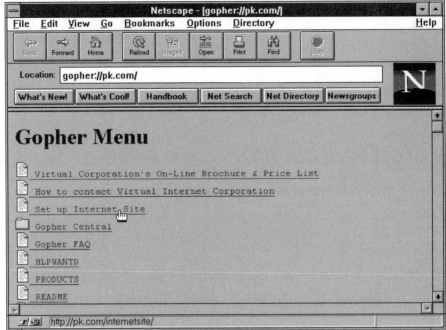

Figure 9-10:
An HTML
anchor in
Gopher alias
names that
creates a
World Wide
Web-style
hyperlink.

You can even use the `<IMG SRC="">` format to place images in your Gopher menu. The following Gopher alias name includes an image:

```
Path=./someotherfile
Name=<img  src="http://www.ncsa.uiuc.edu/SDG/Experimental/anu
art-history/pergamum1s.gif">Welcome  to  Virtual  Corporation's
Gopher Server
Numb=1
```

Figure 9-11 shows this image displayed in Netscape.

Your Internet site may not be complete without a Gopher server depending on the type and format of the information you want to serve on the Internet. Although Gopher isn't the most popular Internet resource, it is an important resource to consider if you want to build a complete Internet presence. If providing files over the Internet is important to you, Gopher even offers some advantages over the World Wide Web and FTP.

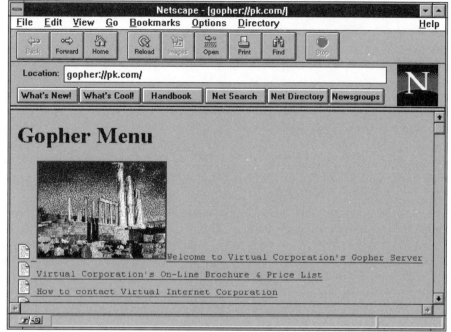

Figure 9-11:
You can add
an image to
your Gopher
menu.

Chapter 10
Creating an Internet Newsgroup

• •

In This Chapter
▶ Understanding the news system
▶ Providing information through Internet news
▶ Integrating Internet news into your World Wide Web site

• •

*I*nternet news, commonly referred to as *Usenet news*, is a simple resource that enables people around the world to carry on conversations and exchange information. The term *news* implies a professional, journalistic source of information, but like television news, Internet news rarely resembles anything professional. The reason is that the vast majority of *newsgroups* (conference areas dedicated to a particular topic) are *uncontrolled,* meaning that anyone who wants to can post a message.

Internet news has, for many people, become one of the primary attractions of the Internet. The uncontrolled nature of the news system is part of the reason for its popularity. Anything — anything at all — can be, and is, discussed on Internet newsgroups. Some newsgroups are strange or useless, but many of them are serious interactive tools that have become indispensable resources for technical and scientific professionals.

This chapter describes the technical function of the Internet news system in terms that are simple and relevant. The chapter also explores ways in which you or your company can establish a presence on the news system and integrate this valuable interactive resource into your World Wide Web site.

The two basic newsgroup types are:

✔ Local
✔ Global

To understand the difference between a local newsgroup and a global one, you need to know a little about how people read newsgroups, how news messages are distributed throughout the Internet, and how the news system operates.

Reading the Writing on the Wall

For too long, reading and contributing to Usenet news was a clumsy, tedious process that was frustrating for all but the most devoted users. The problem was simple: to access Usenet news, a user needed a special program known as a *newsreader*. Most Internet users either didn't have newsreaders or found the programs to be difficult and complicated (your authors included). This situation has changed now that the newer versions of Netscape include a built-in, easy-to-use newsreader.

Accessing the new Netscape newsreader is simple. The built-in newsreader appears automatically when it sees an address that begins with a `news:` `prefix`. You're probably familiar with URL syntax by now, but this prefix may be news to you. We'll discuss the `news:URL` syntax in more detail later, when we show you how to include a link to your news resource on your World Wide Web site.

Before Netscape's newsreader will work, you need to configure it by choosing Options⇨Mail and then News. Your Internet access provider can (and should) give you instructions or otherwise show you how to configure the program. This section is meant to give you an overview of the way in which users will access your news resource; therefore, it leaves out detailed user instructions and newsreader setup requirements.

The `news:URL` prefix has a special meaning that a Netscape Web browser understands. If you enter `news:` in Netscape, the built-in newsreader appears. To access a particular newsgroup automatically, follow the `news:` prefix with the name of the newsgroup that you want to access. The following URL accesses the global newsgroup `news.groups` (see Figures 10-1 and 10-2):

```
news:news.groups
```

Now comes the tricky part. `news:news.groups` is a valid URL, but unlike the URL for your Web site, the `news:news.groups` URL doesn't specify a unique resource on the Internet. Remember that the URL of your Web site is a unique address; whenever anyone on the Internet accesses your Web site, he or she sees the same exact Web page that everyone else sees. With the `news:news.groups` URL, however, each person sees something different and accesses a different news server. A *news server* is a program that maintains newsgroups and news messages and that communicates with newsreaders. `news.groups`, for example, is a global newsgroup that is accessed on each user's local news server. (Think globally, act locally.)

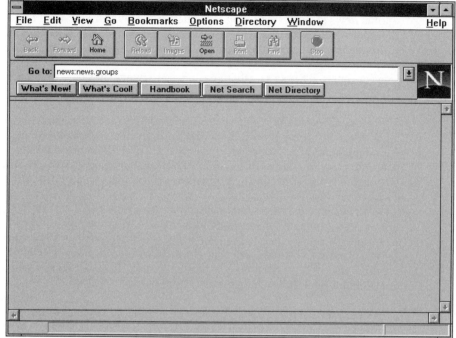

Figure 10-1:
Enter a
news: URL
to access
the
Netscape
newsreader.

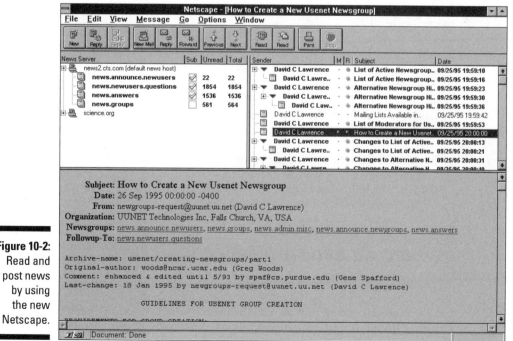

Figure 10-2:
Read and
post news
by using
the new
Netscape.

When a user posts a message to a global newsgroup, that message enters the global news stream, beginning with the news server maintained by the user's Internet access provider. Then the message is distributed automatically to other news servers on the Internet. Not every message posted to a global newsgroup makes its way to every news server, so people who read a global newsgroup don't necessarily have access to every message that's posted to the newsgroup.

For most newsgroups, this situation isn't a big deal. The kinds of conversations that occur on global newsgroups don't require 100 percent reliability. But the unreliable nature of global newsgroups does preclude your company from offering customer support or other important business electronic conferencing through a global newsgroup. The answer is to create a local newsgroup.

A *local newsgroup* is one that exists only on a single news server. Because a local newsgroup isn't distributed globally, like other groups, anyone on the Internet who accesses a local newsgroup sees precisely the same messages that every other person sees. This capability to see the same message on many servers makes it possible to conduct important discussions in which every participant must have access to every message.

To access a local newsgroup, use the more familiar URL format `prefix://server/itemname` (`prefix:` is news:, `server` is the name of the news server on which a local newsgroup exists, and `itemname` is the name of the local group). The following `news:` URL refers to a local newsgroup named `science.org.research`, hosted by the news server named `science.org` (see Figure 10-3):

```
news://science.org/science.org.research
```

Figure 10-4 shows Netscape's newsreader after it contacts the news server named `science.org`. The local newsgroup `science.org.research` is displayed automatically. This newsgroup is a local newsgroup that is accessed globally. (Act global, go loco.)

Thousands upon thousands of newsgroups are available on the Internet, and you may wonder how they got there, especially if you want to create one yourself. The following section answers this question; later sections show you how to create your own newsgroup.

Where do newsgroups come from?

Thus far, we've mentioned news servers only in passing. The reason is that news server software isn't available for personal computers yet, so we don't want to bore you with technical details about which you don't need be concerned. Because you won't be running a news server, understanding that they

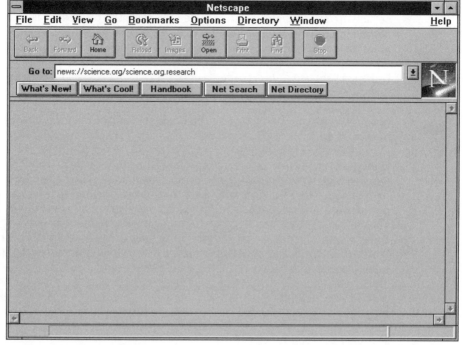

Figure 10-3:
Access
local
newsgroups
by using
the more
complete
URL syntax.

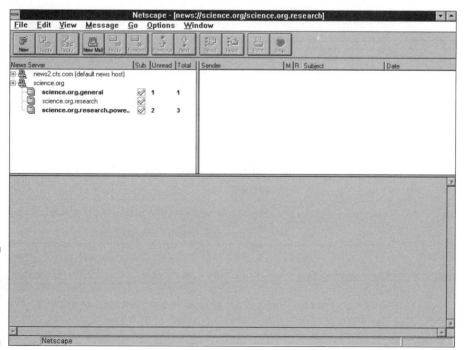

Figure 10-4:
Use local
newsgroups
for reliable
conferencing.

exist and leaving it at that is OK. Let your Internet access provider worry about setting up and running an Internet news server; the procedure is tedious and complicated, anyway, and doing it right requires a high-speed connection and a great deal of disk space.

News servers use *Network News Transfer Protocol* (NNTP) to exchange news messages with other news servers. News servers are sometimes known as *NNTP servers*. Newsreader programs also use NNTP to exchange messages with news servers, effectively fooling the news server by masquerading as another news server.

Understanding how existing newsgroups came into being is useful. To begin with, why do newsgroups have such strange names? The answer is that the people who wrote the first news server software decided to organize newsgroups in categories. The categories were given short symbolic names, such as `news`, `comp`, and `sci`. Any newsgroup whose name begins with one of those category names is considered to be part of that category. This naming convention forms a *newsgroup hierarchy*. The following are a few sample newsgroup names:

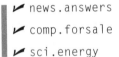

- `news.answers`
- `comp.forsale`
- `sci.energy`

Each newsgroup category serves a particular purpose. Table 10-1 shows the seven major categories that comprise the core of global newsgroups.

Table 10-1	The Seven Major Global-Newsgroup Categories
Newsgroup	*Category Description*
news.	Groups that pertain to the Internet news system itself
sci.	Scientific newsgroups for serious discussions
rec.	Newsgroups for discussion of recreational activities
comp.	Computer-related groups
misc.	Miscellaneous discussion groups (no focus)
soc.	Groups for socializing or talking about social issues
talk.	Debates about controversial topics

Local newsgroups are created by organizations that run news servers. Most universities, for example, have news servers and provide local newsgroups for discussion of campus-specific issues. Internet access providers have local newsgroups to provide technical support or to give their customers a place to talk among themselves.

Local newsgroup names don't need to adhere to the global-newsgroup-naming structure. The Internet access provider Netcom, Inc., provides several newsgroups whose names begin with `netcom.`, such as `netcom.support`. Because these newsgroups are local, not distributed throughout the Internet, they need not comply with the global newsgroup naming scheme.

Global newsgroups are created in two ways, depending on the type of group that is involved. The "official" global newsgroup categories, such as `sci.`, `comp.`, and `news.`, rely on a voting process. The "unofficial" global newsgroup categories, such as `alt.`, rely on anarchy for group creation.

Official newsgroup categories are very strict about new group naming. The unofficial categories, as you might imagine, don't impose any naming restrictions, so names such as `alt.help.with.homework` aren't uncommon.

Move over, Rush Limbaugh and Art Bell: moderated groups

Most newsgroups allow anyone to post anything. The quality of the material in a newsgroup is determined by the quality of the people who participate. This after-the-fact method is a way for quality to be maintained. If a person posts an offensive message, he or she usually receives endless e-mail spouting disapproval, and a great deal of discussion about the offending message often occurs in the newsgroup. The person who posted the message never forgets the flood of angry letters (called *drive-by hatred*) that he or she receives and usually posts more appropriate messages in the future.

Waiting for someone to post an offending message, and then blasting them is, at best, a clumsy way to prevent inappropriate postings; at worst, this method is totally ineffective, and inappropriate postings become the norm for the newsgroup. A special type of newsgroup solves this problem by allowing someone to approve or reject articles before they are posted. This type of newsgroup is called a *moderated* newsgroup.

One person — usually, the newsgroup's creator — is designated as the moderator. Articles posted to the newsgroup are sent directly to the moderator instead of to the group. The moderator reads each message and either approves or rejects it. When the moderator rejects a message, he or she usually sends an e-mail message to the message writer, giving the reason why the message wasn't suitable for posting.

Moderating a newsgroup is an excellent way to maintain a question and answer format or to establish a level of editorial quality. This arrangement also is effective for newsgroups that function as one-way news and information messages. In these newsgroups, the moderator simply rejects all other requests to post messages.

The following section shows you how to create both moderated and unmoderated global and local newsgroups. You should be able to decide by now which type of newsgroup is most appropriate for your needs. A final tip: global newsgroups essentially are public property. You can't control a global newsgroup and, therefore, don't own it, even if the group was your idea.

Giving Birth to a Newsgroup Idea

The idea for a newsgroup can come from anywhere. Often, a newsgroup idea springs from the release of a new product or from a new special-interest group that is discovering Internet news for the first time. Any topic that interests people is a valid newsgroup idea.

After you've given birth to the idea, the group needs a name. Make sure that the name of your newsgroup is interesting and descriptive, because the name of your newsgroup is the single most important factor in determining its content. In a newsgroup called `alt.cold.fusion`, people will expect to read about and discuss advancements in this area of research. Carrying on serious conversations about cold fusion in a newsgroup named `alt.cold.fusion.silly.idea`, however, would be difficult.

Newsgroups can be local or global. A local newsgroup exists only on a single news server, whereas global newsgroups are available on every news server. Messages that are posted to a local newsgroup exist on only one news server, whereas messages that are posted to a global newsgroup propagate around the Internet and are available on many (although not necessarily all) news servers.

Be sure to scan the list of current newsgroups to make sure that your newsgroup name is available and is not already being used for exactly the type of conversation that you have in mind. Also read the newsgroups `news.groups`, `news.announce.newgroups`, and `alt.config` to verify that someone else hasn't recently recommended your newsgroup or one that's very similar to it. If you want to start a moderated newsgroup, consider adding the extension `.moderated` to the end of your group name.

Creating a global newsgroup with the seal of approval

Global newsgroups are created through a voting process. The first step is submitting a *Request for Discussion* (RFD) for your newsgroup idea. Read the newsgroup `news.announce.newgroups` to find a good RFD example, and copy the format when you create yours. Then post your RFD to the following newsgroups:

- `news.groups`
- `news.announce.newgroups`

You also should post the RFD to any other newsgroups or mailing lists that are related to your newsgroup idea. The goal is to elicit discussions by those people who are most likely to use the new newsgroup. Don't overdo your postings, though. Keep the number of newsgroups to a minimum so as to be considerate of others, and never post your RFD to newsgroups that are totally unrelated to your newsgroup proposal.

If you have trouble posting to `news.announce.newgroups`, you can e-mail your RFD to `newgroups@uunet.uu.net`, which will post the RFD for you. You also should look for a message titled "How to Create a New Usenet Newsgroup," which is posted regularly on `news.groups` and `news.answers`.

After you submit your RFD, someone reviews it, and if everything is in order, the RFD is posted to each of the newsgroups that you specify. In response to the RFD, discussion ensues on the newsgroup `news.groups`. After enough time has passed to give people a chance to think about and comment on your newsgroup idea, a *Call for Votes* (CFV) must be posted to these same news-groups. The CFV is posted by you, or the volunteer vote takers. This posting triggers a voting process, the result of which determines whether the Internet community approves or denies your group proposal.

When the time comes for a Call for Votes, send e-mail to the Usenet Volunteer Votetakers (UVV) for advice on how to proceed. The e-mail address is:

`uvv-contact@amdahl.com`

This tedious and involved "official" global newsgroup creation process is a holdover from the days before the World Wide Web. Internet news was one of the only global Internet information resources, and a great deal of energy was expended to keep the newsgroup resource one for serious discussion. Computer network managers who were in charge of administering news servers for universities, research institutions, and government offices were overwhelmed by the task of managing huge volumes of newsgroup traffic. These managers needed a simple way to ensure that their time and network resource wouldn't be consumed by an endless stream of useless newsgroups.

Instead of improving Internet news technology and creating innovative tools to solve these problems, a political solution was devised. If you find this political system to be repulsive and useless, ignore it, and create a local newsgroup or use the `alt.newsgroup` hierarchy. The following section describes how to create an `alt.newsgroup`.

Starting a global newsgroup the alternative way

A way around this tedious voting process exists. One global newsgroup hierarchy — the `alt.hierarchy` — doesn't require public approval for its newsgroups. Many people believe that `alt` stands for *alternative*. The name has taken on that meaning over time, but it originally stood for *anarchists, lunatics, and terrorists*. This hierarchy has quickly become one of the most popular and diverse of the many hierarchies. The `alt.` newsgroups range from `alt.alien.visitors` to `alt.comp.shareware.for-kids`. Forget the phone book; if you can't find something here, it *really* doesn't exist.

Creating an `alt.` newsgroup is simple: just post a message to the `alt.config` newsgroup, suggesting the new group. Also post a copy of the newsgroup suggestion to other groups that are related to the one you want to start, so that discussion of the new group idea can be widespread. If the administrators of Internet news servers like the idea, they will create the new `alt.` group. Be sure to read a few other proposals before posting your own to get a general idea of what a proposal should include.

You also should read a message titled "So You Want to Create an Alt Newsgroup," which is posted periodically on `alt.config` and `alt.answers`. This message provides up-to-date instructions on creating an `alt.` newsgroup.

Forming a local newsgroup

A local newsgroup is created by the organization that controls a news server. Because an organization has total control of the groups that exist on its news server, it can create any group instantly. Contact your Internet access provider to find out whether it will create a local newsgroup for you and, if so, whether users from elsewhere on the Internet will be granted access to the local newsgroup.

When you are searching for a host for your local newsgroup, keep two things in mind:

✔ The entire local-newsgroup concept is somewhat new on the Internet. Don't be surprised if your local access provider has never had such a request.

✔ The name of your local newsgroup shouldn't conflict with the name of a global newsgroup. Identical names may cause serious news conflicts. The news administrator will probably drop your group in favor of the global group.

Until recently, local newsgroups were used only for local discussions, as in the case of a university. Outsiders were prevented from accessing the local newsgroups or simply never tried, because gaining access wasn't easy. Now that Netscape Navigator supports the `news://hostname/groupname` URL syntax, you can host a local newsgroup that people can access globally. It may take a while, however, for the average Internet news administrator to recognize this possibility and adjust his or her news server accordingly. Be patient and be persistent if you encounter a confused response to your request for a local newsgroup. If all else fails, buy the news administrator a copy of this book.

Internet News and the World Wide Web

The newsgroups offer an incredible amount of information and serve as a forum for dialogue about specific topics. Until recently, newsgroups required external client software to access or were very difficult to include as a hypertext link in HTML pages. The newest Web browsers provide several methods that link people who are perusing your Web page to newsgroups that add to the information presented on your page.

Until recently, someone using a Web browser could contact the default news server only by typing `news:` as the URL syntax. Obviously, the word `news:` is not quite enough information to include as a hypertext link in your HTML page, but the times, they are a-changing. You still can use `news:` to access the news default server, but other, more powerful methods now exist.

In constructing a Web page, you can place a newsgroup as a hypertext link in an HTML document by using the following code:

```
<a href="news:alt.surfing">alt.surfing</a>
```

This syntax immediately launches the newsreader built into the Web browser for the person who is currently accessing your Web page and sends that person to the designated newsgroup.

Another method allows you to designate a specific news server with a hypertext link by using the following HTML code:

```
<a href="news://science.org">news://science.org</a>
```

Taking this method one step further, you can link a specific news server and newsgroup to a HTML document by using the following code:

```
<a href="news://science.org/science.org.general">general</a>
```

This method is particularly advantageous when you have a local newsgroup for customer support or product feedback, because it allows you to include a direct link to your local newsgroup within your Web page.

Providing directions to users so that they can access your news resource is even simpler; just give them the news://hostname/groupname URL syntax. You could print the following text on your company brochures or business cards to tell people how to access a local product support newsgroup on the news server server.name.com:

```
news://server.name.com/product.support
```

These new capabilities greatly expand the usefulness of newsgroups and allow you to integrate them into your World Wide Web site easily.

Usenet news is one of the most valuable interactive information resources on the Internet. People enjoy and benefit from the discussions that occur in newsgroups. Starting a new global newsgroup or running your own local group can be an excellent extension to your existing Internet presence. The potential of newsgroups to serve as simple, powerful, global discussion tools is finally being realized now that newsgroups can be accessed directly through World Wide Web browsers.

Part IV

The Essentials
of Life Online

In this part . . .

Living in a wired world requires the development of new skills and abilities. What has long been a comfortable and routine part of life is suddenly complicated and confusing. It's a lot like traveling to a foreign country where things like the money in your wallet and the language in your head cease to have any actual value. The things you've taken for granted for so long — being able to buy food when you get hungry or ask directions when you get lost — are frustratingly just out of reach.

The Internet should feel like home, but it won't until you have mastered a few of the essentials of life online. Acquiring and installing new Internet software for your computer and buying or selling things electronically are examples of the new skills you must develop. Some of the essentials discussed in this part are fundamental, such as learning how to give out your address so that people can locate your Internet site. The topics covered in this part are important for everyone who runs an Internet site.

Chapter 11
Basic Training

*T*his chapter presents some of the things you need to know when running an Internet site. Some things may be basic, such as how to compress and decompress files; others are more advanced, such as information on how to manage a TCP/IP network.

Compressing and Decompressing Files

Quite a few utility programs can make files smaller, making them easier to store or move around. These programs create an *archive file* containing a compressed version of the file or files you compress.

Archive files come in two basic types: the *normal archive*, which can have many different file extensions depending on the program used to create it; and the *self-extracting archive*. To open a normal archive file, users must first *decompress* the file using appropriate decompression software. But a *self-extracting archive* is an executable program that decompresses its contents when you run it — which means that people can decompress your archive files without having to have the correct decompression software.

Following are just a few of the reasons why you may want to compress your files:

- ✔ Save space on your hard drive
- ✔ Compress files into an archive so that they fit on fewer floppy disks
- ✔ Shorter download times
- ✔ Compress files into an archive for backup purposes
- ✔ Place files in an archive to make delivering and installing software easier

Zippy says "Use WinZip"

One of the most used programs on the planet is a small shareware program called PKZIP, which has been around for many years. PKZIP and its partner program, PKUNZIP, are used to compress and uncompress files, respectively.

The PKZIP program uses a special compression formula to make files smaller. Those files are then stored in an *archive file.* The archive file can contain one or more compressed files and often has the extension .ZIP. PKZIP can create both normal archives and self-extracting archives which normally have the file extension .EXE.

Recently, a Windows version of PKZIP, called *WinZip,* was created. This program makes creating compressed archives simple. Using this Windows software program, you can view the contents of an archive or click on files to view, extract, or delete them. The graphic user interface is much easier to use than the old DOS command interface. The WinZip user interface also makes extracting files (uncompressing them from the archive) much simpler.

This program is available all over the Internet. Because it's shareware and can be distributed freely, you can always include a copy with any compressed files you deliver to others. To get you started, download a copy from the source:

```
http://www.winzip.com/winzip/
```

You can find versions for Windows 95, Windows NT, and Windows 3.1.

Installing WinZip

WinZip comes in a self-extracting archive. After downloading it to your hard drive, you can run the file you've downloaded, and the setup process begins automatically.

If you're using Windows 95, you can start the Windows Explorer and double-click on the WinZip 95 icon.

During the Install process, WinZip recommends a directory where the program can be installed. You can either accept this directory or choose a different drive or directory. Next, WinZip asks whether you want to use Express or Custom setup. Unless you have special requirements, the Express setup should do the job. Finally, you are asked to read and agree to the license agreement. (Remember, this program is shareware.) If you do so, the WinZip screen shown in Figure 11-1 appears. Notice that the top of the screen still says unregistered. You are encouraged to comply with the license agreement and register your product.

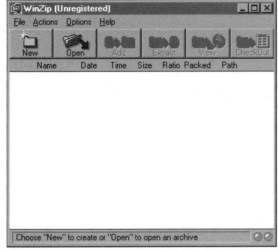

Figure 11-1:
The WinZip screen appears after a successful installation.

Zipping it up

You'll often hear the terms *zip* and *unzip*. *Zipping up a file* is a much more fun way of saying, "Creating a compressed archive." Of course, *unzipping a file* means extracting the file from the compressed archive.

To create a new archive and compress a file or group of files using WinZip, follow these steps:

1. **Click on the New button, shown in Figure 11-1.**

   A New Archive dialog box, as shown in Figure 11-2, appears.

2. **Select a new filename for your archive and the directory in which you would like the file stored.**

   After you do so, an Add dialog box appears.

3. **Select the drive, directory, and files you want included in your archive (see Figure 11-3).**

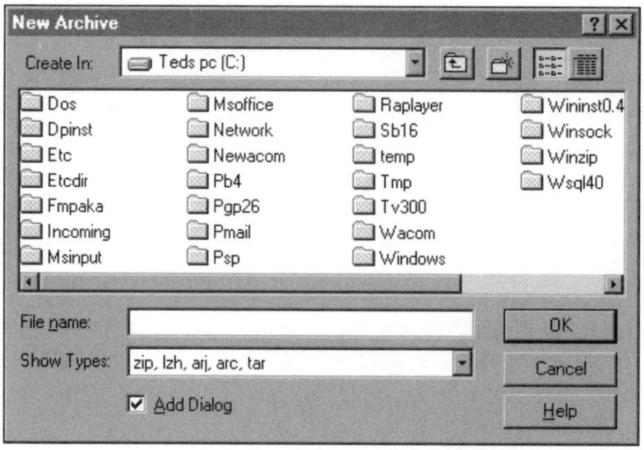

Figure 11-2:
Name your
new archive
and specify
where you
want to
store it.

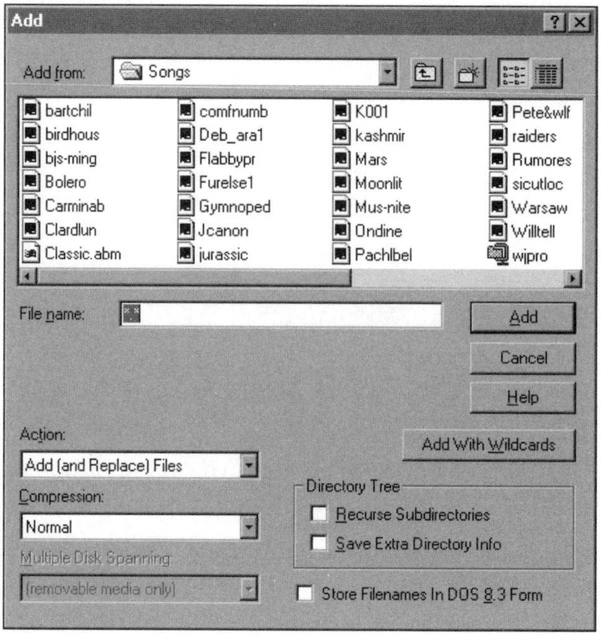

Figure 11-3:
Select the
files you
want
included in
your new
archive.

Select files individually or use a wildcard to select groups of files. The Add dialog box also offers other features you can select to maximize compression or to minimize the compression but increase the compression speed. If you're compressing many files, you may want to increase the compression speed. This decision depends on whether you care about speed or the size of your archive file. If you already have an archive file and you are adding files to it, you can choose options that enable you to replace, refresh, move, and update files in the archive.

4. Click on the Add button to create your archive.

When WinZip finishes creating the archive, the contents of the archive file are displayed, as shown in Figure 11-4.

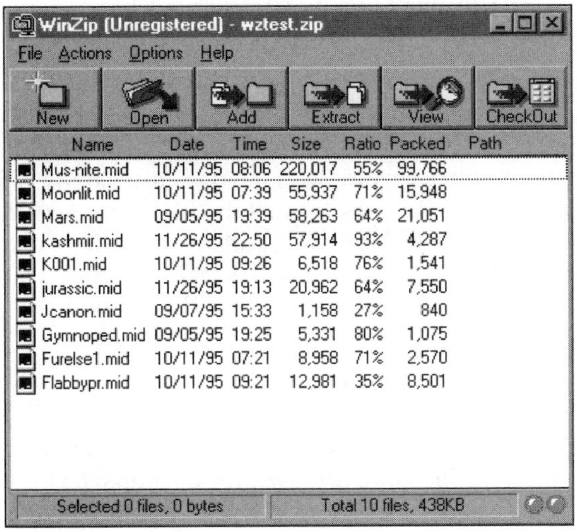

Figure 11-4:
WinZip
displays the
names of
the files
in your
archive.

Name	Date	Time	Size	Ratio	Packed	Path
Mus-nite.mid	10/11/95	08:06	220,017	55%	99,766	
Moonlit.mid	10/11/95	07:39	55,937	71%	15,948	
Mars.mid	09/05/95	19:39	58,263	64%	21,051	
kashmir.mid	11/26/95	22:50	57,914	93%	4,287	
K001.mid	10/11/95	09:26	6,518	76%	1,541	
jurassic.mid	11/26/95	19:13	20,962	64%	7,550	
Jcanon.mid	09/07/95	15:33	1,158	27%	840	
Gymnoped.mid	09/05/95	19:25	5,331	80%	1,075	
Furelse1.mid	10/11/95	07:21	8,958	71%	2,570	
Flabbypr.mid	10/11/95	09:21	12,981	35%	8,501	

WinZip [Unregistered] - wztest.zip
File   Actions   Options   Help
New   Open   Add   Extract   View   CheckOut

Selected 0 files, 0 bytes   Total 10 files, 438KB

Unzipping can be fun

As soon as you select an archive file in WinZip, you are presented with a list of the archive's contents, as shown in Figure 11-4. You can choose to extract any number of files from the archive.

You can configure many different programs so that when they encounter a zipped file, they automatically start WinZip and unzip the file. The compressed file must use a compression type recognized by WinZip. One of the places you can set up this configuration in Windows 95 is in the Windows Explorer. Check out the Windows 95 Help for configuring Explorer to automatically extract files from archives.

In addition to extracting WinZip archives (they have the file extension .ZIP), you can use WinZip to uncompress other types of archives. Some of the programs that create these archives include LHA, GZIP, UNIX compress, and UNIX tar.

Compressing files on the Mac: StuffIt

StuffIt is the file-compression utility predominately used on the Internet for compressing Macintosh files. If you are a Macintosh owner, you may already have StuffIt installed. Most of the software you can download from the Internet is compressed using StuffIt. If you don't have this program installed, we won't tell you to "just stuff it." Instead, here's some help.

Occasionally, files that have been downloaded from the Internet have been specially coded as text. Normally, this coding is so they can be sent through e-mail. If the StuffIt software you download is encoded, you'll need either *UULite* or *DeHQX* (pronounced *dee-hex*). These programs decode your files so that they are ready to run. Which utility you need depends on the type of file you want to decode. A file with the extension .HQX requires a bin-hex utility such as DeHQX. A file with the extension .BIN requires a UUdecode program such as UUlite.

Installing StuffIt

Before you can install the StuffIt program, you need to download it. (See http://www.science.org/internetsite.) If the file you download is encoded, you need to use one of the decoding software products discussed in the preceding paragraph. If you've installed one of these utilities, drop the newly downloaded StuffIt software onto the icon for the decode utility. The decode utility works automatically, and StuffIt is ready to run.

Using StuffIt

If you read the section on WinZip, you know that compression software has many uses. You can compress files into archives for backups, fast deliveries, or sometimes, just to organize your hard drive.

To use StuffIt, whether to compress files for fast delivery over the Internet or just to amaze your friends, follow these steps:

1. **Launch StuffIt by double clicking on the executable file in the StuffIt folder on your hard drive.**

2. **Select File⇨New from the StuffIt menu bar.**

   This step creates a new archive to hold the files that will be stuffed (compressed), as shown in Figure 11-5.

3. **Type in the name of the new archive in the space provided.**

   Again, refer to Figure 11-5. We called our sample archive NETSITE.SIT.

4. **Click on the New button.**

   This step gives you an empty archive with the title Netsite at the top (see Figure 11-6).

5. **Choose Archive⇨Stuff from the menu bar or click on the Stuff button to add files to the empty archive.**

   The directory window opens. Choose the files you want to include in the archive and click on the Add button. The files you select appear in the area on the right side of the window (see Figure 11-7).

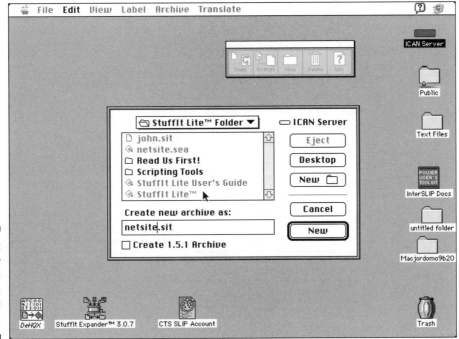

Figure 11-5:
Open a new
archive to
hold the
files that will
be stuffed.

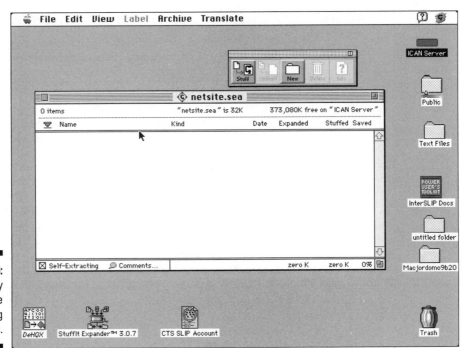

Figure 11-6:
The empty
archive
waiting
for files.

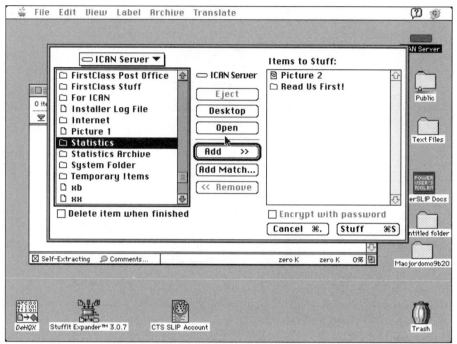

Figure 11-7:
Select files
to include in
the archive.

6. When you select all the files you want in the archive, click on the Stuff button.

The files now appear in the archive window, as shown in Figure 11-8.

7. Choose File⇨Close from the menu bar.

That's it. The files are in the archive, stuffed, and ready for delivery to visitors at your Internet site. Now all you need to do is place the archive in the appropriate location on your hard drive so that visitors to your site know where to find them. Refer to the earlier chapters on the Web, FTP, and e-mail to learn more about how an archive (or file) needs to be prepared and positioned for delivery at your site.

Remember that your visitors will need to know how to decompress your stuffed archive. You need to make allowances for the fact that both Windows and Macintosh users will probably be coming to your site. Make sure that you provide links to decompression utilities at your site. Again, you can find references and links to sites that provide decompression utilities for both the Windows and Macintosh platform at our Setting Up an Internet Site home page:

http://www.science.org/internetsite/

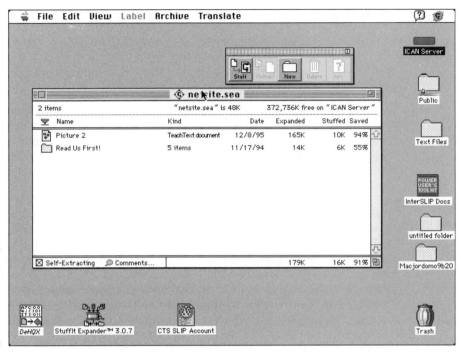

Figure 11-8:
The archive
is filled and
the files are
stuffed.

Letting your users know what files they'll get when they download an archive from your site is a good idea. Eating glass is more fun than downloading a large file with a vague description attached, only to find that the file is not what you wanted. The time taken to download, decompress, and install the file is wasted. That can leave a bad first impression of your site and quickly spread around the Internet.

Basic Network Stuff You Need to Know

Don't skip this section! You may be thinking that this section is not for you because you have only one PC sitting on your desk, not a network. Not true. A *network* is simply one computer connected to another, and the Internet is a big network of computers. Therefore, setting up an Internet site means setting up your computer, no matter what kind it is, to be a network node. The term *network node* refers to any computer on a network.

Preparing your computer to provide information on this global network of computers requires that you know something about how networks share information and what you have to do to make that information sharing happen.

TCP/IP

Information moves across the Internet in small electronic units called *packets*. Packets are like little envelopes sent through the mail. Each one contains an address, just like any envelope would, and some amount of information.

Here's a story that may help you understand how packets work. When a small community in the western United States decided to purchase the London Bridge, it didn't rent out the Queen Elizabeth II to ship it over. Instead, it had the bridge disassembled, stone by stone. Each stone was marked so that the bridge could be reassembled in its new desert home. Then the stones were packaged, so many to a box, and the boxes were sent to their destination.

Packets are kind of like the boxes used to transport the stones of the London Bridge. When you send a file over the network, the file is chopped into many byte-sized pieces. These pieces are arranged in packets, and the packets are sent to their destination. It doesn't matter if the packets follow the same route to their destination. Often, they don't. What is important is that when they all arrive, they are reassembled into their original form. This disassembly and reassembly is a little like the transporter mechanism used in the "Star Trek" series.

All computers on the Internet use a protocol called *TCP/IP* (Transmission Control Protocol/Internet Protocol) to communicate with one another. TCP/IP determines how packets are sent between computers and generally handles all communication sessions between computers on the Internet.

The Net advantage

Remember that the Internet is just a network — one that's no different from a network you would have in your office or possibly at home. And as with all networks, you can do more than just send and receive information on the Internet. Computers on a network can also share resources. Here are some of the resources computers commonly share across a network:

- Printers
- Disk drives
- Files
- Modems

One of the main reasons people started connecting PCs into networks was to share printers. With a network, all the computers in an office can use a printer attached to one computer on the network that is set up to share its printer with the others. The capability to share printers alone makes networks very popular. A company can buy a single, more expensive, high-speed laser printer instead of buying a large number of less expensive, dot-matrix printers.

Only recently did people became aware that their networks were actually capable of much more than acting as a printer-sharing device. Networks can also be used to share disk drives, for example. Individual desktop PCs don't need humongous hard drives if they can share the hard drive space of a large file server computer. (A file *server* is a computer that shares its disk drives with other computers on a network.)

Server computers make their printers, disk drives, files, or other attached devices available to other computers on the network. The shared files or devices are given names by which other network nodes can refer to them. The server computer is then responsible for handling security for the shared devices. For example, the server may allow only certain nodes to share its hard drive while letting all nodes share its printer.

Mount up

When computers on a network use devices shared by a server computer, they are said to be *mounting* those devices. Mounting resources shared by a server gives a computer new capabilities. If your computer mounts a printer, for example, it then has a new printer you can use. A network node can actually mount several printers attached to several computers, as long as each device has a unique name, such as *Laser1* and *Laser2*.

When a node computer mounts all or part of a hard disk shared by a server computer, it appears as a separate drive. A mounted drive is also known as a *virtual drive* because it is not physically located in the node machine. On a Macintosh, the drive shows up with a hard drive name, such as "My Remote Desktop." On a PC, it shows up with a different drive letter, such as D or E. The new drive letter depends on what physical drives you already have installed. Most PCs have at least drives A and C. A CD-ROM, if your computer has one, is normally designated as the D drive.

When a UNIX computer mounts a shared drive, the drive shows up as a separate directory instead of a separate drive. In UNIX, all drives, whether physical or virtual, show up as part of one file system (part of one directory structure).

Figure 11-9 shows an example network. The computers on this network are named MyNode, YourNode, and LymphNode. On this network, drive C on MyNode is a physical hard drive. In other words, it's the real thing. You can feel it, touch it, and hear it spin. MyNode is sharing this hard drive across the network. Both YourNode and LymphNode have mounted this hard drive and call their new virtual drives by different drive letters. In this case, the virtual drives are named E and F, respectively. To unsuspecting users on the YourNode and LymphNode computers, it might appear as though their computer actually has an E drive or an F drive. When users access files from their virtual drives,

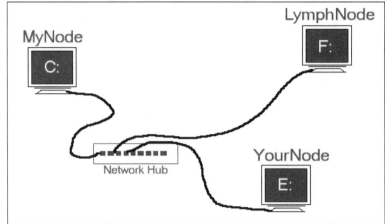

Figure 11-9:
Network
nodes
connected
by a
network.

however, they are actually accessing files over the network on MyNode. If the user on LymphNode deletes a file on the F drive, the file is actually deleted from the hard drive on MyNode.

In Figure 11-9, a printer named LaserPrinter is physically attached to LymphNode. LymphNode is sharing its printer over the network so that MyNode and YourNode can mount it.

Internetworking

As stated earlier in this chapter, the Internet is just a big network. We can't stress this concept enough. Most people think of the Internet as some incomprehensible cyberspace nebula of something or other. Well, it's not. The Internet is simply a network of computers that offers all the capabilities discussed in the preceding section. Sure, this network has a lot of computers attached to it. But that fact makes no difference at all in the way the network is used. If we want to share the hard drive of one of our computers over the Internet (a process called *exporting*), we can. Then, with our permission, someone else can mount the hard drive and use it as a virtual drive. Thousands, tens of thousands, or tens of millions of people could share one common disk drive if doing so was important.

Printers function in the same way on the Internet as they do on a *local area network* (computers networked within a single location), so you can export them to the Internet. This capability presents an interesting possibility. If you shared your printer over the Internet, anyone could mount that printer and print documents on it. For you, this phenomenon would be like receiving faxes from people except that the faxes would be laser-quality and printed on plain paper.

If you work with someone remotely, you may want to share a disk. This disk could be accessed by both you and your remote partner. This setup would keep you from having to use file transfer utilities to move files to and fro and also end the confusion of having more than one copy of a file floating around — which can make figuring out which file contains the latest revisions difficult.

Simply getting connected over a network will not allow you to share and mount disks and printers — you need special software called *NFS software.* NFS stands for Network File System. You can find both commercial and shareware software packages that allow you to set up NFS. These software packages use WinSock or MacTCP to allow them to communicate over the Internet.

Your computer may already be connected to a network. If your network is connected to the Internet, you can mount drives and printers on your local network or over the Internet using software programs such as PCNFS by SunSoft or OnNet by FTP Software.

IP Addressing

As we mentioned previously, every computer connected to the Internet has an IP address. Because these addresses are used in much of your Internet software, understanding how IP addresses are assigned is important. IP addresses are assigned in two ways:

- ✔ Permanent IP address assignment
- ✔ Dynamic IP address assignment

If you use SLIP to connect to the Internet, an IP address is permanently assigned to your machine. Whenever you connect to the Internet, the same IP address identifies your computer. When setting up programs that need your IP address, you can simply type in this permanent address.

If you connect to the Internet using the newer connection protocol, PPP, your IP address may be assigned in two ways. Your IP address may be permanently assigned to your machine, just as with SLIP connections. Or it may be assigned using something called *dynamic addressing*, where a new IP number is assigned each time you connect. Some PPP servers are set up to dynamically assign IP addresses to PPP clients that connect. When an IP address is dynamically assigned each time you connect to the Internet, you need to update your software configuration with the new IP address. When using your site to run server software, dynamic addressing can be a serious problem.

If your IP address is dynamically assigned, you can't give people the IP address of your machine for connection purposes one day and expect the address to work the next time they want to connect to your machine. You should discuss the different options for assigning IP addresses with your service provider when you set up your account.

One way around the problem of dynamic IP addressing is to apply to the InterNIC for a *domain name*. When you have your own domain name, your access provider can assign any IP number it wants. The access provider is responsible for routing your Internet traffic to your machine. Internet users contact your machine by name and won't be concerned with what IP number your machine has.

Managing with SNMP

Your PC can manage a network of computers or even act as the *network host* that connects your network to the Internet. To establish a PC as a network host, you should install a program known as SNMP, or *Simple Network Management Protocol.* (There's that *protocol* word again.)

Castle Rock Computing has a version of SNMP for Windows called SNMPc. You can order this software online by logging into `http://crc.castlerock.com/`. SNMPc can manage networks with 2 to around 10 or 15 computers; it wasn't designed to handle huge networks.

SNMPc software has the following hardware and software requirements:

- 386 PC running at a minimum of 33 MHz
- At least 8MB of memory
- At least a 20MB hard drive
- VGA color display
- Mouse
- Microsoft Windows 3.1 (Contact Castle Rock Computing to find out if the software will run on Windows 95.)
- WinSock 1.1

SNMPc makes managing your network extremely simple. It uses icons to show what devices or computers are connected and creates a map of your network *topology.* If you have seen a geographical topological map, you know that it shows all the mountains, hills, valleys, and streams for a geographic area. A network topology is a map of the connections and devices that make up the network. With SNMPc, you can either create this map manually or let the program create it for you automatically.

SNMPc also lets you know the status of all the devices connected to the network. The SNMPc software contacts each device (a process called *polling*) to determine whether it is online and happy. You can determine how happy a device is with a *threshold setting.* Think of this setting like a pain threshold. For example, a network node may take a full minute to respond to a poll from the SNMPc software. Your threshold setting may show that after 30 seconds, the node is definitely not happy. (Happy is a relative term.) Changing a threshold setting tells the network what it should put up with in terms of performance.

When a computer, or network device, such as a printer, is not operating within expected parameters, the SNMP software starts sending reports to the network manager. This way, network performance problems or machine problems can be corrected quickly. A message a network manager might expect would be:

```
Laser Printer 1 has exceeded connection timeout limits.
```

Meters, called *health meters*, let you know how healthy, or happy, each device is, based on its threshold settings. Using event filters (similar to the new mail filter in the Pegasus e-mail client discussed in Chapter 5), you can tell your computer to react to threshold conditions returned by SNMPc when it polls the devices. For example, if a printer goes down, you can have the SNMPc software send a numeric page to the system administrator.

SNMPc (and other SNMP versions) manage all the devices attached to a network as *objects.* These objects include computers, printers, disk drives, CD-ROM drives, and any other external add-on hardware. SNMPc keeps track of these objects in a special database known as the MIB, or *Management Information Base.*

If you're a programmer, you may be interested in knowing that you can talk to the SNMPc program through DDE (*Dynamic Data Exchange*). With this Application Programming Interface, you can share network information through any DDE-ready program. For example, a Microsoft Excel spreadsheet or a Microsoft Word document can log network information using DDE.

Security

Security is one of the most talked-about topics related to the Internet. This book covers some of the ways information can be transmitted across the Internet using military-grade encryption, but how safe is your computer from hackers trying to break in?

The answer is probably the opposite of what you may expect. The simpler a computer is, the harder it is for a hacker to break in, and a PC is pretty simple. UNIX workstations, on the other hand, sometimes have as many as a hundred different programs running, each one providing a potential means of entering the computer.

You don't need to provide special security precautions for a PC connected to the Internet. Here are some of the reasons why:

- You cannot log in to a PC like you can log in to a UNIX workstation.
- Unlike UNIX machines, PCs do not have special administrative accounts that allow access to all the files on the computer, no matter how sensitive.

Of course, PCs are very simple devices to break into if someone tries to break in from your desktop, not from the Internet. If you leave your computer unprotected on your desktop at work or at home, anyone can walk up to it, turn it on, and access all your information.

PC protection

You can take some steps to thwart the *walk-up hacker,* however. This most dangerous kind of hacker could be your toddler, who is learning to use a keyboard with the bang-here-bang-there technique, a colleague who "just needs a couple files," or your teenager, who decides to delete the company financial records to make room for the latest version of Doom.

The easiest way to protect your computer is to unplug your keyboard from the back of the computer and lock it in the desk drawer. You can also consider buying a special keyboard drawer with a keyed lock. Alternatively, some computers have a key lock, which, when locked, does not allow input from the keyboard.

Another option is to use a password-protection device. Some newer computers allow you to require the user to type a password as soon as the computer is turned on, although leaving your computer on all the time makes this scheme fairly useless. You can also set most screen savers to require the user to enter a password before restoring the screen. Screen saver passwords are only moderately secure because rebooting the computer bypasses this security. Also, most people have the time setting for the screen saver set for a long period so that they don't have to constantly type in their password, which also makes accessing your files easier for a hacker.

Use good common sense to protect your PC from accidental or malicious "walk-up" break-ins. Here are some do's and don'ts:

- Do back up your computer data often.
- Don't leave your passwords lying around on scraps of paper.
- Don't use obvious passwords that anyone can guess.
- Don't tell anyone your password.
- Do change passwords often, but don't write them down.
- If you have sensitive information, follow some of the steps discussed above for protecting your computer or look into other security measures.

If the information on your PC is sensitive and needs to be protected, you can find programs available that will encrypt the files on your hard drive using *military-grade RSA encryption.* RSA Data Security, Inc. offers a set of utilities called RSA Secure that makes encrypting files, entire directories, or your whole hard disk simple. Check out this company's Web page:

```
http://www.rsa.com/
```

Firewalls and proxies

One strategy used by many large corporations to protect their computer networks is to install a *firewall.* A firewall is a computer, free of any secure information, that acts as a gateway to less secure machines. The firewall machine normally has extra security software installed to warn of potential break-ins or to thwart potential hackers. Some of the security precautions include

- Dial-in call back: This feature prevents people from logging in when they call in. Instead, it calls them back and then allows login.
- The *iron box:* This device is a trap for hackers. It gives them a modified shell account and some bait files. While the hacker is hacking around, the iron box traces the hacker's location.

Firewalls have only one problem: They make working on the network extremely difficult for people with machines behind the firewall. If your machine is behind a firewall, you can't use the normal Internet software the same way all your friends are. Because your software can't communicate directly with the Internet, your Internet programs are configured to communicate to the Internet through a proxy. The word *proxy* means "stand-in."

Proxies are not available for all Internet programs, and they are often more expensive than standard programs. Furthermore, if you find a proxy for an Internet program you want to use, you must also convince your company's computer department to run the server version of that proxy application on the firewall machine.

As we mentioned earlier, if you are running a PC or Macintosh computer, you don't need to place it behind a firewall. This level of security is effective only for more complex computers. Many value-added Internet access providers, even the largest ones, still use proxy software and firewalls to limit your access to the Internet. This fact is something you should consider carefully when deciding to use one of these services for your Internet access — remember that the quality of your Internet experience is entirely under their control.

The 5th Wave   By Rich Tennant

"No, thanks. But I would like one more chance to see if I can make my connection to the Internet work the right way."

Chapter 12

Setting Up a Secure Environment for Online Sales

*E*very Internet site needs the capability to conduct secure and reliable online commerce. After they establish secure environments, not-for-profit organizations can receive electronic donations, product manufacturers can sell directly to consumers, and service companies can collect fees. Creating a secure sales environment isn't difficult, but it can be expensive. To simplify the process, this chapter gives you a solid overview of the technology required and explains each step involved in setting up a secure environment.

This chapter covers no single solution; instead, we give you the foundation that you need to decide which solution is right for you. The specific product manufacturer or Internet shopping mall service provider you choose will give you a great deal of support and guidance after you write a check. You can expect quality technical support to be included with the service or product fees that you pay to your service provider.

If the thought of spending money to gain security support makes you a little queasy, remember that if you're generating online sales or contributions to your cause, you're making online money. Making money on the Internet takes money, so dive right in and do it!

Introduction to Encryption

Encryption means to scramble information into a form that's entirely unreadable by human beings. (Many books on encryption achieve this goal without actually being encrypted.) The purpose of encryption is to prevent unfriendly or untrustworthy people from reading the encrypted material. Encryption forms the heart of all Internet commerce, and you need a working knowledge of encryption to understand the technology that you use to generate secure online sales.

Following are a few encryption terms that you need to know:

- ✔ The study of encryption is known as *cryptography.*
- ✔ Unencrypted information is called *plaintext.*
- ✔ Plaintext is encrypted with an *encryption key.*
- ✔ The encrypted result is called *ciphertext.*
- ✔ Ciphertext can be decrypted only by a *decryption key.*

Code-breakers — software that is able to gain unauthorized access to information by figuring out the code that was used to encrypt text — repeatedly guess the decryption key until they stumble upon the right one. The number of possible decryption keys used in a particular encryption determines how difficult the encryption is to break. In this way, encryption is sort of like a combination lock; the more digits in the passcode, the better the lock. The number of possible decryption keys used to encrypt a piece of text is referred to as *encryption strength.*

Encryption techniques

Two basic types of encryption are used: secret key and public key. *Secret-key encryption* relies on a single key for both encryption and decryption. The secrecy of the key is of critical importance in this type of encryption. *Public-key encryption* uses a different key for decryption than it does for encryption. The two keys form a *key pair,* in which one key — the private key — is kept secret and the other — the public key — is made available to the public. Any message encrypted with the public key can be decrypted only by the corresponding private key. This technique allows for reliable encryption without needing to use a secret key.

Secret-key encryption

As mentioned in the preceding section, when you use *secret-key encryption* (a password), the encryption key also is the decryption key. Secret-key encryption is inherently vulnerable because in addition to sending the encrypted message to the recipient, you must send the secret key (password). If the secret key isn't communicated securely, the whole point of encrypting the message is lost: Unauthorized users can get their hands on the key and thus decipher the encrypted information. If you have a secure way to communicate the secret key, however, why bother with encryption in the first place? Why not send the message (plaintext) unencrypted through the secure communications link used for the secret key?

Using secure communications is much easier and safer than using a secret key. Code-breakers during World War II found out how simple it was to decode almost all the encrypted information by simply figuring out the password. Today, with modern, powerful, computers on the desktop, breaking passwords is a relatively simple task for anyone interested in that sort of thing. The alternative is to use public-key encryption (discussed next).

Public-key encryption

Public-key encryption uses a pair of keys: a public key and an associated private key. The owner of a key pair distributes the public key to the general public. Anyone who wants to send an encrypted message encrypts it by using the recipient's public key. The recipient uses the corresponding private key to decrypt the messages. This technique ensures that only the owner of a private key can decrypt the messages encrypted with the public key.

Ideally, everyone will eventually have a public key/private key pair. This combination will be the only way privacy is ensured, especially when online shopping becomes a part of everyday life. When just about everyone has a key, millions or even billions of keys will exist. People need a simple way to find and use the public key owned by the person or company to which they want to send a secure message; they must have *public-key directories,* centralized databases of public keys. These directories are a little like phone directories, yet more. You find the listing of the person you want to communicate with in the directory, and then you learn their public key so that you can communicate with them securely (in a private manner using encryption).

Not only will people have public and private keys, software products requiring secure communication will also have keys. Very soon, all Web sites will use public-key encryption for secure online Web communications. This same capability is being built into e-mail software, FTP software, Usenet news software, and banking applications.

Authentication

Encryption guarantees privacy; *authentication* verifies the identity of the party with whom you communicate. Creating a secure communication link with someone doesn't do much good if you really aren't sure who is on the other end of the link. Without authentication, you have no way of being certain who or what organization is sending an encrypted message. Perhaps an impostor is using someone's computer. Imagine the problems that could arise if the U.S. military accepted and carried out any orders that arrived encrypted without first verifying that the orders came from the President. Authentication has been a part of important military command messages for many years. So, you can see that without authentication, encryption solves only half of the security problem.

Authentication is accomplished through the use of a *digital signature* (electronically encrypted authentication). In the same way you sign a letter, or memo, you can apply a digital signature to the encrypted message. The term *signature* can be a little confusing. A digital signature is not a graphic picture of your actual written signature; think of a digital signature as a special electronic watermark.

Public-key encryption works well for the creation of digital signatures because:

- ✔ Information encrypted with a public key can be decrypted only by the corresponding private key.
- ✔ Information encrypted with a private key can be decrypted only by the corresponding public key.

You can digitally "sign" an encrypted message by using your private key to encrypt a message. Then someone must use your public key to decrypt the message. If the message can be decrypted using your public key, it has to be from you. The recipient of your message has established the authenticity of your message, that you really sent it, by using your public key.

Once again, the need for official public-key directories becomes apparent. You have a public key. How do you know where it came from? Creating an official, and trusted, public-key directory gives one more level of trust and authentication when using a digital signature. You can feel confident that the message you have just decrypted using a public key is in fact from the person who you believe sent the message if you can check a public directory. Unfortunately, this trust issue can only be taken so far. At some point you just have to believe, within reason, that you can trust the public key you've been given.

One way to further authenticate your message is to authenticate the key you have in your possession. You do so by using a *key certificate*. A key certificate is a digital document that attests to the ownership of a public key by a particular person or organization. Key certificates are issued by *Certificate Authorities* (CA), which are, in turn, authenticated by a higher authority. At the top of the authentication hierarchy (the most trusted people in the world when it comes to keys) is a private company entrusted to be the keeper of the keys, so to speak. Only after verifying the key certificate for a particular public key can you be reasonably certain that the key belongs to the person or organization that appears to be using it.

The *Public Key Certificate Standards* (PKCS), the Internet standard that deals with public keys, states that every digital signature must point to a certificate that validates the public key of the signer. This setup makes it possible for software such as Netscape's Navigator or secure e-mail software to authenticate digital signatures automatically by contacting the appropriate CA and viewing the corresponding official public-key certificate.

With all this talk about business on the Internet, a great idea may be to start a new Certificate Authority. The assignment and management of key certificates and corresponding public-key directories soon will be a critical path necessary for all secure Internet communications. Contact RSA Data Security, Inc. at `http://www.rsa.com/` for more information about starting your own CA.

Public-key certificates create confidence in the authenticity of certified public keys. Two or more certificates may be linked in such a way that the certificates certify the authenticity of the other certificates. This link is known as a *certificate chain*. This chain continues from certifying authority to certifying authority until you reach the company or organization considered most trusted.

To obtain a public-key certificate, you first must generate a public-key pair (see "The secure World Wide Web server" later in this chapter for more information on this topic). Then you must send the public-key part of the key pair to an official CA, along with proof of identity, such as a notarized copy of your driver's license. After validating your identity, the CA sends a key certificate verifying that the public key has been registered and is officially recognized as belonging to you. (The section "Getting a digital ID and public-key certificate," later in this chapter, provides a little more detail on this process.)

The CA then maintains your public key in a public-key directory and gives a copy of your key certificate to anyone who requests one. If your private key ever becomes compromised, the CA can add your key certificate to a *Certificate Revocation List* (CRL), which invalidates the previously certified public key.

World Wide Web Security

With its simple graphic interface, the World Wide Web is now the home of the Internet marketplace. Most of the encryption technologies discussed in this chapter focus on making the World Wide Web a secure place to transact business.

A typical World Wide Web sales transaction might work something like the following:

- Joe Smith views an online catalog and finds things that he wants to buy.
- He accesses a secure order form in which he enters the items that he wants to purchase, along with his credit card information.

> ✓ He transmits the order and payment method information to the secure server, where a program is set up to verify the payment method.
>
> ✓ The company notifies Joe Smith that his order has been accepted and tells him when to expect the shipment of goods or how to access online goods or services.

This typical transaction involves four main components:

> ✓ The unsecure online catalog
>
> ✓ The secure World Wide Web form
>
> ✓ The secure World Wide Web server
>
> ✓ An electronic payment method

The next sections explore these various elements as they relate to secure business transactions on the Web.

The online catalog and Web order form

You can find many excellent books that show you how to create online catalogs and Web order forms. Also check out Chapter 17 for some hints on adding some hot features to your Web pages. Using some of the features in that chapter, you can create an online catalog that actually builds the order form while the customer views the catalog. After you establish a secure environment, the information on your order form will be transmitted securely. The idea of transmitting form information securely is now being used by some banks.

For a good example of a securely transmitted form, check out Wells Fargo Bank's On-Line Banking page at `http://www.wellsfargo.com/`. Figure 12-1 shows the bank's site certificate. This certificate is your way of authenticating your connection to the bank. As you can see in Figure 12-1, the site certificate is issued by a Certifying Authority.

The secure World Wide Web server

Not all Web servers are created equal. Shareware Web servers run on just about all computer platforms but usually don't include any type of encryption capability. Other Web servers, such as Netscape's Commerce Server, provide secure communications by using a *secure sockets layer* (explained in "Using Secure Sockets Layer," later in this chapter).

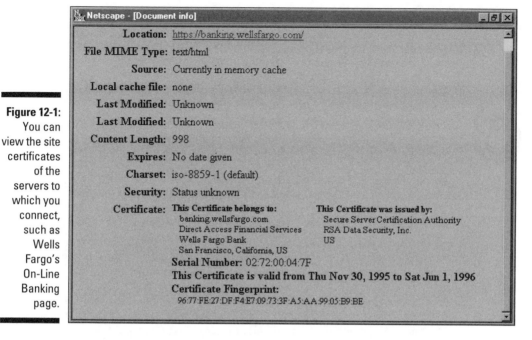

Figure 12-1:
You can
view the site
certificates
of the
servers to
which you
connect,
such as
Wells
Fargo's
On-Line
Banking
page.

After purchasing and installing a secure Web server, you need to perform some setup functions to activate its security capabilities. Most important, you need a public key/private key pair for the server to use. This key pair is known as the servers' *digital ID*. Typically, secure Web server software includes utilities that generate a public key/private key pair and a certificate request that a CA will accept. (For a background discussion on key pairs, certificates, and CAs, refer to "Authentication," earlier in this chapter.) If your secure Web server doesn't provide such a utility, contact the company that sold you the software and ask how to go about generating these keys.

If you're using a digital ID for authentication, your digital ID incorporates your host name. This way, the URL of a site includes the same host name as the digital ID. Web browsers such as Netscape Navigator automatically verify that the host name matches the one embedded in the digital ID and display a warning if a discrepancy is detected. For detailed information on how to set up your site to use a digital ID, see:

```
http://www.verisign.com/pr/pr_ns_secure.html
```

If you plan to run a Netscape Commerce Server or a Netscape News Server, you need to obtain a digital ID from VeriSign. For now, VeriSign is the most trusted Certifying Authority. VeriSign is a private company that manages many of the authentication management techniques described throughout this chapter.

Getting a digital ID and public-key certificate

If you operate or are planning to operate a secure Web server, you should apply to VeriSign for your digital ID. For information that is specific to your Web server, contact the VeriSign Web page at the following URL:

```
http://www.verisign.com
```

Processing your request for a digital ID takes about a week, so plan to apply for a digital ID before you try to open your Internet shop.

Follow these steps on the path to obtaining a digital ID:

1. **Install your secure Web server software, and name your site.**

2. **Create a Distinguished Name for your Web server.**

   Follow the instructions that come with your Web server to create a Distinguished Name. This name is the trusted name of your server.

3. **Document your Web server.**

   This documentation includes a letter that identifies the *webmaster* (Web administrator) for your site and a "Proof of Right to Use" the Distinguished Name. Detailed information and complete text of a sample letter are included on the VeriSign home page. After you've filled out this letter, send it with your application.

4. **Based on the Distinguished Name that you chose, generate an RSA Key Pair (public/private key pair).**

   Your Web server documentation tells you how to perform this procedure.

5. **E-mail your application to VeriSign, requesting your digital ID.**

   The appropriate e-mail address for your application is listed on the Verisign home page, `http://www.verisign.com/`. The VeriSign Web page lists specific e-mail addresses for each type of secure Web server.

6. **After you submit your request, mail a signed authorization letter with your payment arrangement, such as credit card number or purchase order.**

   Send the letter to this address: VeriSign, Inc., 2593 Coast Avenue, Mountain View, CA, 94043, USA.

7. **After you receive your digital ID, follow the instructions in your Web server to install it.**

For additional information on obtaining digital IDs and public key/private key pairs, you can contact RSA Data Security, Inc. at:

```
http://www.rsa.com/
```

Using Secure Sockets Layer (SSL)

Secure Sockets Layer (SSL) is the most popular protocol that provides security and encryption for all communications between a client and a server. To provide this security, authentication of the server is always required, and the option to authenticate the client also exists.

Software developers use the Secure Sockets Layer when writing programs that need to communicate securely at all times. Unlike the security built in to secure Web servers, programs using SSL have public key encryption for all data communication.

One of the main advantages of the Secure Sockets Layer is the fact that it is indeed a layer — in other words, application programs, such as FTP or the World Wide Web, run on top of it. All the security is negotiated between the client and the server program before even one byte of data is exchanged by an application program, so all the data is sent securely.

The Secure Sockets Layer enables a special type of security known as *channel security*. Channel security provides three basic advantages:

- ✔ The communication channel used by your program is always secure. After the Secure Sockets Layer negotiates the connection by exchanging keys, all transmissions are secure.

- ✔ You always know to whom you're talking because the channel (communication session between two computers) is always authenticated between the client and the server. This type of authentication is the same that we discussed earlier in this chapter, except this is done automatically by programs.

- ✔ The transport protocol (TCP/IP) provides *reliability*; you can depend on the fact that messages that are sent reach their intended destination. Macintosh computers include a message integrity check.

The Secure Sockets Layer provides a comforting level of security. Having security built in to your programs rather than having to think about security yourself is easier. This option is certainly better than not having any security at all. Netscape Communications was the company that proposed this standard to the *Internet Engineering Task Force* (IETF), the Internet standards body. But even before the IETF accepted the Secure Sockets Layer, SSL was included in Netscape products such as Netscape Navigator and the Netscape Commerce Server.

To see the site certificates that Netscape Navigator supports, choose Security Preferences from the Options menu. The site certificates are listed there, as shown in Figure 12-2.

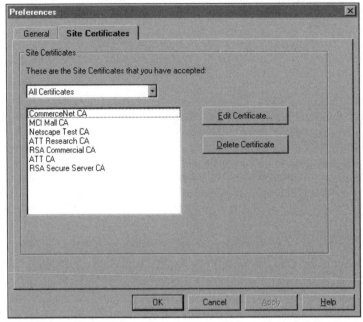

Figure 12-2:
View the
Netscape
Navigator
site
certificates.

The site certificates in Version 1.1 of Netscape Navigator are *hard-coded*. Version 2.0 and later versions allow you to update the site certificates that you want to recognize as trusted by you. In programs such as Netscape, in which the end user is responsible for the last word in authentication, the user must specify which site certificates Netscape uses to authenticate its secure connections.

Using HTTP over SSL

TCP/IP applications use different ports for communicating. These ports are *software communication ports,* not any type of plug on the back of your computer. (Think of a software communication port as being more like an address than a physical entity.) When data arrives on a computer from the Internet, the TCP/IP software knows which application will handle the incoming data. TCP/IP knows which application based on the port number listed in the address that accompanied the incoming data. You may already know that the World Wide Web (HTTP) uses port 80. You sometimes see the port number listed as part of the URL, `http://www.science.org:80/`.

A special port is set aside for HTTP over SSL. In other words, when your Web server receives requests for data over this special port, the Web server knows to return the requested information using the Secure Sockets Layer. Thus, your World Wide Web pages are transmitted securely. The special port number is port 443. Web documents that use this special secure port have the URL prefix `https://` rather than the standard `http://`. The *s* in `https://` stands for *secure.*

Not all Web browsers and servers currently support the `https://` URL. The `https://` URL will most likely gain significant industry support, however, and appear regularly in the future. Before you begin using this URL type, you should make certain that the Web server you are contacting supports the `https://` prefix.

This URL may or may not catch on. We wanted to let you know about it in the event that you do run across it. No discussion of secure communications would be complete without discussing HTTP over SSL.

Secure Hypertext Transfer Protocol

SSL is not the only protocol available for ensuring security and encryption on the World Wide Web. One alternative is the *Secure Hypertext Transfer Protocol* (S-HTTP), developed by EIT in early 1994. S-HTTP is distributed commercially by Terisa Systems, a company co-founded by EIT and RSA Data Security.

An extension of the familiar HTTP protocol, S-HTTP hasn't gained as much popularity as the Netscape SSL approach. Unlike SSL, S-HTTP supports both public-key technology and the traditional shared-secret (password) technology, but its implementation of public-key cryptography is quite different from that of SSL. S-HTTP does not require the client (the person who has a Web browser) to have a public key.

Some of the features of S-HTTP are

- ✔ Capability to authenticate clients
- ✔ Capability to authenticate servers, including support for a hierarchy of site certificates
- ✔ Support for digital signatures to authenticate the messages that are sent
- ✔ Support for differing levels of security, based on the needs of the application
- ✔ Secure communications through corporate firewalls (computers set up to protect networks from prying pranksters)

On the other hand, some of the features and advantages of SSL are

- ✔ Ease of implementation (doesn't require any special Web-based programming)
- ✔ Increased client/server security through hiding the entire communication session, not just the transaction

- ✔ Better server authentication
- ✔ More reliable client/server communications, because SSL is part of the underlying communications layer

Both the SSL and S-HTTP technologies offer security for World Wide Web transactions. Which protocol will emerge as the dominant technology is still uncertain. You have to pay more attention to this issue if S-HTTP becomes the standard; you'll be required to create pages that are specifically designed for secure communications.

Electronic payment methods

Ah, a suitable ending to this chapter. One of the main reasons for setting up a secure environment for online sales is to collect the money. Boy, that term's ready for the scrap heap. Who uses money anymore? Electronic financial transactions are quickly replacing hard currency both online and on the street. You can use your ATM card for just about everything now. Credit card companies are moving to create "smart cards" that have chips embedded in them to process quick cash debits.

The Internet presents an entirely new set of challenges related to collecting money from customers. One of the biggest concerns about online sales has been security of credit card transactions. But as many people have argued, this fear is overblown. After all, you risk your credit card number every time you hand it to a store clerk, waiter, or waitress; leave it with your travel agent; or print it out on some type of mail-in order form. Given current computer security, online transactions — even without security — probably are safer than most of the other credit card transactions that you make every day.

What makes Internet transactions scary for people is the apparent anonymity of the transactions. The buyer probably doesn't know the person who's receiving the credit card information. But the same argument can be made about mail-order transactions. Authentication (discussed in the section "Authentication," earlier in this chapter) takes some of the fear out of anonymous electronic transactions.

After the fear is gone, however, the question of how transactions are carried out over the Internet remains.

Credit-card transaction systems

The simplest and most obvious way to transact business over the Internet is to have customers pay for goods and services by providing their credit card numbers. Many companies are working diligently to make this method the most secure type of transaction that can possibly take place on the Internet. Visa and Microsoft have teamed to develop a technology called *Secure Transaction Technology* (STT) to facilitate secure electronic payment systems.

Visa and Microsoft also have extended SSL to create *Private Communication Technology* (PCT). PCT provides better authentication than Secure Sockets Layer by extending it but remains 100 percent compatible with the SSL standard.

After you know that credit card information can be transmitted securely, you have to figure out how to handle the rest of the transaction. VeriFone, Inc., a supplier of Transaction Automation system solutions, has a suite of products to deliver end-to-end (buyer to seller, seller to bank) solutions for processing payment transactions over the Internet. The company's products include an electronic wallet for consumers (a little like a debit or ATM card for the Internet), a virtual point-of-sale terminal (cash register) for merchants, and an Internet gateway (way to make a payment) for Internet shoppers. These products go beyond simply accepting credit card transactions; they offer a complete solution for vendors that want to accept online transactions. These solutions can take a transaction from the buyer's order through credit card approval at the bank.

Verifone's system is not limited to credit cards; the company's software can handle many of the new electronic payment forms discussed in the following sections. Check out the company's Web page at:

```
http://www.verifone.com/
```

Electronic money

Another option for a secure Internet sales environment is the use of electronic-money technology. Because you can't pay for things on the Internet by shoving dollar bills into the floppy drive slot on the front of your computer, a way to pay for things needed to be created. Of course, one way would be the use of plastic money (credit cards). With credit card transactions, however, you have a certain amount of uncertainty. Is the card good? Will it be good when the transaction goes through? Is the card being used fraudulently? The answer to these uncertainties is a relatively new concept called electronic money. *Electronic money* has some advantages over traditional credit card sales and is worth investigating.

Several companies offer secure electronic-money systems for the Internet. One such company is DigiCash, which uses digital signatures to authenticate digital cash. DigiCash does so by having the user's computer generate a random number. This random number becomes the note and can be sent using electronic mail or a World Wide Web form. The vendor receives the note and submits it to DigiCash which credits the vendor's account with electronic cash. This electronic cash is a little like a Las Vegas poker chip. The vendor can choose to "cash in" the notes whenever he or she wants the real, hard, cash.

For those of you worried about the privacy of your personal finances, a technique called *blinding* keeps the bank from knowing who generated the note. Using blinding, these electronic transactions are just like cash transactions. They can't be tracked.

For more information, see the DigiCash Web site:

```
http://www.digicash.com/
```

CyberCash is an electronic-transaction-processing company that has a few twists. Unlike other companies, CyberCash doesn't require consumers to have a relationship with CyberCash to use the system. Consumers simply need to download the CyberCash Wallet software, which is freely available from the CyberCash Web site. This software creates the link between the consumer, the seller, and their respective financial institutions.

To receive CyberCash from people on the Internet, you set up accounts directly with CyberCash. These accounts are non-interest-bearing holding accounts. Digital cash can be transferred into or out of the account. CyberCash also enables you to set up financial transactions on an as-needed basis, such as to transfer money from one person to another through the Internet. For more information, check out the CyberCash Web site:

```
http://www.cybercash.com/
```

Other electronic-money systems are likely to emerge. Watch these developments with interest because the future of privacy in electronic commerce is at stake. All types of companies currently conduct online sales by using combinations of all the technologies discussed in this chapter. Visit some of the online malls and shopping networks to see how Internet sales are being handled today.

Some companies charge a fee to accept and process transactions for you. We don't recommend using such companies if you can help it. If you consider doing business with one of these companies, make sure that you read all the fine print in the contract; you may find some real eye-openers.

Chapter 13

Advertising Your Site

- -

In This Chapter

▶ Listing your Internet site in online indexes

▶ Advertising your Web page

▶ Marketing your Internet site offline

- -

Setting up an Internet site doesn't guarantee overnight popularity. Internet users need to know about your site before they'll visit. The main key to introducing your Internet site to potential users is simple: Be yourself.

Meeting others on the Internet is a lot like meeting people when you move into a new apartment building. When you move, you can go door to door introducing yourself; meet people in the laundry area; send cards to the neighbors; or throw a barbecue. Similarly, you can advertise your Internet site in many ways:

✔ Add your site address to directories.

✔ Register your Web home page.

✔ Join mailing lists like those described in Chapter 6.

✔ Post messages in the newsgroups.

Just as you can make new friends in many ways when you move to a new location, you can make new enemies in many ways, too. Throwing loud all-night parties is a sure way to acquire a few enemies in your new neighborhood. On the other hand, you may acquire a few friends this way, too. The Internet is just a big neighborhood. If you respect the other members of the community, they'll generally respect you. If you fill people's mailboxes with junk mail or other garbage, you'll make friends with some people and make enemies of many others.

This chapter shows you how to make your presence known on the Internet. With some tact and common sense, you'll have lots of Internet friends in no time.

Graduating from Being Known to Being Famous

There's making your site known and then there's making it famous. Before you launch your cybermarketing attempt, ask yourself, "Do I want my site to be known or to be famous?" If your Internet site offers resources that are meant to be used by a small group of people, being known may be enough. On the other hand, if your goal is to reach as many people as possible on the Internet, you want your site to become famous.

Being famous, of course, always has its price. In the case of a famous Internet site, you have to work to keep your site fresh and exciting. Just like movie stars, Internet sites have to keep taking on new roles to stay in the public eye.

If you want to transcend being known and enter the realm of being famous, try to become a cool site. Several pages on the Web offer a "cool site of the day." Getting chosen as a cool site can take you from hundreds of accesses a day to tens of thousands (see "Being chosen as a cool site of the day" later in this chapter).

Make sure that you are ready for success. If you don't have the hardware or software to handle a heavy load of people trying to access your site at the same time, you may find yourself with an overloaded machine.

If you do have an overloaded machine, don't just turn it off. A better idea is to create a small, text-only Web page stating that your page cannot be accessed due to unforeseen success. Give users your e-mail address, and ask them to visit again when things aren't so hectic.

Becoming infamous on the Internet is much easier than becoming famous. Many new words have been coined over the Internet; one of the better ones is *netiquette*, taken from *Net* and *etiquette*. Because the Internet has no rules — only guidelines — you need to become familiar with the netiquette of your area of the Internet, just as you would have to learn the customs and protocols if you moved to a new country. Be sensitive to cultural differences. Take the time to learn the customs and protocols of a particular group of Internet users before advertising your site in their general direction.

Knowing Your Audience

Whether you want your site simply to be known or your goal is to have the hottest site on the Internet, you have to know your audience. Not knowing the people for whom you're creating your site is like trying to paint in the dark.

Defining Internet audiences is now the subject of scrutiny by some of the top marketing agencies in the world. Even Nielsen, famous for its TV ratings, has joined the game. Internet users are literally as diverse as the cultures of the world. The studies conducted by advertising companies and organizations such as Nielsen help define who is using the Internet and for what purpose.

On the Internet, the one thing that you can count on is the fact that everything's changing. By *everything*, we mean:

- ✔ The profile of the average user
- ✔ The number of people connected
- ✔ The type of Internet access that people are using
- ✔ Hardware technology
- ✔ Software products

In the past, the Internet was the domain of young, predominately male computer-whizzes. In early 1995, 88 percent of the people online were young males. But this statistic is changing faster than you can say, "The regional Bell operating companies and cable companies are offering Internet access." By the end of 1995, the Internet audience had already changed to include as many women as men. Not only are both genders evenly represented, but people of all ages are getting into the Internet action.

As the use of the Internet becomes more mainstream, people are receiving e-mail from their octogenarian grandparents. Just the other day, a six-year-old told us that he has his own home page, that he connects to the Internet by using PPP, and that he uses Netscape as a Web browser. At the age of six!

Clearly, your potential audience (everyone in the world) is a lot different than your intended audience. When deciding how to advertise your Internet site, think about the needs, inclinations, and perspectives of your typical user. Identify your site with key words or phrases that will appeal to your audience. But don't forget that smart six-year-old kids will wander by your advertisement once in a while. Attractive graphics, alluring animations, and exciting sound effects will catch their attention, and they'll show their parents.

Adding Your Site Address to Directories

The cliché "If you build it, they will come" may be true for baseball fields but not for Web pages. If nobody knows that you have a Web page, that's exactly who will visit it — nobody.

Just as you can advertise your business by putting your phone number in the local Yellow Pages, you can advertise your Web site in Internet directories — which are simply the digital equivalent of telephone books. Every directory is different, but one thing's certain: If you can't find it in one of the Internet directories, it probably doesn't exist.

Table 13-1 lists some of the directories that you may want to investigate. The table lists the starting points, search utilities, and indexes where you may want your page to be listed.

Table 13-1 Directories and Starting Points that Welcome Web Forms	
Site	*URL*
Yahoo	http://www.yahoo.com/
ElNet Galaxy	http://www.einet.net/
Lycos	http://www.lycos.com/
WebCrawler	http://www.webcrawler.com/WebCrawler/SubmitURLS.html

Many cities have home pages highlighting local businesses that have World Wide Web sites. Contact your local Chamber of Commerce and ask whether you can be included in its home page. If your city doesn't have a Web site, consider starting one for it. You may give City Hall the impetus that it needs to start its own project — especially if you include information on your page that supports the mayor's opponent in the next election.

Internet white pages

How many times have you grabbed the phone book to look up a number? You've always depended on the white pages for quick access to phone numbers in your area. Now you have the same access to e-mail addresses. Although you can find Internet phone books in book stores and at newsstands, the white pages that we're talking about are electronic and located on the Internet. Just as you get telephone books that cover different regions and/or types of listings, you can find different types of Internet white pages. Some white pages include local listings; some provide school listings; and some, such as the Singapore White Pages (shown in Figure 13-1) cover a specific region.

You can reach the Singapore White Pages at the following address:

```
http://sunsite.nus.sg/cgi-bin/sgp_wpages
```

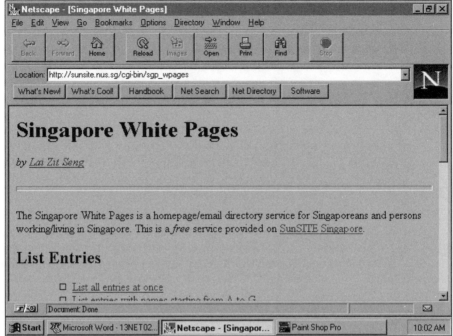

The Internet also has university and special-interest white pages. You can find student directories, for example, by going to a university's home page and then looking for a link to its directory of students and faculty members. Many universities provide such a link somewhere in their Web pages.

If you're a member of a club, organization, church, or community group, consider having your Web page included in its white-pages directory. Being listed in organizations' directories helps get your Web pages seen by the people who are interested in seeing you succeed. If your group doesn't have a directory, recommend that it start one by explaining all the benefits that the group will receive from Internet exposure.

The World Wide Yellow Pages

What would white pages be without the yellow pages? Although many versions of white pages are available on the Internet, the World Wide Yellow Pages (a product of Home Pages, Inc.) is a single resource. The directory uses the following address:

```
http://www.yellow.com/
```

When you post your own listing on the World Wide Yellow Pages' list of online businesses, people can find you by searching for your entry's heading or for your business name or location. Businesses can place a listing in the World Wide Yellow Pages for free. You can enter all types of information about your business by using the directory's Web form.

Four11

Four11 is an organization that allows you to enter your personal contact information for free. Contact information can include phone numbers, e-mail addresses, and Web home page addresses. You and others on the Internet then can search the database, which currently contains a half-million entries. Figure 13-2 shows the result of a search on the family name *Coombs.*

Your directory listing can direct other users to your home page, to your company's home page, and to other ways of contacting you either at home or at the office. Four11 also offers a very convenient way of creating a personal Web page. You can create a new Web page right over the World Wide Web.

The Four11 directory services address is:

```
http://www.Four11.com/
```

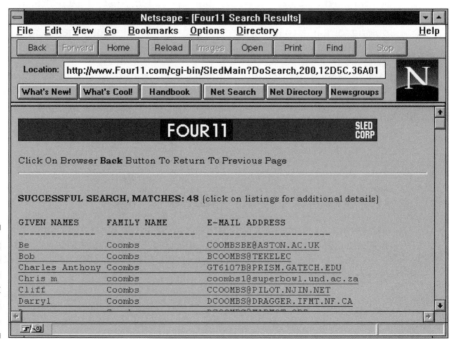

Figure 13-2:
Find people
on the
Internet fast
by using
Four11.

Who's On-line

Who's On-line is a noncommercial database that allows you to add personal contact information by profession or activity. People who use this search utility can query on different criteria and eventually come across your home page.

One of the key requirements for being listed in this resource is your résumé. Upon receiving your résumé, Who's On-line considers listing your home page in its hypertext resource by profession.

If you want to add a page to Who's On-line, contact its Web page at the following address:

```
http://www.ictp.trieste.it/Canessa/ENTRIES/entries.html
```

Be patient. You may have to wait as long as a couple of weeks for your listing to appear.

Community of Science

If you or your organization is involved in science or research, you can get a listing in the Community of Science database. This database lists academic qualifications, publications, degrees, and more.

The Community of Science also allows membership in the organization at the university or corporate level. For more information, check out its home page at the following address:

```
http://medoc.gdb.org/work/info/cosinfo.html
```

The fee for belonging to this organization is pretty high — about $6,000 a year. (Did we say "pretty high"? There's nothing pretty about a fee that high!) Ask your academic or scientific agency to purchase support for the entire organization.

Getting Exposure

Most people create a home page on the Web because they want other people to see and respond to it, so making sure that your home page gets the right exposure is important. No single strategy for obtaining this exposure is best. To be successful, you need to find people to create links to your page, get your pages indexed in search utilities, advertise your site, and work hard to make sure that the content is interesting enough for people to want to visit. The preceding section of this chapter discusses one way to lead people to your site: getting listed in online directories. In this section, you find more ways to get your page out in the open.

Linking up

The trick to making a Web site successful is establishing as many links to it as possible. A *link* is a reference to your site that's located on someone else's Web page. This linking capability is why the Internet is often confused with the World Wide Web — it's a huge interconnection of links that form a vast web. The more connections to your page, the greater the chance that your page will be seen. Getting links can be fun — so much fun that in a few years, you'll probably see bumper stickers declaring that "The Person with the Most Links Wins."

Contact as many people as you can on the Internet, and ask them to create links to your page. If the following sources have Web pages, don't hesitate to ask them to create links from their pages to yours:

- ✔ All your friends
- ✔ Your access provider
- ✔ The city in which you live or work
- ✔ Your school
- ✔ Web indexes and directories

One of the most popular Web search utilities, Yahoo, contains guides for creating links. In Yahoo (http://www.yahoo.com/), click the link that says World Wide Web, and you'll see links to all sorts of beginner guides.

Being chosen as a cool site of the day

The universe of World Wide Web publishing rewards excellence in Web pages in two ways. (Gaining this recognition is like an actor winning both an Oscar and the People's Choice Award.) One way of being rewarded is simply being successful. If thousands of people flock to your site because your pages are interesting, informative, fun, or attractive in some way, that accolade is the best that you could hope for. The other measure of excellence is being included in Glen Davis' Cool Site of the Day (see Figure 13-3).

Check out this page at the following address:

```
http://cool.infi.net/
```

Figure 13-3:
Glen Davis'
Cool Site of
the Day can
make you
famous.

Being named one of Davis' Cool Site of the Day pages can give your page enormous exposure. Many pages that have been recognized as a Cool Site of the Day are visited by tens of thousands of World Wide Web surfers in a single day.

Posting to newsgroups

Newsgroups were among the first popular gathering places on the Internet — so popular, in fact, that the words *newsgroups* and *Internet* once were almost synonymous. A newsgroup is one of the many discussion areas available on the Internet. Newsgroups originally were formed (and still are formed today) to enable users to share information or carry on electronic dialogue about anything and everything. When you tell people in newsgroups that you have an online presence, you automatically increase your visibility.

Certain newsgroups work better than others as places to post the announcement of your new Web page. Begin with general newsgroups that were specifically created for posting announcements. One recommendation is the `comp.infosystems` hierarchy of newsgroups, at the following address:

```
comp.infosystems.www.anounce
```

Figure 13-4 shows a common newsreader program that can be used to post messages to newsgroups. When you write your posting, tell newsgroup readers a little about what to expect when they log in to your Web page. Remember to include your URL.

Following are some guidelines to keep in mind when you post to newsgroups:

✔ Post messages to newsgroups that have the same focus as your page.

✔ Read the newsgroup before you post to it. Reading posts that are completely unrelated to the information being posted to the newsgroup is aggravating.

✔ Don't post the same message to hundreds of similar newsgroups.

✔ Don't advertise specific items the way you would in a magazine or newspaper; save specific product or service information for the people who are interested and seek out your online presence.

✔ Newsgroups archive their messages, so your posting will be erased after a period of time. The more active a newsgroup is, the quicker the messages disappear. Posting to a newsgroup one time doesn't guarantee that your message will be around forever.

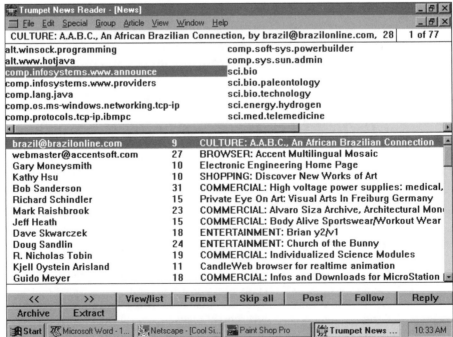

Figure 13-4: Use your newsreader to post announcements to newsgroups.

> ✔ Make sure that your posting and the content of your Web page will appeal
> to the audience of a particular newsgroup before you post your message
> with that newsgroup. When you post to alt.wolves, for example, don't
> post a "Humans Against Wolves Home Page" message unless you're
> looking for a fight.

Pushing Your Product

Whether you're marketing fresh lobster from Maine, tours of the Holy Land,
coffee from Hawaii, or rare books from your attic, you can sell it on the Internet.
You don't have to be a big mall, such as the Internet Shopping Network, to be a
big success. The Internet has been called the great equalizer; you have just as
much opportunity to sell your products in this electronic village as the big guys
do. You just have to have a few tricks up your sleeve.

Advertising your automated mailing list

Information is one of the hottest products going on the Internet. After all, isn't
this the Information Age? If information is your product, you need to know how
to distribute it.

A great way to distribute information is to create an automated mailing list —
which is nothing more than a vehicle that enables people to sign up to receive
your information automatically or participate in e-mail conversations. More and
more people subscribe to automated mailing lists every day. The Seidman
OnLine mailing list (run by Robert Seidman), for example, has more than
15,000 subscribers.

Following are three significant ways to increase participation in your mailing list:

> ✔ Tell newsgroups about your mailing list. (When you are working with a
> newsgroup, follow the guidelines in "Posting to newsgroups" earlier in
> this chapter.)
>
> ✔ Mention the mailing list on your home page.
>
> ✔ Advertise your automated mailing list on the World Wide Web by telling
> people (on your home page) how to subscribe.

You can look at Yahoo's list of mailing lists at the following address:

```
http://www.yahoo.com/Computers/Internet/Mailing_Lists/
```

Advertising your anonymous FTP site

Anonymous FTP sites are wonderful places to store shareware programs, files of information, or any other type of electronic information. If you decide to run an anonymous FTP site, you'll find that advertising it is simple. Archie, started in the late 1980s at McGill University, is a search utility that checks a database of file information and then catalogs file information from both anonymous FTP sites and Gopher (see Figure 13-5).

To learn more about Archie, see the Archie page at Yahoo:

```
http://www.yahoo.com/Computers_and_Internet/Internet/Archie/
```

Adding your FTP site to the Archie database is simple. Just find the Archie server nearest you, and send e-mail to the administrator. The Archie page at Yahoo can help you do so.

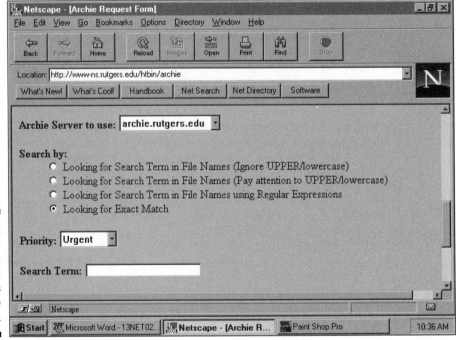

Figure 13-5:
Search
Archie using
tools such
as this
World Wide
Web form.

Using Other Marketing Tricks

"What good is sitting alone in your room?"

This line from the musical *Cabaret* says it all. What good is setting up an Internet presence that no one knows about? Remember that not all the marketing for your Internet presence is online. In fact, the most effective way to get people to log in to your site is to tell them about your site personally.

Word of mouth

Tell people that you are online. You are the best marketer of your information. You probably will have to give some lengthy explanations (or occasionally wave your hands) as you describe the World Wide Web or the Internet to people, but you may be surprised by the number of people who want to learn more. Most people now understand the concept of e-mail, and they may think that e-mail is all that the Internet offers. Other people picture the Internet as being a giant bulletin board. Telling these people that you are online sometimes leads to interesting discussions.

A side benefit of discussing your online presence with others is the fact that they learn that you keep up with the times and use the resources around you to succeed. Of course, having someone grab a pen (if they can find one), paper (other than the restaurant napkin), and then write out h-t-t-p-:-/-/ can be time-consuming and frustrating; by the time he's written everything down, he may have lost interest. Try combining word-of-mouth advertising with printed materials.

Printed materials

Online advertising hasn't yet replaced printed advertising; printed materials are still a very effective way of telling people that you have an Internet site. Putting your URL on your business card makes finding you online fast and simple — no one has to struggle to find a pen, paper, and a place to write down your information. In fact, always include your e-mail address and URL in all your print advertising. The following list offers additional suggestions for advertising your Internet address:

- Run small advertisements in appropriate media.
- Add your URL and e-mail address to coffee mugs, pens, floating key chains, and so on.
- Add your home page URL to greeting cards. You may be surprised how much closer contact you maintain with distant relatives and friends from long ago when you find out that you're not alone in cyberspace. Aunt Marsha and Uncle Herb may have e-mail and a home page, too.

Postcards

Postcards don't sound very high-tech, do they? But we included them in the "Printed materials" section for a reason: we're talking about *electronic* postcards. For a fun and interesting way to tell friends and clients about your new presence on the Net, send them electronic postcards. Point your Web browser to the following URL:

```
http://postcards.www.media.mit.edu/Postcards/
```

To send a postcard from the preceding site, follow these steps:

1. **Choose a postcard from the postcard rack of famous paintings.**

2. **Type an appropriate message.**

3. **Supply the recipient's address.**

4. **Click on the Submit button.**

The recipient of your postcard receives an e-mail message stating that he or she has been sent a postcard. Instructions on retrieving the postcard are given. The recipient logs in to the Web site listed earlier and enters the password. The picture you chose then appears, followed by the text of your message. Your friends can view a postcard for up to 30 days before it's deleted from the system.

This service is free, and it's fun. Getting one of these cards is always a special treat. We're sorry that we don't have a figure that illustrates one of these postcards. We asked Monet for permission to use one of his paintings, but he didn't respond to our e-mail.

Telephone conversations

The telephone remains one of the most important business tools in the world; the Internet hasn't replaced it yet. But the problem with the phone is the fact that most people use it only to talk to people during business hours or to leave messages. You should take advantage of current telephone technology to direct people to your more interactive technologies. Your company's interactive voice-response system (you know — the electronic voice that answers the phone) can offer electronic alternatives for customers who are looking for information about your Internet site. You could use an outgoing message such as this:

"If you want further information, you can browse our World Wide Web site at [address] or download the most current specifications from our FTP site at [address]. You also can contact the sales department directly through Internet Phone by connecting to the IRC server at [address]."

Millions of people still use the telephone to transact business, provide information, and talk with friends. No reason exists as to why you shouldn't take advantage of this old technology to direct people to your exciting online presence.

Chapter 14

Hooked on the Internet

· ·

In This Chapter

▶ Running your Internet site with dial-up accounts

▶ Looking at the direct-connect alternatives

▶ Examining the future of networks

▶ Looking at national Internet access providers

▶ Looking at local Internet access providers

▶ Examining public data networks and access to the Internet

▶ Using online services to access the Internet

· ·

*T*he Internet is all about getting connected. All the wonderful Internet software won't do you much good unless you have an Internet connection. In this chapter, you learn about some of the ways that you can get connected. You also learn about some exciting technologies that are on the horizon.

Connecting to the Internet

Setting up an Internet site entails many topics. Following are a few of the things that you may be concerned with:

✔ What kind of connection do you need?

✔ Which access provider should you use?

✔ How can you connect more than one computer to the Internet?

✔ How can you have more than one e-mail address if you have only one account with your access provider?

How you actually create your Internet connection and the type of service that you use are two of the most important issues that arise after you decide to set up an Internet site. Hardware connections — the way that your computer physically connects to the Internet — affect both the way you experience the Internet and the way the Net surfer experiences your Internet site. Which Internet provider you choose should depend on price, options, and whether your Internet site will have room to grow and expand.

More and more businesses have several computers on a local area network. The new goal for these networked computers is to get Internet access and e-mail. Creating the type of connection to offer these services is not always an easy task. Sometimes, it takes "getting physical."

Getting Physical

Connections are comprised of three major divisions:

- Dial-up *shell accounts* (no IP connection)
- Dial-up *SLIP and PPP connections* (IP-connected)
- *Dedicated connections* (connected all the time with an IP connection)

You also can connect to the Internet in other ways — for example, by using a cellular-phone connection or satellite telephones — but regular hard-wired connections are the most common.

Beam me down, Scotty

Satellite TV has been around for quite a few years. All those dishes on housetops and in back-yards can now be used to collect Internet information beamed directly via satellite.

One of the most time-consuming, bandwidth-intensive tasks on the Internet is moving large amounts of information, such as Usenet news. Every day, megabytes' to gigabytes' worth of Usenet news must be transferred to computers all over the Internet.

Using satellites, which are capable of one-way communication, is an excellent way to move this kind of information to your computer without tying up your network connection. Special ser-vices now download Usenet news, e-mail, and your favorite Web pages daily via satellite for only a fraction of what you would pay to receive this information via your normal access provider.

Most people don't want to receive all the Usenet news or have only a few Web pages to down-load. Depending on the needs of your Internet site, keep satellites in mind as an option for large amounts of data transfer. For more information, you can contact Northern California Interna-tional Teleport, Inc., at the following site:

`http://www.pagesat.net/`

She Sells Seashells Down by the Cybershore

Shell accounts were among the first types of accounts available to the public on the Internet. Using a shell account, you dial into your access provider, log in, and end up staring at a UNIX prompt (%>). Some shell accounts present a user menu, but most of them leave you wondering what to do next. If you don't mind learning a few UNIX commands, this kind of account still is useful for many tasks (see Figure 14-1).

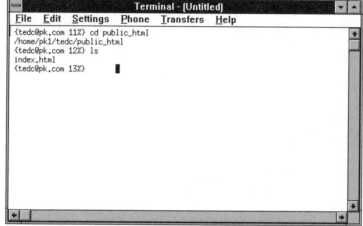

Terminal - (Untitled)

File   Edit   Settings   Phone   Transfers   Help

```
{tedc@pk.com 11%} cd public_html
/home/pk1/tedc/public_html
{tedc@pk.com 12%} ls
index.html
{tedc@pk.com 13%}
```

Figure 14-1:
Shell accounts often are used to access Web publishing accounts.

UNIX allows each user to have a *home directory,* which is both a starting point and a private file-storage place for each user. When you log in to a shell account, you start in your home directory, where you can keep personal files, e-mail, and other directories of information. Using a shell account is common if you are going to set up a Web publishing account with your access provider.

A Web publishing account has a special directory; the files you store in the directory are available via the World Wide Web. Your access provider either creates your Web publishing directory or asks you to create the directory, giving it a particular name (such as public_html). You can then publish your World Wide Web pages in that directory.

The UNIX command for creating a directory is:

```
mkdir <directory name>
```

UNIX is case-sensitive. You can use long directory names and directory names in which the words are separated by periods (for example, `www.info.files`).

To move files to and from your shell account, you need to use either an FTP program or one of the common file-transfer protocols, the most common being Zmodem. If you have a shell account (or expect to have one), the access provider can identify the type of file-transfer utilities used.

If you are using the Windows Terminal program to transfer files, you cannot use Zmodem to transfer your files. You can, however, use Xmodem or Kermit.

It ain't a banana peel, but you can slip on it

If you are going to access the Internet through a UNIX shell account, you may as well get everything out of it that you possibly can. One thing that you can do is fake an IP connection. This way you'll have the best of both worlds.

Using only a shell account, you can gain graphical access to the Internet, which means that you can use graphical programs (such as Netscape) to access the World Wide Web. Remember that accessing the Internet this way isn't the most common method, but it is a little trick that you may want to keep up your sleeve. One of the programs that allow you this kind of access is a free program called SLiRP. The home page for this program is:

```
http://www.wit.com/~danjo
```

SLiRP emulates a SLIP (Serial Line Interface Protocol) account. See the section on IP connections for more information about SLIP accounts.

ISDN Is UP

A phone-company high-speed connection that is beginning to sweep into the hearts and hard drives of many people is *ISDN* (Integrated Services Digital Network). With an ISDN card in your computer rather than a modem and with a specially installed ISDN line, your computer can communicate at 56.6 kilobits per second (even up to 64 Kbps).

If you find this information meaningless, compare it with another meaningless number to see whether you can make sense of it (physicists make these comparisons all the time). The fastest commercial modem that operates over normal telephone lines communicates at 28.8 kilobites per second (which is twice as fast as the 14.4 fax/modem most of us have). The ISDN line communicates twice as fast as the 28.8 line. Have you noticed a trend here?

You can achieve speeds faster than 28.8 by ordering U.S. Robotics's new Sportster modem. This company has achieved speeds greater than 32.2 by making changes in the transfer software. If you have a U.S. Robotics Sportster modem, you can buy an upgrade chip for very little money. Contact the following URL: `http://www.USR.com/`

One really great feature of ISDN is its availability for different platforms. ISDN cards are available for PCs, Macs, and even Amiga computers. You'll be happy to know that some ISDN PCMCIA cards are made to fit into most laptop or notebook computers. If you own a high-end UNIX workstation, you haven't been left out in the cold; ISDN cards are available for UNIX workstations, too.

ISDN isn't new. Actually, the technology is more than six years old, but it's just now becoming commercially available. Part of the reason is that the telephone companies are just now installing the hardware needed to support ISDN. Special switching equipment and special ISDN phone lines also have to be installed.

Another nice feature of ISDN is the fact that it supports a concept known as *bandwidth-on-demand*. Rather than maintain a fixed amount of bandwidth during your connection, you use bandwidth (amount of available transmission space on the phone line) only when you need it. This feature allows for more efficient use of the telephone network.

Call your local telephone company and your Internet access provider to see whether ISDN is available in your area. The telephone company may offer ISDN, but your access provider may not. Someday soon, phone companies and access providers everywhere will offer ISDN.

ISDN is a digital phone service rather than the traditional analog connection used by older telephones. The only thing special about ISDN is the speed at which it allows your computer to communicate. You may be charged a per-minute online rate for this service, so check with the phone company before you choose ISDN as your dedicated connection (see "I'm Dedicated" later in this chapter for more information).

If you're interested in getting ISDN access, you want to get an ISDN Terminal Adapter (modem). Contact the following URL for more information on 3com's product:

`http://www.3com.com/`

I'm Dedicated

A dedicated connection to the Internet means that your connection — whether it's a telephone line or a fiber-optic ATM (Asynchronous Transfer Mode) connection — is always open. Your access provider has a dedicated connection to the Internet, and you can have the same open connection to your access provider. The fee for this connection varies, depending on the following factors:

- ✔ Your access provider's fee for a dedicated connection (normally based on the modem speed).
- ✔ Your phone company's charges. (If you are using a residential phone line, this charge is the cost of a single local call.)

After you have a dedicated connection, you can run all the server software discussed in this book, creating a complete Internet site right from your computer.

Your computer establishes a PPP connection with your access provider (see the next section, "AAA, BBB, CCC, . . . PPP"). The connection stays active all the time. If you use some of the commercial PPP packages, your computer and your access provider reconnect if your line goes down. This capability can be very important if you're selling products or services online. You don't want that sinking feeling of getting up in the morning, staring over your coffee mug at the modem, and suddenly realizing that only two of the four lights on the face of the modem are lit, meaning that the thing is disconnected.

AAA, BBB, CCC, . . . PPP

If you have a modem, a PC, and a desire to be on the Internet, PPP is the most common type of Internet access available. *PPP* (Point-to-Point Protocol) sets up a network connection between your machine and your access provider's machine. Without a network card or any special hardware, your PC or Macintosh can be connected to a network by using PPP software.

You may wonder how this access is different from SLIP access. PPP really isn't a whole lot different. PPP is a newer technology that does a few more whiz-bang things behind the scenes that you should never have to care about.

If you are given the choice between SLIP and PPP, choose the newer PPP technology. PPP will hold you in good stead until technology takes us to the next step. You'll find that most access providers have standardized on the PPP software, which can handle more types of connection options. But this isn't really important to the person trying to get connected.

PPP, where are you?

Hunting around the local computer shack's software bin may have you scratching your head. Hmmm — no PPP. Some commercial PPP applications are available, but you probably won't find one with *PPP* in its name (for example, BlunderSoft's PPP). Normally, you can find PPP — at least in commercial packages — in software that has names such as Internet Starter Kit or Internet Direct Connect Kit.

A common shareware version of PPP is available from a company called Trumpet (see Figure 14-2). Installing Trumpet's TCPMAN software allows you to connect to your access provider by using either SLIP or PPP.

Before you begin hunting all over the place for the Trumpet software or a commercial package, you should talk with your access provider. Many access providers offer their own proprietary connection software or a preconfigured copy of the Trumpet software.

Remember that the programmers who develop shareware products depend on your licensing fees for both their livelihood and for funding of future development programs. Remember to license your shareware software products.

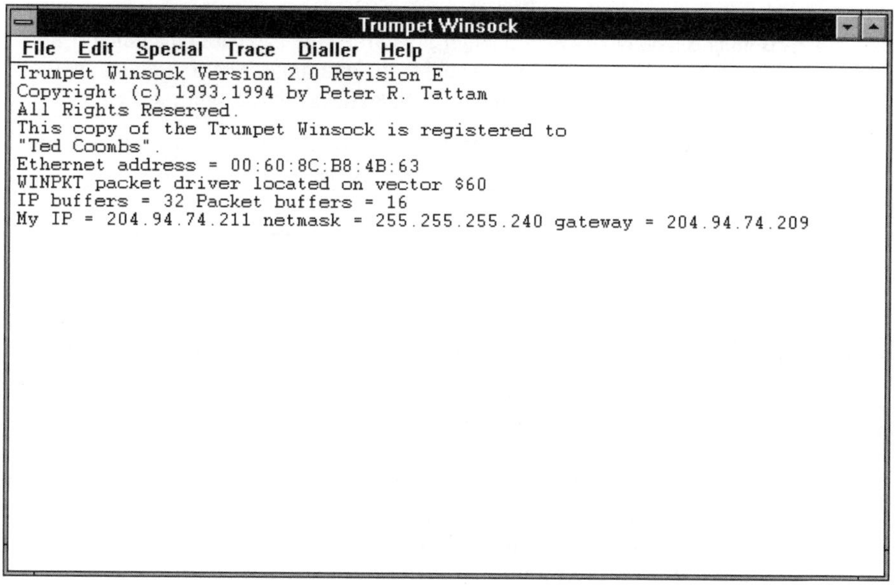

Figure 14-2:
Trumpet's
TCPMAN is
commonly
used to
connect PCs
to the
Internet.

```
─                          Trumpet Winsock                          ▼ ▲
 File  Edit  Special  Trace  Dialler  Help
Trumpet Winsock Version 2.0 Revision E
Copyright (c) 1993,1994 by Peter R. Tattam
All Rights Reserved.
This copy of the Trumpet Winsock is registered to
"Ted Coombs".
Ethernet address = 00:60:8C:B8:4B:63
WINPKT packet driver located on vector $60
IP buffers = 32 Packet buffers = 16
My IP = 204.94.74.211 netmask = 255.255.255.240 gateway = 204.94.74.209
```

Configuring PPP

You need information from your access provider to set up PPP. This information is nearly the same whether you are setting up the Trumpet software or another PPP implementation.

Most access providers have the parameters for configuring PPP already set or provide detailed information on how to set the parameters correctly for accessing their machines. Table 14-1 explains the configuration parameters.

Table 14-1	PPP Configuration Parameters
Parameter	**Description**
IP Address	The address of your computer when it's connected to the Internet. In some cases, you may have a fixed address. In other cases, when you use some versions of PPP, you are assigned an IP address when you log in.
Netmask	A road sign to the computer, telling it whether your packets should stay on your local network or be forwarded somewhere else on the Internet.
Name Server	The IP address of the computer that matches domain names with IP addresses.
Default Gateway	An important parameter if you are on a network that is connected to the Internet; it tells your computer which machine is the gateway to the Internet.
Time Server	An unimportant parameter that specifies which machine keeps track of the local time.
Domain Suffix	The parameter for your own domain name.

Frame Relay

Until ATM makes its way into the mainstream, the alternative for high-speed access to the Internet at a reasonable price is a technology called *frame relay*, which is an interface standard similar to ATM. In a frame relay, information is sent in fixed-size packets called *generic packets*. When the packet sizes are fixed, you can improve the efficiency to the point at which frame relay is equal to other high-cost connection alternatives, such as X.25.

Frame relay is optimized for traffic that is *protocol-oriented*. Remember that HTTP, FTP, and Telnet are all protocols. So frame relay has been optimized for this type of program interface — in other words, it is fast and efficient. Frame relay is available in two speeds: 56K and 384K. A 56K line is twice as fast as a 28.8 modem.

The monthly fee for this high-speed dedicated access is reasonable. The phone company charges a flat monthly fee for the service, and normally, your access provider tacks on its own monthly fee. For less than $400 a month, you can have dedicated high-speed access to the Internet.

For more information on where to purchase frame-relay hardware, contact the following URL:

```
http://www.group.com/prods/main.html
```

X.25

X.25 sounds like something out of *Star Wars* ("Hey, I need an X.25, R2D2"). This high-speed networking technology is available almost anywhere around the globe. Where frame relay is not available, X.25 is a viable alternative.

Some of the strengths of X.25 networking are

- X.25 is available globally, through both public and private means.
- X.25 uses a packet-switching approach.
- X.25 handles bursts of traffic — the norm on most networks — well.
- One of the advantages of X.25 and frame relay is a virtual-circuit connection.
- X.25 has built-in error correction.

Most of the time, you need to install a leased line. At least one company, however, provides a product that allows connection to an X.25 network over a dial-up line. NetcomHighway runs at T-1 rates over leased lines; one current drawback is the fact that Netcom Highway runs only on UNIX. In the summer of '96, this product will be available for Windows NT.

For more information on NetcomHighway, contact the following URL:

```
http://www.group.com/prods/main.html
```

X.25 is a technology that most likely will fall by the wayside. With both frame relay and the eventuality of ATM, the limitations of X.25 mean its eventual demise. Two of those limitations are its high cost (due to extensive protocol handling) and its limitation to T-1 speeds.

ATM

The future is here today — almost. Asynchronous Transfer Mode (ATM) technology most likely is the network technology that the Internet will adopt for the future. Right now, the Internet can transmit a limited amount of information. The technology behind the Internet is now almost 30 years old. The original designers were excited when only a thousand computers were attached. Now, however, the network is beginning to struggle under the massive amounts of data that are being sent over it, and it will struggle even more in the future because of sound and graphic data.

Information on the Internet is transferred in *packets* — not little zip-lock bags, but little software containers. Each packet contains varying types and sizes of information, which makes it nearly impossible for hardware (chips and so on) to deal with these packets. Hardware likes information in predictable sizes and shapes. ATM technology packages all the data in predictable byte-size packets (53 bytes, to be exact). If you think this arrangement sounds similar to the way that frame relay works, you're right. The major difference between the two technologies is the fact that ATM is a hardware solution with higher possible speeds.

Hardware can handle data switching and routing much faster than the current software system. ATM will solve this current bottleneck. You can connect to your local phone company's ATM switch right now for about $8,000 a month. At this price, ATM is not an option for most people (at least, not for computer-book authors). But stay tuned. This excessive cost will not always be the case, and changes probably will occur sooner rather than later. When fiber optics connects all homes, this technology probably will enable gigabit-per-second network speeds (that's 1,000,000,000 bits per second, which is about 69,444 times faster than a 14.4 modem).

If you are a network administrator in a fairly large company, consider starting your own ATM network in-house. The necessary hardware is fairly reasonably priced. You may want to wait before connecting to the phone company's switch, though — especially because not many other ATM networks are available to talk to yet.

Talk with your service provider about your Internet site and what you hope to accomplish with it. Be aware that access providers are eager to sell you the most expensive, latest, greatest service that they have going. Sometimes, the best strategy is to start small and grow. You may find that you don't need the power of frame relay, no matter how fast and slick it is. After you're connected, however, going back to a slower connection is hard. On the other hand, you don't want to limit people's access to your site. You have to walk a fine line in making this decision.

Using your access provider's services, you can set up many of the services that you need to run your Internet site. Thereafter, a dedicated connection of some kind will allow you to use your own machine as the Internet server. This setup gives you a great deal more flexibility. You then have to watch cost and speed in making a decision to install high-speed access.

After you decide which direction you want to take in connecting to the Internet, you can choose an access provider that provides that type of connectivity. Make sure that you talk to several providers about your decision; some providers may offer alternatives that work better or are more cost-effective than other providers' services.

What Are the Gotta-Haves?

To set up a site on the Internet, you must have a way to present your information. The most popular way is the World Wide Web, so we think it's safe to say that you must have a World Wide Web account. A nice-to-have for your Web account is a Web page served by a secure S-HTTP server.

Your potential customers also must have a way to contact you. In this case, business gets turned around a little. An e-mail account is probably a must-have. The nice-to-haves are things such as a phone and an address. If you're on the go all the time and not stuck in an office, you still can run a successful online business. Using a palmtop computer and RadioMail, a wireless e-mail connection, you can keep in touch from anywhere. See the following URL: http://www.radiomail.net/

You can find hundreds of Internet access providers around the country and probably in the city where you live. For information, see "Local Internet access providers" later in this chapter or simply look in your local newspaper.

Finding the Right Access Provider

If you think that competition among long-distance carriers is fierce, just wait until the competition for your Internet access reaches fever pitch ("Save 50 percent on file transfers to your friends and family!"). Unlike long-distance service — in which the only factors are price, call quality, and whether you watch "Murphy Brown" — Internet access is rich with feature choices.

Internet access providers fall into two basic categories: Internet-only providers (as CompuServe likes to call them) and private data networks that also provide access to the Internet. How much access to the Internet either type provides is a prime consideration when you're setting up an Internet site.

National Internet access providers

Most of the access providers are limited to their local area. Others cover a limited area, such as a single U.S. state. Only a few national Internet access providers exist. Of these, Netcom was one of the first.

Netcom

The largest national Internet access provider is Netcom On-Line Communication Services, Inc. This service provides Internet access to most of the major urban areas across the United States.

Netcom offers several levels of service. A personal dial-up account includes the following:

- World Wide Web
- FTP
- Telnet
- Usenet news
- Full Internet access

Netcom also offers frame relay, dedicated T-1, and ISDN connections.

Netcom has developed its own custom graphic user interface to the Internet services, called NetCruiser. This award-winning point-and-click interface is excellent for the Internet consumer or tourist, but it probably is not the best account if you are going to set up an Internet site. Instead, talk to a Netcom representative about some of the company's commercial accounts.

Netcom has full World Wide Web publishing accounts. This service enables you to keep your Web pages on the Netcom machine so that people have high-speed access to them 24 hours a day.

Netcom is one of the premier national Internet access providers that has come up through the ranks. The company began as an Internet access company and built its business on providing the best possible service. Other networks may have the backing of billion-dollar telecommunications companies, but none of them has the experience with Internet-access providing that Netcom has.

You can reach Netcom at 800-353-6600, or you can contact the company at its World Wide Web site:

```
http://www.netcom.com
```

SprintLink

Talking about Internet access without talking about the backbone is tough. SprintLink is the main national Internet trunk throughout the United States. In other countries, you have a different provider for your Internet backbone.

Contact Sprint directly for its access fees. The company does not provide access for individual accounts; you must be on a network that connects to the backbone or to an access provider. Sprint limits its services to these larger customers. If you are going to be setting up an Internet site that will resell Internet access, Sprint is the company to call. See the following URL: `http://www.sprintlink.net/`

Local Internet access providers

When you're deciding on a local access provider, make sure that the provider has a point of presence within your local calling area. A *point of presence* (POP) is the number that you dial into if you are using a dial-up account. A quick call to the operator can confirm whether the access number is local to you. This information becomes particularly important if you are having thoughts about a dedicated dial-up line from your home. If the call isn't a local call, you'll be charged by the minute. This can run up quite a bill if you leave the line open 24 hours a day.

We use a local Internet access provider: CTSNet of San Diego, California. CTS has one of the world's largest World Wide Web publishing services. The company offers the FTP drop-box, Gopher publishing, and many other services described in this book. CTS currently offers normal dial-up accounts, dedicated 28.8 lines, ISDN, and T-1; it eventually will offer frame-relay accounts. See the following URL: `http://www.cts.com/`

Running a few tests

Before you rush out and sign up for your Internet account, test the quality of service; if the service is bad, you have to live with it. Find out what your provider's local call-in number is and then call it, using your normal voice telephone. Try calling at different times of the day to see how often the line is busy. Doing business with a popular access provider is great, but not if it means that you can't get online when you need the access most.

Call the provider's tech support number a couple of times and ask questions such as, "What's a POP?" (pronounced *pee oh pee*). See how the support staff responds to you. If a staff member puts you on hold or if a supervisor says that he or she has to look up the information or refer the question to the owner, you should think twice about signing up with that service.

Shopping around will pay off

Comparison shopping pays off. You can find as many different payment programs as Internet access providers. Some providers will give you unlimited access time for a single monthly fee. This is one of the best deals you can get. Others have an incredibly complex set of rules, guidelines, and charges. Following are a few hidden costs that you should watch for (not paying attention to these points can mean an unexpected addition to your monthly bill):

✔ *Disk-use charges.* Find out what your free disk allotment is and stay within it. If you need more disk space, purchasing it ahead of time is best. Going over your disk-use allotment can be costly.

✔ *Bandwidth.* A limit on how much traffic is allowed into your account. Each person who accesses your account takes up a certain amount of bandwidth. Bandwidth is an issue if you have a World Wide Web or FTP account. Most access providers pay for a certain amount of access to the Internet from their access provider. Because access providers pay for a limited amount of bandwidth, they pass the cost of additional bandwidth on to you. Again, purchasing excess bandwidth ahead of time is best if you're going to need it.

✔ *Monthly, daily, or weekly access-time limits.* Some accounts give you a flat 20 hours of access time and allow you to spend it however you want; others give you two free hours a day and charge you extra if you go hogwild someday, downloading all the cool software that you've read about. Very few access providers have unlimited connect times unless you have a dedicated account. Once again, be careful to buy what you need.

✔ *Extra fees for domain-name service; FTP; Telnet access; or other services, such as aliases.* Most of these services require one-time setup. Many access providers like to charge monthly fees for these services, which require nothing extra from them after setup. You have to shop around and decide how many little things you will allow a provider to charge you for. Some access providers bill once for domain-name service; others milk you over a lifetime.

Before you sign up, check with other customers of the service. A good place to find out who the customers are is to go to the access provider's home page. Assuming that the provider provides a Web publishing service, it probably provides links to its Web publishing customers' pages. Calling these people is a better shot than asking for references.

One reason why it pays to shop around is the fact that more and more access providers require you to sign up for a minimum of three months or sometimes for as long as a year in advance. Getting any kind of refund usually is out of the question. Before you tie yourself to an access provider, getting to know that provider and the type and quality of service that you can expect is a good idea.

If you are setting up your Internet site, you probably don't want to change access providers midstream. One thing that you may want to do is run a credit check on the business. Dun and Bradstreet offers this service online. Make sure that the business looks as though it will be around to continue providing service.

If you have concerns about any of these issues, using one of the national service providers, such as Netcom or Network MCI, is a safe bet.

Online services

Millions and millions of people are accessing the Internet by using online services such as CompuServe and America Online. These services are not really the way to set up an Internet site. We discuss them because they are such an important part of being online. Knowing what services these services bring and how you might want to use them to increase your presence on the Internet is also important.

CompuServe

CompuServe is one of the grandfathers of online services, having connected computers over a public network for more than 20 years. Over the years, the service has built up one of the largest online information-database systems around. CompuServe's database of shareware, for example, is unmatched.

CompuServe isn't the Internet, but by no means is it small-time. The service connects nearly three million computers in most countries around the world. Following are some of CompuServe's strengths:

- ✔ Easy-to-use e-mail
- ✔ Simple file transfer
- ✔ More than 2,000 databases of information

Once a stand-alone network, CompuServe offers Internet access to its users. The service's Internet software company — Spry, Inc. — has created World Wide Web software for CompuServe customers.

In the fall of 1995, CompuServe brought its Electronic Mall to the Internet. The Electronic Mall, which was one of the pioneering attempts to set up shop online, began about 11 years ago. In this move to the Internet, CompuServe is offering to help clients set up World Wide Web home pages that are served by a Spry Secure S-HTTP server (see Figure 14-3). You can make financial business transactions securely in the CompuServe Electronic Mall.

CompuServe is aggressively pursuing the integration of its network into the Internet. The service now offers PPP access via 28.8 modems and soon will offer ISDN service with speeds to 64 Kbps. This integration into the Internet will take awhile, and you should ask questions when setting up this service to make sure that it will do everything you need it to.

For more information, you can go to the following site:

```
http://www.compuserve.com
```

America Online

America Online (AOL) has certainly moved agressively into the world of Internet access. Touted as the easiest user interface, America Online has more customers than any other service. It offers access to the Internet using a Web browser. At the writing of this book, America Online was in discussions with Netscape Communications regarding the use of the Netscape Navigator.

If you're going to set up an Internet site, AOL may be an option to consider. America Online has a large number of subscribers, so you may want to consider AOL as an additional avenue for selling a product or service. Many companies now offer their service on both the World Wide Web as well as the online services such as America Online.

Figure 14-3:
CompuServe offers World Wide Web access.

Other types of Internet access providers

National and local Internet access providers and the online services are not the only types of Internet access providers. Free nets offering free Internet access have popped up in cities all over the place. You may want to consider all types of alternative services when setting up an Internet site.

Free nets

Several communities around the world offer their citizens free access to the Internet. Free nets, for the most part, don't provide the type of access necessary to run an Internet site — PPP access, Web server accounts, or any of the other types of server programs that you need to run any type of Internet business. You can do a few clever things with an e-mail-only account, however, so don't rule out this type of service completely.

Make sure that you read the acceptable-use policy when you sign up with a free net; it may have restrictions on commercial use of its network. This commercial use may not apply to not-for-profit or educational organizations, however.

Cooped up with the co-ops

Another type of Internet access provider — the Internet co-op — has become popular recently. One of the first such co-ops, called The Little Garden, is in the San Francisco Bay area. Since the inception of that service, other co-ops have formed all over the place. If co-ops are available in your area, they may be able to provide competitive service.

Car 54, where are you?

Wireless Internet access is going to be more and more popular. For now, most wireless service is limited to e-mail. As we said earlier, however, e-mail-only accounts are not to be underestimated. Running a good e-mail information server on your mobile PC can give you a powerful Internet presence. Add collateral services, such as fax capability and the paging services offered by the wireless carriers, and you have quite a business arsenal.

UUCP-only accounts

UUCP-only accounts are inexpensive, and they offer a little more than just e-mail; they also offer a Usenet news feed. This way, if you are providing your service via e-mail, you can use the newsgroups to make your service known.

UUCP accounts download your e-mail and any newsgroups to which you subscribe directly to your computer. This arrangement enables you to keep online time to a minimum and your access charges low. The average online time for a UUCP-only account is about three hours per month.

UUCP (UNIX to UNIX Copy) is a protocol that has quite a bit of built-in communication and file-transfer capability. Your computer dials into a special UUCP account, using the UUCP program on your computer; then a completely automated session takes place, transferring mail and news to and from your computer. The great thing is that you can set up this transfer to take place in the middle of the night so that you can read your morning e-mail over coffee without having to log in anywhere.

Other ways to find Internet access

Listing all the various access providers would take another book the size of this book. You can, however, find an online list many pages long in Yahoo (one of our favorite Internet indexes). Here is the URL:

```
http://www.yahoo.com/Business_and_Economy/Companies/
Internet_Service_Providers/Internet_Access_Providers/
```

Using this list is a bit of a catch-22: How can you see the list if you don't already have access? Local libraries often provide Internet access to the public; you may be able to peruse the list there. You'll look smart with your copy of *Setting Up An Internet Site For Dummies* tucked under your arm. (If the librarian tries to wrestle it away from you, you can donate your copy and buy another one or you can make the library get its own copy.)

Another place where you can get temporary Internet access is in a cybercafe or coffee shop. As long as you're not living in Nowhere, USA, your town may be sporting one of these newest fads. This new type of coffee shop allows customers to peruse the Internet while chugging down overpriced steamed milk and coffee. The owners of these stores often can provide a wealth of information on local access providers and the price of tea in China.

Last, but not least, you can sneak into your kids' room at night and use their account. Be careful, though; they may have booby traps.

Setting up an Internet site is way cool and new-wave now, but someday soon, an online presence will be a necessity, whether you're a pizza shop, Joe's Bait and Tackle, Fishee Boat Mortgage and Finance, or a head of state. When people let their fingers do the walking, they'll be walking across their keyboards right to your Internet site.

Part V

Preparing
for the Future

In this part . . .

The Internet is changing very quickly, but the change is not a magical one. The Internet is just software and telecommunications services linking computers together. Aside from political change, only two things affect the Internet: new software technology and new computer communications services.

When viewed from this perspective, preparing for the future of the Internet is simple. New computer software will enable new Internet services, and faster, more reliable communications technology will pave the way for new software. This part analyzes the future of the Internet and suggests ways to prepare for it. The exciting second-wave of the World Wide Web brings us all a few steps closer to the promise of a single, seamless interface for the Internet.

Chapter 15

The Second Wave

*T*he World Wide Web is generally what people think of when the word *Internet* is mentioned. This exciting graphical world took off dramatically with the release of the first graphical Web browser, Mosaic. Soon after, in December 1994, Netscape released its new graphical browser, known as Netscape Navigator. Since then, a flood of companies has been providing information for users surfing the Net.

Till now, the limitations of the Web — mainly its lack of true interactivity between users and providers — were all too apparent. If you have had a great deal of exposure to the Web, you know that it has consisted simply of billboards, large banners of text and pictures that seem to zip by as you surf the Web. Becoming overwhelmed by the flood of often useless information doesn't take long. But the days of passive viewing on the Web are over, and with the development of exciting new tools and browser capabilities, the Web is on the verge of a second wave.

All Hail, Java

Java is a new multiplatform language developed by Sun Microsystems. Many companies that are serious about the Internet have endorsed and licensed Java. Sun often describes Java this way: "Write once; run anywhere." Cute saying, but what does it mean?

Typically, a programming language must be compiled for the particular platform for which it will be used, such as Windows, UNIX, or Macintosh. A program that is compiled for Windows cannot run on a Macintosh machine. The dream of the Internet information providers, of course, is that, as users surf around to different Web sites, they can encounter and immediately begin using computer programs, whether they use Windows or Mac operating systems. These programs could be multiuser games in which the user can interact with other users in a dynamic Web environment, programs that allow a user to write checks from his or her bank account, or endless other applications. Because the programs would not be resident on the user's hard drive but would be downloaded at the time of use, the software providers can update programs and not have their users experience any version-compatibility problems.

The cross-platform capabilities of Java make these advancements possible over the Internet. Using Java, someone who is providing information on an Internet site can develop interactive programs that can communicate with anyone who visits his or her Web site, using any type of computer operating system.

Internet appliances

Having an Internet appliance doesn't mean that you can hook your refrigerator up to the Internet, but it's close. Many companies are proclaiming that with the new age of Java, users will be able to purchase inexpensive systems — say, $200 to $500 — that can be connected to the Internet so users can run programs written in Java. If users did have this capability, these systems would not need a huge hard drive capacity because users could contact Web sites and download the programs only when needed. Instead of having to purchase the newest version of Microsoft Word, for example, you could contact the Microsoft Word Web site and begin using the program that is downloaded to your machine temporarily. The proponents of this exciting new system would expect you to pay, of course — possibly a monthly or per-use fee. Whether this particular Internet appliance scenario becomes reality depends on whether several technical and economic hurdles can be overcome.

Java for programmers

If you are an experienced programmer familiar with C++, you should be able to begin programming in Java in a relatively short time. You can find general information about Java at Sun's Web site:

```
http://java.sun.com
```

Inspired people can begin working with the Java language by downloading the Java Developer's Kit at the same Web site.

Netscape's New Navigator

Since its founding, Netscape has pursued the strategy of continually integrating new HTML extensions into its new client browser software before any other company does, so as to maintain a technological lead. Some of the most exciting capabilities of Netscape's newest browser allow for the integration of Java applets, inline plug-ins, and JavaScript. These new features hold the promise of making the Web a true completely interactive environment.

Java applets

Can you imagine switching to a new Web page and finding a ticker tape of stock quotes running across the top? You will. This technology may sound like an AT&T commercial, but new tools known as *Java applets* now allow for animation in Web pages and many other exciting possibilities.

You can find an interesting Java applet that involves scrolling news information at the following Web site:

```
http://www.cnet.com
```

A Java applet is a small program, written in Java, that is downloaded to your computer when you contact a particular Web site. You can design the Java applets to start a musical tune when a user clicks on a particular hypertext link or to begin an animation when a Web page is first loaded. The hangman game in Figure 15-1 illustrates a Java applet that is downloaded to the user's computer through the Internet and then executed.

The functional and aesthetic capabilities that Java applets can add to a Web site appear to be endless.

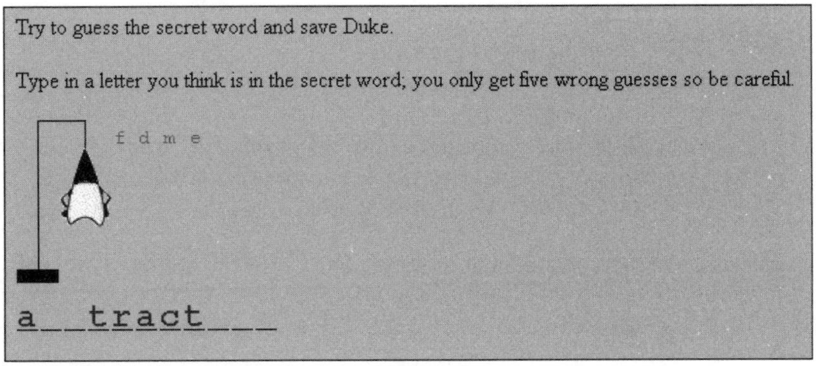

Figure 15-1:
The user attempts to determine the secret word in five guesses.

Try to guess the secret word and save Duke.

Type in a letter you think is in the secret word; you only get five wrong guesses so be careful.

f d m e

a _ _ t r a c t _ _ _

Plug-in developers

Skilled programmers can begin to develop their own plug-ins by using Netscape's Plug-Ins Development Kit, which is available at the following Web site:

`http://www.netscape.com/comprod development_partners/plugin_api/`

A complete step-by-step guide to plug-in development, created by `SCIENCE.ORG`, is posted on the Web at the following location:

`http://www.science.org/netscape/ plug-ins/`

After reviewing the information presented at these two sites, you should be well on your way to creating your own inline plug-ins.

Inline plug-ins

Inline plug-ins allow for complete programs to be executed within the Netscape Navigator browser, similar to the way different programs operate in a Windows environment. The programs are called "inline" plug-ins because they work right in the Netscape Navigator window — as though the plug-in had extended the capabilities of Netscape itself. A user can download a plug-in program, and when he or she contacts a particular Web page, that plug-in immediately launches the program within the Netscape Navigator browser window.

The companies rushing to produce inline plug-ins include Macromedia, which has created a plug-in called Shockwave for its Director multimedia software; Intuit, which has created a plug-in for Quicken; and Progressive Networks, which has developed a Real Audio plug-in that is capable of receiving sound in a continuous stream rather than requiring users to download an entire sound file and then play it.

JavaScript

Netscape has developed its own scripting language, *JavaScript*, to be integrated within HTML documents. JavaScript serves as an interface to the inline plug-ins and Java applets; it also enables you to develop basic programs within the HTML code for a particular Web page. You can run JavaScript applications in the newest versions of Netscape Navigator.

Netscape has developed a complete guide to the JavaScript language. You can find this guide at the following Web site:

```
http://www.netscape.com/comprod/products/navigator/⟳
version_2.0/script/script_info/
```

This language is designed to be easy to use by anyone who is familiar with HTML code. After reviewing the guide, you should be able to begin integrating the JavaScript language into your own Web sites.

LiveWire

Netscape Communications has created an exciting program called LiveWire which works with Netscape Navigator Gold to provide a dynamic system for generating Web sites. Creating your own Web pages has never been more simple or powerful. The LiveWire system also offers features that make running a Web site more simple and efficient. Rather than just creating Web pages, you create *network applications* that are managed by LiveWire. These applications consist of HTML pages, Java applets, inline plug-ins, and Java programs that run with your HTTP server. An advanced version, LiveWire Pro, adds relational database connectivity. This means you can now create your own database applications using this simple-to-use tool. LiveWire is a great, efficient tool for anyone who provides information on a Web site.

Microsoft's Internet Products

Although Netscape took an impressive lead in the Internet computer industry, Microsoft is by no means out of the game. Microsoft has taken a very aggressive attitude toward exploiting the potential of the Internet. The company has matched each of the new Internet development tools developed by Netscape with a competitive version. In fact, Microsoft led the pack in the easy-to-use Web creation tools. Internet Assistant is an add-on software tool that turns Microsoft Word into a Web-page creation tool and a Web browser. Users can now use the familiar formatting tools of Microsoft Word to create Web pages. Using the Internet Assistant-enhanced Microsoft Word is easier than typing in all the HTML yourself. To use this tool effectively, you still must know HTML basics. Expect to see Internet connectivity integrated into all the programs in the Microsoft Office suite of products.

In competition with Netscape's LiveWire system, Microsoft has produced Internet Studio for developing World Wide Web content, integrating many of the new dynamic tools such as Java applets. In competition with JavaScript, Microsoft is promoting VB Script for the World Wide Web. Using VB Script, a pared down version of Microsoft's Visual Basic programming language, you can write programs that run across several platforms. VB Script also allows you to link and automate OLE objects and Java applets.

Microsoft will leverage its new capabilities in the area of 3-D multimedia animation to bring a new generation of Web authoring tools, including VRML, the Virtual Reality Markup Language. Expect to see the Microsoft implementation of VRML to support VB Script, Java, and C++. For more information contact:

```
http://www.microsoft.com/intdev/tech.htm
```

Last, but certainly not least, in competition with Netscape's Navigator browser, Microsoft has developed Internet Explorer. One of the differences between the Netscape Navigator and Microsoft's Internet Explorer is that Microsoft has decided to offer the Internet Explorer unconditionally free. This is also true of the Windows 95 add-on (previously planned as a Windows 95 upgrade) simply called Internet Add-on.

The race is on among Netscape, Microsoft, and many newcomers. The winner remains to be seen, but the benefit to users and Internet providers is that such intense competition will serve to push the Internet ahead faster technologically — with competitive prices for both users and Internet providers.

If you are interested in providing information at an Internet site by using the Web, you can't ignore these new tools and features. Netscape's and Microsoft's tools, such as LiveWire and Internet Studio, should allow you to develop content for a Web site easily and manage it more efficiently. Take the time to learn at least one of these tools.

New features such as Java applets and inline plug-ins offer untold capabilities. If your goal is to design a Web site that has exciting content — one that people will come back to again and again — you need to take a close look at these new features.

Chapter 16

The Interactive Global Village

*T*he Internet today is a harsh, technical, often unfriendly environment; it's untamed. But already, we're seeing glimpses of the Internet's potential. When the roar of technical computer jargon subsides and the unfriendly and sometimes backward Internet technology matures, you'll sense that something very important is about to happen. The human race is on the verge of a critical decision about the future.

The Internet has the potential to create and sustain a global, interactive village. The draw of global commerce and the newfound capability of the average person to participate in it over the Internet constitute a force of unfathomable magnitude.

What will the future global interactive village look like? Who will control it? Where will its laws come from, and who will enforce them? We have no assurance that the Internet will continue to be democratic, defined by the values of its users. Amidst all the questions and uncertainty one thing is certain: The Internet changes all the rules.

Before the Internet took off, the world was already moving toward being a global village. World travel and global satellite communications have for decades influenced the emergence of worldwide social awareness. The Global Agreement on Tariffs and Trade agreement (GATT) took shape and was turned into law while the Internet was just starting to grow.

You can be sure that the politicians and business leaders responsible for GATT weren't thinking about the emergence of a single, worldwide, interactive data network. The communications technologies that these leaders had in mind were telephone, television, and radio — good, traditional media controlled by economic superpowers. The Internet adds an unexpected twist to global free trade, placing individuals and small businesses on a level playing field with the rest of the electronic world.

These large issues may not be the ones you've thought about lately. But, with the level playing field created by the Internet, you're now capable of true global commerce right from your living room. Gaining an understanding of social issues, global economics, and some of the new legal issues facing people connected to the Internet will help you become a more integrated part of the Internet global village.

Enough Hype — Now, Some Real Examples

Everyone says that the Internet is a major force of social change, but where's the proof? Endless Internet hype is overwhelming, not to mention annoying. We wanted to know exactly why the Internet will change everything, so we looked for good examples and convincing reasons. The following sections present a few examples that impress us.

Science, education, and the Internet

Scientists and students realize truly remarkable advantages from the Internet. One resource that has been in the news lately is The Visible Human Project, a large set of digital images that show every detail of human anatomy one millimeter at a time. You can access the project, which includes both male and female anatomy, at the following URL:

```
http://www.nlm.nih.gov/extramural_research.dir/
visible_human.html
```

The simple existence of such a project can be taken as proof that the Internet represents something very important to the scientific and educational communities. The project is very important, but not for the reason that you may think. Human anatomy has already been mapped with the techniques of The Visible Human Project, so the anatomical insights aren't what is scientifically important.

To science, The Visible Human Project represents the opportunity to incorporate a precise electronic anatomy model into all kinds of biological research. Now new software can be written, giving researchers around the world an interactive biology laboratory in which they can conduct endless experiments. The potential of such an interactive biology lab is limited only by the capabilities of the computers and the software that make it possible.

Someday, software will simulate the flow of blood, the function of the organs, and the activity of the brain so accurately that scientists can use a virtual visible human to conduct meaningful experiments. In a strange way, the people who donated their bodies to science for the sake of The Visible Human Project are being brought back to life in cyberspace. Imagine the potential impact on the methods of science that a simple visible-rat project with a sophisticated interactive research lab could have.

The benefits to education also are rooted in the development of new software. Automated multimedia teaching programs could augment the ability of high-school biology teachers to educate and inspire students. The difference between a real scientist conducting important research and a student of science will increasingly be determined by the kind of software that each uses to view and interact with the global pool of scientific data.

This discussion brings up an interesting point: Should scientists working in interactive research labs use their World Wide Web browsers to access the labs? We don't think so. Even with some of the new World Wide Web features, a Web browser is not the right tool for serious scientific research, and it may not even be the right tool for interactive remote learning. Watch the development of new visible-human-project software to see how much, if any, of it works in a Web browser.

Another exciting Internet science project involves the entire field of astronomy. The Hubble Space Telescope has helped renew interest in astronomy, but its impact has been much more significant as a result of NASA's use of the Internet. Via NASA's Web site, you can download astrophotographs taken by the Hubble, sometimes within hours of their transmission back to Earth. The NASA Web site is located at this URL:

```
http://www.nasa.gov/
```

One NASA Internet project that we recently learned about allows students on the ground to control experiments aboard the space shuttle while it is in orbit. We can only imagine the ways in which the future international space station will be used via the Internet. Space scientists and students of the space sciences have already benefited greatly from the Internet. New Internet software promises to change the ways space scientists conduct their research and the methods students use to learn about scientific discoveries.

When you create your Internet site, include links to NASA and other important Internet resources. These links will make your site more interesting and support the work of the people adding important educational content to the Internet. An additional thing you can do is to add your own thoughts about such projects.

Interactive shopping

We were skeptical at first about the potential of Internet shopping; would it really be anything more than glorified television shopping? Several things, however, have convinced us that interactive shopping offers more than that.

First, the Internet Shopping Network (`http://www.internet.net/`) has reported a significant increase in sales, due primarily to overseas (outside the United States) shoppers. This trend makes a great deal of sense, if you think about it. Although many Americans live just around the corner from a physical shopping mall, people in other countries (especially developing ones) don't have this luxury; their shopping options are severely limited. The Internet Shopping Network offers an excellent solution.

Along with enabling retailers to reach the overseas market, the Internet has proved to be an excellent selling vehicle for retailers that offer unique or specialty items. If a product is hard to find in the real world, the Internet is the place to sell it. In fact, specialty retailers generated impressive sales even before the Web offered security features. People who wanted to purchase specialty or hard-to-find items were willing to take the chance that a hacker might intercept their credit card numbers, or more often, found alternative ways to send their payments.

A new technology called a *digital ID* (described in detail in Chapter 12) promises to make Internet shopping as simple as clicking on the ad for the product that you want to buy. Web browsers such as Netscape's Navigator soon will supply customers' digital IDs (if they have those IDs) to merchants automatically after those customers decide to make a purchase. This setup means that you will no longer have to fill out a long form and type your credit card number each time you make a purchase.

Assuming that Internet shopping becomes this simple, what does this type of shopping mean for Internet advertising, and what effect will this advertising have on global culture? For one thing, a well-designed and compelling advertisement could directly generate sales for a product. Today, the actual sale is far removed from the advertising that generates interest in a product. Jason, as a kid, wanted to purchase sugar-filled treats immediately upon seeing advertisements for them on television. Actually, he wanted the treats to materialize magically in front of him at no charge, because he wasn't old enough to work, but you get the general idea.

If you create an Internet site that includes online sales, you will be confronted with two specific areas of concern, advertising and selling. Advertising and purchasing will become interactive, with sales being generated instantly when the right ad is placed in front of the consumer at just the right time. In the future, your customers will use a personal network agent that can filter out ads that don't interest them. Network agents are being developed that will be able to describe customer interests and buying habits to automated advertising generators so that they can dynamically create ads that will appeal to a specific customer. You will want to stay abreast of agent technology so that you can make maximal use of this technology to further target your customer base.

These newly-developed, intelligent advertising-generation programs may even have access to credit ratings and current bank-account balances of customers viewing your advertising. More likely, your Internet commerce site will access an Internet credit agency that doesn't reveal confidential information, but does track (and score) the purchasing habits of your potential customer. This type of automatic credit checker is a little scary to the average consumer. The Big Brotheresque loss of privacy will enhance personalized and targeted advertising at the expense of consumer privacy. As the developer of an online store, you have to weigh the pros and cons of using such systems.

No matter what happens, Internet shopping will have a unifying effect on global society. Currency differences have no meaning on the Internet, and for the first time, the shopping experience will be identical no matter where you live.

Internet customers will come from every part of the world. Therefore, international shipping and Internet file-transfer technology will become key to the infrastructure of global Internet commerce. Whether a product is a physical item or an electronic document, getting it to international customers will be an essential strategy decision for businesses.

Government machinery improvement

A great deal of talk has been generated about the potential of the Internet to create a true democracy. Our system of government in the United States is a representative democracy; we elect representatives to make decisions on our behalf but really don't have any direct input on key issues. A true democracy would allow its citizens to vote on any issue electronically, and the majority would rule.

The very thought of a true democracy is scary. Imagine the power of the popular media in such a society. Just as a creatively designed advertisement could persuade you to make an immediate online purchase, the right news coverage of a terrorist attack could provoke a vote for retaliation and war against the terrorist country. Calm, sensible, and wise thought is something that we expect from our representatives before they make decisions of this magnitude, and when they demonstrate these skills, we realize the benefit of our form of government.

Although switching from a representative democracy to a true democracy may not be a viable idea, what is certain to develop in the future is a set of political Internet tools that will change the way in which we interact with our representatives. Through the Internet, we will be able to inform our elected officials of our opinions, as well as track their performance through access to voting records and multimedia political archives. Keeping abreast of government activity will be very simple, and real facts about government actions will be available at our convenience.

Some local, state, and federal agencies already provide this type of information on the Internet. You may be able to find information about your representatives on the Internet today. Rather than give you the specific Internet addresses for the politicians that we like, we'll simply suggest that the information is out there and that you can find it easily by using any of the Internet search utilities. We look forward to the time when better political Internet software gives us real-time updates on government activity. Browsing through hundreds of pages of information on the Web is ineffective and tiring, and it does nothing to encourage involvement in the political process.

Ideally, the net effect of these changes will be positive. Interactive Internet government presents the possibility of a more accessible, more sensible governing process; it could (and should) revolutionize the way that the government and the governed relate to one another.

Virtual communities

One exciting development is the emergence of virtual communities. Entire towns are organizing to establish a presence on the Internet. The city of Blacksburg, Virginia, for example, worked in cooperation with Virginia Tech to create the Blacksburg Electronic Village. You can visit this impressive creation at the following address:

```
http://www.bev.net/
```

Clearly, the electronic village has helped bring together the people of Blacksburg; also clearly, they were pretty together to begin with. Many more virtual communities are beginning to spring up and grow around the world. If your area doesn't have one yet, share this book with others and generate momentum to start your own virtual community on the Internet.

The desire to associate and conduct business within our own communities seems to be human nature. Becoming part of the online community can and will bring the same sense of camaraderie, and with it trust, relationships, and business. As in any community, the responsible store owners are the ones that help shape the neighborhood.

Another interesting trend in community development is the emergence of Internet coffee shops. These establishments, which are appearing in all parts of the world, offer Internet access along with a hot cup of java and a friendly atmosphere. Internet coffee shops are a great way to build real-world relationships surrounding the Internet.

The fact that these events are occurring simultaneously around the world is an intriguing indication of a growing shared experience. The Internet is quickly becoming a common cultural thread that could work to bridge the gaps between dissimilar cultures. Right now, people throughout the world are doing exactly what you're doing: learning how to create a presence on the Internet and trying to understand what it means for the future. You now have something important in common with a growing percentage of the rest of the world.

Virtual workplace

You may already be one of the millions of Americans who telecommute. If so, you know how significantly telecommuting changes your life. Although you may still be in the employ of a company, you're empowered to create your own work environment and develop your own work habits. This opportunity can be a challenging proposition, but the rewards are well worth the extra initial effort required to get your bearings and develop good telecommuting skills.

The benefit to companies also is significant. Studies have shown that worker productivity increases when effective telecommuting practices are put into place. Telecommuting has become such a mainstream and important effort that even the State of California's transportation department, CalTrans, is involved in research on ways to implement telecommuting practices in California companies. Recently, the idea of a paperless office has engaged the imaginations of companies everywhere. According to *Wired* magazine, the hype about the paperless office is over; now companies are excited about the idea of an officeless office.

We view the idea of virtual corporations and the widespread use of telecommuting as being of pivotal importance to the future of work. People should be able to live in the cities of their choice and work for companies that they believe in without worrying about geographical distances and time wasted commuting to and from work.

As you may expect, the growth of the Internet has added momentum to the telecommuting movement. One of the barriers to effective Internet telecommuting is the lack of a file-transfer standard for the Internet. Working with other people via the Internet is very difficult without a simple way to share computer files, such as spreadsheets and word-processed documents. This situation will change very soon, as a new Internet file-transfer service becomes available. Watch our site for more information:

```
http://www.science.org/internetsite/
```

Internet Programming

The Internet and all its applications are made available by Internet software. This special software is no more difficult to build than traditional software is, and anyone who has computer programming experience can build it. We've watched as Internet programming has evolved from laboratory experiment to corporate technology to its current Web-oriented phase. The programming hasn't changed a great deal in that time, although some new toys have become available.

New developments in Internet programming technology will be some of the most important keys to the future of the Internet and to the world that it helps create. Companies such as Sun Microsystems, Netscape, and Borland are making this essential technology available right now. Most of the major software developers are licensing the Java programming language, as shown in the following list:

- Java by JavaSoft at `http://www.javasoft.com`
- JavaScript by Netscape Communications at `http://www.netscape.com`
- Java Applets on the Web by Netscape Communications and Microsoft at `http://www.microsoft.com`
- CORBA in Java by Iona Technologies at `http://www.iona.com`
- Java programming tools by Powersoft at `http://www.powersoft.com`

We can't emphasize enough how important Internet programming technology is to the average Internet user. This technology shouldn't just be for technical people who get paid to write Internet software; everyone who uses the Internet should be able to program the network. Creating new Internet software enables you to express yourself electronically; it's a fundamental capability of the new interactive world.

Anyone setting up an Internet site needs to become familiar with Java and learn more about some of the exciting standards that will change the way software communicates. For more information on Java, point your Web browser to `http://java.sun.com/`, and for more information on CORBA, point to `http://www.omg.com/`.

Trust us: Internet programming tools that are right for you will come along. Don't be afraid to experiment with new Internet programming technology to find out whether it meets your needs. If you ask, most software companies will allow you to evaluate their software. Another good way to test-drive Internet programming tools is to buy a book about the software before you decide to explore it further. Either the book will make sense to you (meaning that the software will, too), or it won't. Don't give up the search, however, because Internet programming is in your future.

Part VI
The Part of Tens

The 5th Wave   By Rich Tennant

"NOW, THAT WOULD SHOW HOW IMPORTANT IT IS TO DISTINGUISH
'FERTILIZING PRACTICES' FROM 'FERTILITY PRACTICES' WHEN
DOWNLOADING A VIDEO FILE FROM THE INTERNET."

In this part . . .

This part of the book is the most fun. The Part of Tens chapters highlight ten things that we thought you would like to know about but that didn't fit anywhere else in the book. First are ten Internet add-ons you can't live without. Running a killer Internet site means using tools that make it simple. The better your tools are, the better your site will be.

Then, you find more than ten additional sources of information that show you where to go to learn more and to stay informed of new Internet technology. Finally, this part has ten JavaScripts you can add to your HTML pages.

Chapter 17

Our Ten Favorite Internet Add-Ons

In This Chapter

▶ The software that helps make it all happen

▶ Inline plug-ins

▶ Digital camera

*T*he Internet is only a connection. What you do with that connection is what counts. After you're connected, everything, that is, all the software you use, can be considered an add-on. We have some favorites we want to share with you. We're certain that more exciting software will continue to be developed. Feel free to share your experiences with us. After all, the Internet is all about networking!

WSArchie

WSArchie is a client program that searches the Archie database for files in anonymous FTP sites. This Windows Archie client, written by David Woakes, makes navigating the many hosts and directories a snap. In fact, you can interface this program with your FTP client so that when you find the file that you want, you can simply double-click on the file to start the download process. You can download (and then install) the WSArchie software from the following URL:

```
http://dspace.dial.pipex.com/town/square/cc83/
```

To use WSArchie, enter the name of the file for which you are looking; select the Archie server that you want to use; click on the Search button; and wait while Archie creates a reply. Navigate the hosts and directories in the search results by clicking on the rows and columns (see Figure 17-1). The filenames change as you click on different host or directory names.

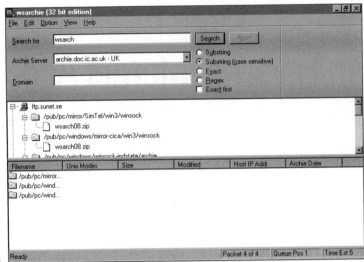

Figure 17-1:
Navigate
hosts and
directories
by clicking
on the host
or directory
names.

For more information on WSArchie, you can contact David Woakes by e-mail at the following address:

```
David@maxwell.demon.co.uk
```

Paint Shop Pro

Many of the things that you can do on the Internet involve graphics. You may want to view, edit, convert, or enhance graphic files to display them in World Wide Web pages, for example. One of the finest shareware tools that we have used for manipulating graphics is Paint Shop Pro, by JASC, Inc. You can use this product to draw or paint pictures, retouch scanned photos, and convert documents from one graphic type to another. In many ways, this program is similar to the popular commercial software, Corel PhotoPaint.

Paint Shop Pro allows you to do the following:

- Capture a *screen shot* — that is, save a picture of whatever's on your computer screen at the moment. (Many of the figures in this book are screen shots, for example.) With Paint Shop Pro, you can capture the full screen or a specific portion of the screen.

- Create .GIF files with invisible backgrounds — this type of background is widely used for creating Web pages.

✔ Use a full set of brushes, pens, spray cans, and special effects to paint and draw on new or existing graphics.

✔ Save images in a graphic format used by fax machines.

✔ Save or convert files in 20 formats, including Sun Raster and Macintosh.

✔ Convert and browse many files at the same time.

✔ Add high-quality text to your images.

✔ Use built-in scanner support that enables you to bring graphic images into Paint Shop Pro right from your scanner.

Paint Shop Pro is a breeze to use. Unlike many graphics editors, the program allows you to open multiple documents at a time and then view or edit them. This feature makes manipulating animations simpler by letting you see several graphics next to one another.

Paint Shop Pro is a shareware 16-bit software package that can be downloaded from the following FTP site:

```
ftp://ftp.winternet.com/users/jasc/
```

If you register the shareware and pay the cost, a 16-bit patch can be down-loaded and installed.

Inline Plug-ins

One of the hottest new trends hitting the Internet is the use of inline plug-ins. An *inline plug-in* is a way to run a program that is executed within the Netscape Navigator Web browser environment. This is similar, yet different to the Netscape helper applications. A *helper application* is a program that starts when a file that needs this program is encountered by Netscape. For example, video is not handled within the Netscape browser. Instead, helper applications would launch allowing you to view the video. Inline plug-ins also launch an application, although you may never realize it. This application runs within the Netscape browser, appearing as though Netscape itself had this ability. The multimedia capabilities this new feature provides are only beginning to be realized.

Every day, new companies announce the release of inline plug-ins that can be incorporated into Web browsers. Check out the following URL, where Netscape posts all the current inline plug-ins that are available:

```
http://www.netscape.com/comprod/products/navigator/⏎
version_2.0/plugins/index.html
```

Plug-in software now allows something known as streaming. *Streaming* is when data is sent over the Internet and is viewed or played while the data is being transferred. Streaming keeps you from having to wait for long files to download before viewing, or listening to them. Some of the most exciting plug-ins currently available include Shockwave, for viewing animations; VDO, for viewing real-time video streaming; Real Audio, for real-time audio streaming; Amber, for viewing Adobe Acrobat documents; and WebFX, for viewing and moving around in a virtual graphical environment.

The key to a successful Internet strategy is creating a Web page that users find to be entertaining and useful. After you install and use some of the plug-ins described in the next few sections, the immense multimedia and interactive capabilities that you can add to a particular Web site should be obvious. The Web is undergoing significant changes, and to remain in the lead, you should begin experimenting with new features such as plug-ins to enhance the Web part of your Internet strategy.

The inline plug-in feature can be used only in Netscape Navigator 2.0 version or greater.

Inline plug-in installation

You install an inline plug-in in basically the same way that you do the other programs that you decompress and install throughout this book. First, download the desired inline plug-in, and run the setup program, which should successfully install the plug-in. If you are currently running the Netscape Navigator, restart it. To make sure that Navigator recognizes the plug-in, you may select Help⇔About plug-ins. All the plug-ins that have been installed are listed.

For Netscape Navigator clients to recognize MIME files that the plug-in is capable of viewing, you need to place a .DLL file in the following directory during installation:

```
C:\Netscape\Program\Plugins\*.DLL
```

This file should be placed automatically by the plug-in during its installation. If you have any difficulty with the plug-in, the .DLL file is probabaly in the wrong location.

When you first install the Navigator client, the Program subdirectory contains only two other subdirectories: one labeled Navigator, and the other labeled java. The Plugins subdirectory is created during the first plug-in installation that you do, and the appropriate .DLL file should be copied to this subdirectory. All additional plug-in installations should copy their specific .DLL files to the Plugins subdirectory.

After you download and install a particular inline plug-in, you can check to make sure that the Navigator client recognizes the new MIME files that the plug-in is capable of viewing. In your Netscape Navigator client window, click on Help in your menu bar and select About Plug-ins in the pop-up window that appears. The browser should display the supported file types, as shown in Figure 17-2.

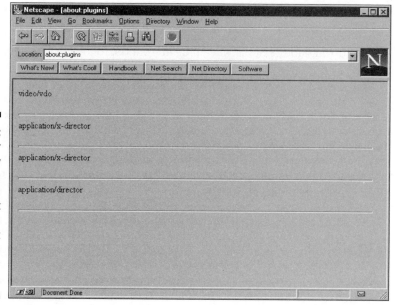

Figure 17-2:
The browser window shows the MIME file types that the plug-ins support for this particular client.

Remember that MIME was created to handle multimedia. Macromedia Director is one of the most popular multimedia content-producing software products. With it, you can create powerful director and x-director movies and animations. The MIME files that plug-ins support in Figure 17-2 include the various director and x-director animations produced with Macromedia Director and video/vdo produced with the VDOLive server software. If the .DLL file for a particular plug-in is not located in the Plugins directory, the particular MIME file does not appear when you choose the About Plug-ins command.

Shockwave

One of the most popular animation programs in the computer industry is Macromedia Director, which has sold more than 250,000 copies. The Shockwave inline plug-in allows users to view Macromedia Director animations within the Netscape Navigator Web browser. (See "Macromedia Director" later in this chapter for information on creating animations.)

The implications of this new feature should be apparent. The Web is no longer a static billboard of information; now it can contain animations that begin when a user visits a particular Web page or when a particular user event occurs, such as a mouse click over a particular image on your Web page.

You can download the Shockwave plug-in from the following URL site:

```
http://www.macromedia.com/
```

After you download and install the Shockwave plug-in, you can view several Web sites that use it. (You'll find those sites listed in the Shockwave Gallery at the preceding URL.) When you first view the various "Shocked" sites, a static gray image appears while the animation is loaded. You must wait a couple of minutes for some animations to execute. If no animation appears after some time, try reloading the same page.

VDOLive

Can you imagine a customer logging into your Web site and seeing a welcome video that guides him or her to particular locations for technical support, sales, or administration? The new VDOLive plug-in promises this exciting new capability. VDOLive uses various techniques to produce reasonably good video, using the small bandwidth that currently exists for most Internet users. With a 28.8 modem, the user should be able to view a decent video image. You can download the VDOLive plug-in from the following Web site:

```
http://www.vdolive.com/
```

After installing the plug-in, you can view a sample video at the following URL:

```
http://www.vdolive.com/plugvdo1.htm
```

At this particular Web site, you should see the image shown in Figure 17-3. With the various bugs that still exist, you may have to reload the Web page to get this image to appear.

Figure 17-3:
The image that indicates where the video will appear.

To begin the video, simply right-click on any part of this image. Then you should see either play or stop selections. Select Play; the image should turn black except at the bottom, where you see the status of the loading image and the reception percentage (see Figure 17-4).

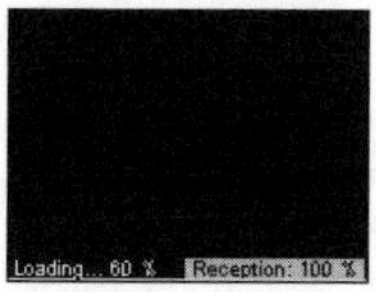

Figure 17-4:
After you select play, the image should indicate that it is loading and display the current reception percentage.

After the image is loaded, the video begins to play. VDOLive offers a new dimension to creating a dynamic, interesting, and useful Web site by adding the capability to view videos.

WebFX

Now you can enter a virtual graphical world within your Web browser. The new WebFX plug-in allows the user to operate in a VRML (*Virtual Reality Modeling Language*) world environment in which the user can navigate through a 3-D world while being able to interact with the environment. For example, clicking on a picture of a lamp could make the lamp suddenly appear illuminated. You'll love playing with this plug-in; download it from:

```
http://www.paperinc.com/wfxstep1.html
```

Various Web sites allow you to move around in a 3-D virtual environment. One of the most interesting 3-D environments is the MTV Cube, which shows people morphing from one to another in one of Michael Jackson's videos, "Black and White." This dynamic VRML demo is located at the following URL:

```
http://www.paperinc.com/vrml/models/mtv/mtv.wrl
```

If you installed your WebFX plug-in correctly, the environment within your Netscape Navigator should look like Figure 17-5, although downloading this Web site takes several minutes.

Figure 17-5:
This VRML environment, viewable with the WebFX plug-in, allows you to navigate to different views.

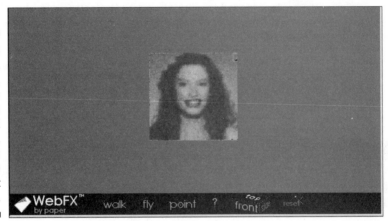

After you go to this site, you can move around in three modes (listed at the bottom of the VRML field): walk, fly, or point. Point your mouse at the mode that you want to use and click on it. Walking allows you to move through the virtual environment as if you were walking through it. Flying allows you to "leave the ground" and fly through the environment. Pointing allows you to interact with objects displayed in the 3-D world.

After you select a mode, you can begin navigating and moving around. Using the keyboard in Fly mode, for example, you press *A* to move in to the object; press *Z* to move away from the object; and press the arrow keys to turn right or left or to view up or down.

In addition to the navigation selections at the bottom of the screen, you can choose among options including Headlight, Bank When Flying, and Chat Status. You can find these various additional navigation options by right-clicking anywhere in the VRML environment to display the navigation menu (see Figure 17-6). Then you right-click on the desired feature to access the second set of menu selections.

Figure 17-6:
This navigation menu allows you to select viewing options at a particular VRML-enabled Web site.

After you have a feel for this exciting new viewer capability, you can check out many of the other VRML sites that you can view with the WebFX plug-in. The sites are listed at the following URL:

```
http://www.paperinc.com/wrls.html
```

Seeing what other people are doing should give you some ideas on ways to incorporate this feature into your own Web site. For more information on creating a 3-D environment for your Web page, you should contact the WebFX site:

```
http://www.paperinc.com/
```

Adobe Acrobat Plug-In

Adobe Acrobat is a sophisticated document generator and viewer that works with Portable Document Format (.PDF) cross-platform-compatible files — that is, you can create, open, and read them either on a PC or a Mac — because they are generated in a PostScript format that either platform can use. The .PDF files also are easy to create using some of the other Adobe or Adobe-compatible products. Amber is an Adobe Acrobat plug-in that allows users to view and print .PDF files within a Netscape Navigator browser window.

The Amber plug-in offers numerous features: enabling the .PDF documents to connect to other Web sites, providing maximum file compression for documents, and providing immediate page display while additional pages are being downloaded. With the Amber plug-in, you can begin providing beautifully formatted information in the form of Adobe Acrobat files at your Web site.

You can download the plug-in from the following URL:

```
http://www.adobe.com/Amber/
```

After downloading and installing the plug-in, you can view a variety of Adobe Acrobat files. Be careful when you use versions of this program that are in the *beta* (test) stage; some of the files in your Web browser may fail. You should not have any problems with the Adobe Acrobat file located at the following URL (see Figure 17-7):

```
http://www.adobe.com/cgi-bin/byteserver3/Amber/Times.pdf
```

Figure 17-7:
Here's an
Adobe
document
viewed
using the
Amber
plug-in.

VRML Design Tools

By creating a VRML Web page, you can create a 3-D world that visitors can navigate using the VRML plug-in described in the section "WebFX."

Caligari, Inc. offers several VRML tools, including TrueSpace 2, Fountain, and TrueSpace S/E. You can download these VRML authoring tools from the following URL:

```
http://www.caligari.com/
```

After installing one of the authoring tools, you can begin to generate your own virtual world environment at your Web site. The Fountain software is designed to create VRML worlds that can be made available on the Web immediately. Figure 17-8 illustrates the starting screen for the Fountain software.

Figure 17-8 shows numerous tools that change the particular viewing and navigation mode used for the viewing capabilities. These are the same navigation capabilities found in the WebFX plug-in. For generating your own VRML environments, this program has numerous features, described in Table 17-1:

Table 17-1	VRML Features
Feature	**Description**
3-D rendering	Creates 3 dimensional images.
Object generation	Creates graphic "objects" users can interact with.
Capability to paint surfaces	Creates pictures on the surface of 3-D objects.
Material characteristics	Gives the graphic objects attributes when the user interacts with them.
2-D and 3-D object imports	Create graphics in other programs and import them.
Object links to URLs	Create World Wide Web links to other pages by clicking on graphic objects. This is useful for advertisements.

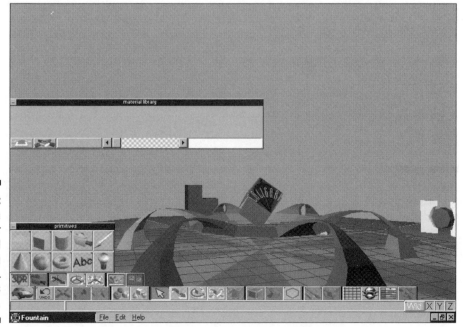

Figure 17-8: Fountain is a tool for viewing and generating VRML environments in the Web.

Using these VRML authoring tools gives you a new capability to provide interesting content to your Web site.

Electronic Book Technologies

Electronic Book Technologies is a company that offers products for publishing large or graphics-intensive documents. These products use a programming language called SGML (*Standard Generalized Markup Language*).

The HTML (HyperText Markup Language) language is only a subset of SGML that is currently used to contact HTTP (HyperText Transfer Protocol) servers that define what we know as the Web right now. In other words, HTML doesn't offer the power or reliability of SGML. Also, unlike SGML, the HTML language is constantly changing, which means that a document you create today may not open or display properly tomorrow.

The products offered by Electronic Book Technologies are ideal for people who want to provide large documents on CD-ROMs or over the Internet. Given the constantly changing HTML standards, trying to keep up with all the changes would make producing this material a nightmare. Electronic Book Technologies offers a DynaWeb server (see Figure 17-9) that allows a document to be generated

Figure 17-9:
This is a Web page produced with the DynaWeb server.

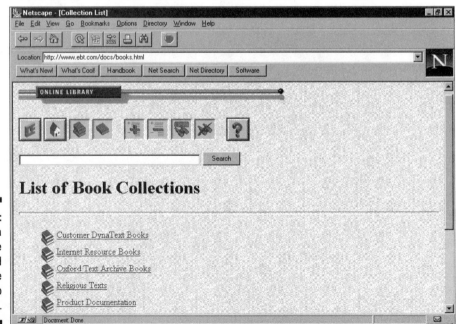

in SGML and then converted to HTML for distribution across the Internet. Therefore, the next time Netscape advances new HTML standards, you won't have to redo all the pages in a 200-page online document.

Another desirable feature of the DynaWeb server is its capability to provide a search tool within the Web document. Because the DynaWeb server is reading the information from the more powerful SGML, rather than from HTML, it provides this powerful search utility for any document.

Electronic Book Technologies will soon offer a plug-in that should allow you to view SGML-produced documents within an HTML Web browser. This feature will keep you from having to convert the SGML to HTML before viewing the document. Keep checking for more information at the following URL:

```
http://www.ebt.com/
```

Digital Cameras

If you want to display pictures on the Internet, you can bypass a scanner by using a digital camera. Instead of saving an image on traditional film, a digital camera saves an image as digital information that you can download to your computer's hard drive.

One of the highest-quality, most affordable digital cameras is the Dakota DCC-9500 (see Figure 17-10). To learn more about this cool digital camera, call 800-52-FOCUS and tell them that you just read about the Dakota in this book.

After you install the Dakota camera software, shown in Figure 17-11, onto your computer, you can download and review all the images currently in the camera's memory. You can then save the image files of the pictures you want to keep and delete all the others.

Figure 17-10:
The Dakota DCC-9500 is a high-quality, reasonably-priced digital camera.

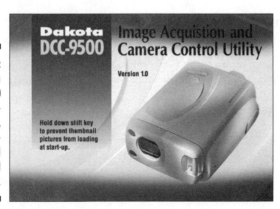

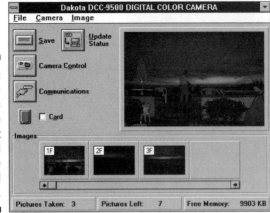

Figure 17-11:
Use the
camera's
software to
view recent
pictures and
then save
or discard
them.

The digital camera allows you to take pictures with three levels of detail.
Higher-detail pictures require more memory and limit the number of pictures
that can be saved in the camera's memory. Using Normal detail, you can store
40 images; using Fine mode, you can save 10 images; and using Superfine mode,
you can save 5 images.

If you expect to take a significant number of pictures, you can purchase
memory-expansion modules to increase the camera's memory capability.

Macromedia Director

Macromedia Director software is used to generate animations that can be
viewed in Web documents by users who have downloaded the Shockwave
plug-in (described earlier in this chapter). Director is one of the simplest,
most powerful animation software packages currently available for creating
multimedia content.

Director uses several design tools that allow you to manipulate objects easily,
thereby producing animations as simply as possible. When you create an
animation, you first place all the items that you want in your animation in the
Cast window. These items might include graphics, text, sound or music,
buttons, and colors. The images in Figure 17-12 represent the various scenes
that appear in a particular animation.

Figure 17-12:
Use the Cast window to enter all the items that will be in the animation.

After you enter all the various items in the Cast window, you go to the Score window (see Figure 17-13), which allows you to indicate at which particular frame each cast object will appear in the final animation. The Score window has a top row of numbers that indicate the frames of the animation. The column of numbers indicates the cast-member objects, and the additional boxes below each frame number indicate the display status of each cast member during that particular frame of the animation.

Figure 17-13:
The Score window indicates where each object is in each frame of the animation.

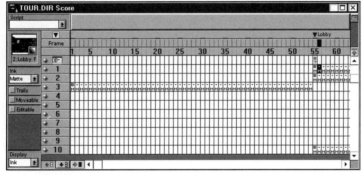

After you assemble the cast objects in the desired frame display within the Score window, you're ready to play the animation, using the control panel shown in Figure 17-14. You can stop the animation at any time to make corrections in the Cast and Score windows.

Figure 17-14:
Use the control panel to display the final animation.

After you develop a Director animation, you must use the Afterburner software to compress the animation so that it can be uploaded to an HTTP server for users who have the Shockwave plug-in. You can download the Afterburner software from the following Web site:

```
http://www.macromedia.com/Tools/Shockwave/
```

At this Web site, you also can find an online guide for developing content that will be provided on the Web for viewing with the Shockwave plug-in. This is an indispensible guide to Shockwave authoring for the World Wide Web.

Chapter 18

More Than Ten Places to Go for More Information

*T*he Internet is the greatest source of information (next to this book) on creating a successful Internet presence. This chapter serves as a guide to the many places that you can go for help or inspiration.

We begin our list of URLs with the places where many people start: the indexes and search utilities. These resources are great to look into when you aren't sure where else to go.

Search Utilities, Indexes, and Directories

The Internet has become so vast that navigating it effectively would be nearly impossible without indexes, guides, databases, and search utilities. You can use these resources to find documents, people, and other online resources. The list in this section is not exhaustive, but chances are that you will find some favorites here and stick with them.

Yahoo is the best directory on the Net; it's easy to use, and well-edited for content. The URL is:

```
http://www.yahoo.com/
```

Four11 is the white pages directory for the Internet. The URL is:

```
http://www.four11.com/
```

Lycos is the largest search database on the Internet. Databases of different sizes are available. Lycos tends to return too much information. The URL is:

```
http://www.lycos.com/
```

InfoSeek is a commercial search utility. For a free demo, see the following URL:

```
http://www.infoseek.com/
```

WebCrawler, a Web crawler utility, is great if you want everything and the kitchen sink. The URL is:

```
http://www.webcrawler.com/
```

555-1212.com is a simple and fast way to find companies, organizations, products, and services on the Net. The URL is:

```
http://www.555-1212.com/
```

Online News and Publications

Many excellent publications are available on the Internet. Some of these publications have been available as print magazines for quite a while; others are new and available only online. By reading the magazines listed in this section, you can stay abreast of everything that happens in the quickly changing world of cyberspace.

HotWired Magazine covers cutting-edge technology and should be on your reading list. The URL is:

```
http://www.hotwired.com/
```

The *San Jose Mercury News* is the best online newspaper. Their URL is:

```
http://www.sjmercury.com/
```

Science, published by the American Association for the Advancement of Science, is one of the major scientific journals. Their Web site is located at the following URL:

```
http://www.aaas.org/
```

Nature, another major scientific journal, is located at the following URL:

```
http://www.nature.com/
```

CNN Interactive, which is as good as the broadcast version of CNN, is located at the following URL:

```
http://www.cnn.com/
```

Software Sources

One of the keys to a successful Internet site is having all the right software. Some of the software is *freeware,* which is free to everyone. Some of the software is *shareware;* you pay for it after you try it, but only if you like it. We encourage you to pay the license fees to the developers of shareware because the payments promote further development.

Finally, some Internet software is available in the traditional-commercial software market. The sites listed in this section have some of all three types of software.

Make sure that you read any file named README, INSTALL, or MANUAL before attempting to install any software. A mistake as simple as omitting -d from a PKUNZIP command can cause the software not to work. In addition, the installation process is not the same for all software.

Ultimate Collection of WinSock Software is one of the best sources of freeware and shareware for Windows. The URL is:

```
http://www.tucows.com/
```

Virtual Shareware Library is a library of all types of shareware programs, not just Internet software. The URL is:

```
http://www.shareware.com/
```

Walnut Creek CDROM is a superb online software resource. The URL is:

```
http://www.cdrom.com/
```

The Association of Shareware Professionals provides access to members' shareware products and other information about shareware. The URL is:

```
http://www.asp-shareware.org/
```

Software.net (pronounced *software dot net*) is the best source for commercial online software sales. The URL is:

```
http://www.software.net/
```

Windows 95 is the best Windows 95 site on the Net. The URL is:

```
http://www.windows95.com/
```

Business on the Internet

Running a business on the Internet is one of the fastest-growing facets of today's world. This section lists some resources that will guide you in setting up your business on the Internet, maintaining it, and marketing it.

Here is our Setting Up An Internet Site page:

```
http://www.science.org/internetsite/
```

Yahoo's Business Directory page is a superb search engine. Its URL is:

```
http://www.yahoo.com/Business_and_Economy/Business_Directory/
```

Internet Marketing Archive page is an excellent resource. Its URL is:

```
http://www.popco.com/hyper/internet-marketing/
```

U.S. Government Organizations

The government giveth, and the government taketh away — and government sites are one of the greatest information sources that your tax dollars can buy.

In your Internet ventures, you may need to contact the Patent and Trademark Office. Its URL is:

```
http://www.uspto.gov/
```

Anyone starting a small business can profit from the information and resources offered by the Small Business Administration On-Line. Its URL is:

```
http://www.sbaonline.sba.gov/
```

The Department of the Treasury has helpful information. Its URL is:

```
http://www.ustreas.gov/
```

NASA (one of the best spots on the Net) is a fascinating site. Its URL is:

```
http://www.nasa.gov/
```

You will probably want to contact The White House some day. Its URL is:

```
http://www.whitehouse.gov/
```

Legal Resources

Cyberspace has created an entirely new place to practice law. This time is an exciting and challenging one for the legal profession, and new precedents are being set daily. We are seeing only the beginning of this new system of justice. In an information society, leaving your legal wherewithal to the lawyers is no longer enough. The sites listed in this section provide a wealth of noncommercial legal information. (We hope that you don't need the commercial kind.)

Cornell Law School's Legal Information Institute provides excellent information. Its URL is:

```
http://www.law.cornell.edu/
```

The WWW Virtual Law Library is an awesome resource. Its URL is:

```
http://www.law.indiana.edu/law/lawindex.html
```

Want to contact The Copyright Website (the name says it all)? Its URL is:

```
http://www.benedict.com/
```

Legal Care for Your Software is a guide for software programmers and publishers. Its URL is:

```
http://www.island.com/LegalCare/
```

Yahoo's Law page offers helpful information. Its URL is:

```
http://www.yahoo.com/Government/Law/
```

Internet Organizations and Services

Who are the people behind the screen who make everything happen? The list includes task forces, research committees, clubs, societies, agencies, companies, and private individuals. This section lists some of the organizations that help maintain the vital databases, information, and order of the Internet.

The Internet Engineering Task Force is an excellent resource. Its URL is:

```
http://www.ietf.org/
```

Contacting InterNIC Registration Services is mandatory in setting up an Internet site. Its URL is:

```
http://rs.internic.net/
```

The Electronic Frontier Foundation has much to offer. Its URL is:

```
http://www.eff.org/
```

This URL offers a popular list of access providers:

```
http://www.yahoo.com/Business/Corporations/↩
Internet_Access_Providers
```

Publishing-Related Sites

We're a little partial to the two URLs listed in this section. IDG Books Worldwide, Inc. has been influential in bringing the Internet to the people. We are pleased to be able to bring you *Setting Up An Internet Site For Dummies* through IDG. If you have ever thought about writing a book — or if, after reading this book, you just know that you could have done better — you should contact a literary agency. Waterside Productions is the best.

IDG Books Online:

```
http://www.idgbooks.com/
```

Waterside Productions:

```
http://www.waterside.com/
```

Chapter 19

Ten JavaScripts to Spice Up Your Web Page

*J*ava is a new programming language, written by Sun Microsystems, that is taking the Internet by storm. This new language is compact, fast, and efficient. More than anything, software written using Java will run on almost any computer. Java's slogan is "Write once, run anywhere!"

Programmers use Java to write full applications or mini-applications, called *Java applets*, that run in Web browsers. The only problem is that Java is a very complicated programming language. If you're not an expert programmer, you can't write Java programs. To solve this problem and make the power of Java accessible to you as an Internet site developer, Netscape and Sun Microsystems created *JavaScript*. JavaScript is a simpler version of Java that you can embed in the HTML source of any World Wide Web page.

If you currently run a Web site or intend to create one soon, then JavaScript is an important technology for you to explore. JavaScript is so important to the creation of Web pages that we're dedicating an entire chapter to it. Following are ten sample Web pages that integrate HTML and JavaScript to achieve effects that are impossible using HTML alone.

To try one of the samples, create a new text file using your favorite text editor, such as Notepad or TeachText. Type in the sample exactly as it is shown. Save the file as text-only and be sure to name the file with a .HTM file extension. Open the file using Netscape Navigator 2.0 by choosing File⇨Open. If everything works okay, the Web page appears in the Netscape Navigator window, with the special effect we describe.

The scripts in this chapter illustrate the basics of the JavaScript language and suggest specific ways in which you can use JavaScript to enhance typical Web pages. These examples should work with Netscape Navigator version 2.0 or greater, though a few of the scripts might not work on your computer due to changes made after this book was written. If you have any trouble using the scripts shown in this chapter, contact the following Web site for updated scripts that will work:

```
http://www.science.org/internetsite/
```

Achieving Status

Drag your mouse over any of the links (the highlighted and underlined text that you click on to surf the Web) on a World Wide Web page and then look at the bottom of the browser window. In the bottom of the window frame, you'll see the URL to which this link will take you. Figure 19-1 shows a URL in the area along the bottom.

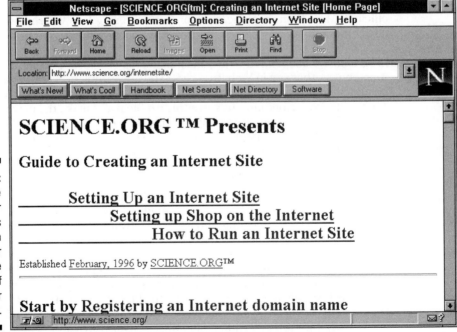

Figure 19-1:
Netscape
Navigator
displays
information
to the user
at the
bottom of
the browser
window.

Netscape Navigator usually displays the message okay. Wouldn't it be much more interesting if the message were *"This link takes you to Netscape's Web site so you can download Navigator"*? In Netscape Navigator, the bottom part of the window, where messages appear, is known as the *status area*. Using JavaScript, you can easily provide a custom message in the status area when someone drags a mouse over a link on your page.

One thing to keep in mind when you type these examples is that JavaScript is case-sensitive. Be sure that you type capital letters where they belong; otherwise, these examples won't work.

To create a custom message for a particular link on your page, you have to include some JavaScript in the anchor syntax. Normally, an anchor looks like this:

```
<A HREF="http://www.science.org/">SCIENCE.ORG</A>
```

With JavaScript added to display a custom message in the status area, the same anchor looks like this:

```
<A HREF="http://www.science.org/"
onMouseOver="window.status='SCIENCE.ORG Home Page';
return true">SCIENCE.ORG</A>
```

Notice these five elements in the preceding code line:

- ✔ onMouseOver
- ✔ window.status
- ✔ The equal signs
- ✔ The single quotation marks around SCIENCE.ORG Home Page
- ✔ The semicolon after SCIENCE.ORG Home Page

Netscape Navigator uses onMouseOver to indicate that the user has moved the mouse pointer over a certain area on the Navigator window. In the preceding example, onMouseOver tells Navigator to display a message in the status area only when the mouse pointer is moved over a link. When the mouse pointer is not over a link, nothing special should happen.

onMouseOver is a Windows *event*, a notification from Windows that something has occurred, such as the user has moved the mouse over a link. Windows sends event messages when users open or close windows or click the mouse, and when hundreds of other events occur.

JavaScript uses `window.status` to refer to the status area. To display a message in the status area, use `window.status` followed immediately by the equal sign (=). For example, the following tells Navigator to display `SCIENCE.ORG Home Page` in the window status area:

```
window.status='SCIENCE.ORG Home Page';
```

JavaScript requires the single quotation marks around the message and the semicolon (;) at the end of the line. The following code uses HTML and JavaScript to create the page depicted in Figure 19-2.

```
<HTML><HEAD>
<TITLE>Window Status Example</TITLE>
</HEAD><BODY>
<H1>Window Status Example</H1>
<A  HREF="http://www.science.org/"
onMouseOver="window.status='SCIENCE.ORG  Home  Page';
return true">SCIENCE.ORG</A>
</BODY>
</HTML>
```

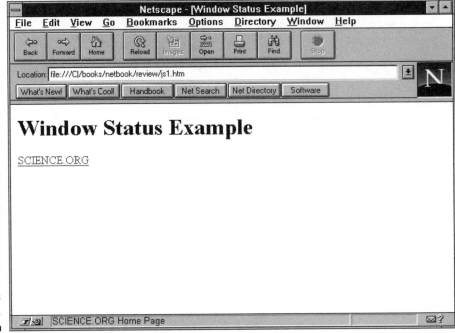

Figure 19-2:
JavaScript gives you control over the message displayed in the status area.

In the preceding example, `onMouseOver="window.status='SCIENCE.ORG Home Page` causes the custom message `SCIENCE.ORG Home Page` to appear in the status area when a user moves the mouse over the link.

Notice in the example the double quotation marks just before *window.status* and after *return true*. The custom message that falls in the middle is surrounded by single quotes. We have very good reasons for using the single and double quotation marks. Just be sure to type the text exactly as it is shown or the Web page won't work the way that it should.

Staying Alert with Java

How would you like to have an Alert dialog box pop out of your World Wide Web page? By using JavaScript, you can cause a pop-up dialog box to appear on the screen to display a message. The *Alert* JavaScript function displays an Alert dialog box (see Figure 19-3) that stays on-screen until the user clicks on OK or presses Enter.

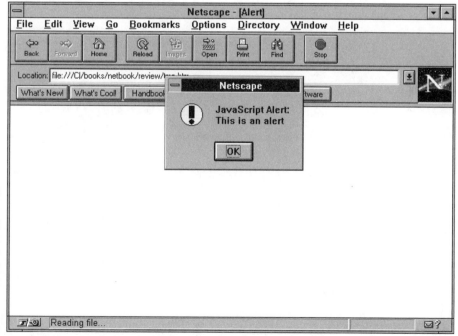

Figure 19-3:
The Alert dialog box is a convenient way to get the attention of the user.

An Alert dialog box warns users that they have done something wrong. This dialog box is particularly useful when your World Wide Web page contains a form. A form is an area of a Web page that allows the user to enter data or select items from list boxes, radio buttons, or check boxes. If you've never created a form before, don't worry; there's not much to it when you use the HTML syntax. (*HTML For Dummies,* written by Ed Tittel and published by IDG Books Worldwide, Inc., provides comprehensive coverage of HTML if you want more information.)

The following is an example of a simple form with a JavaScript function that checks to see whether users entered a value in the text-entry box. If not, Netscape displays an Alert dialog box, informing the users that they must enter a name in the form.

```
<HTML><HEAD>
<TITLE>Alert Example</TITLE>
<SCRIPT>
function checkit(theform){
    if (theform.Name.value.length == 0){
    alert("You must add a name")
    theform.Name.focus()
    return false
    }
theform.submit()
return true
}
</SCRIPT></HEAD><BODY>
<FORM METHOD="Post" ACTION="" name="pform">
Name: <INPUT TYPE="text" NAME="Name" SIZE="12"
            MAXLENGTH="35">
<INPUT TYPE="button" VALUE="OK"
            onClick="checkit(document.pform)">
</FORM></BODY></HTML>
```

This example includes an HTML tag you may not recognize. The <SCRIPT> and </SCRIPT> tags surround JavaScript *functions* in your HTML page. The JavaScript code checkit() is called a *function*.

Figure 19-4 shows the result of this JavaScript example when the user forgets to type in a name in the form. The alert function displays a message and allows the user to click on OK to continue.

The most challenging part of using JavaScript is learning the various functions and key words. Netscape Communications Corporation provides complete documentation for the JavaScript language at the following URL:

```
http://www.netscape.com/comprod/products/navigator/
    version_2.0/script/script_info/index.html
```

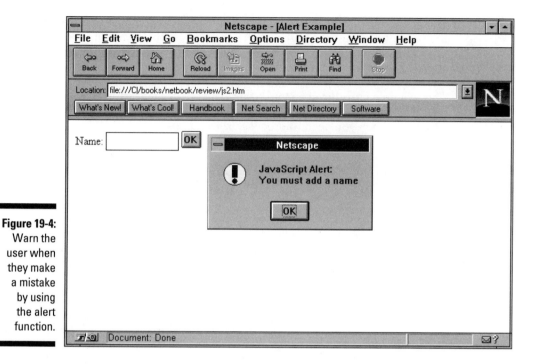

Figure 19-4:
Warn the user when they make a mistake by using the alert function.

Adding Data Promptly

Customizing your pages for your readers is fun. You can prompt for information from your Web page in a Prompt dialog box. For example, you can prompt for a person's name and then write a message to that person in your page, personalized with his or her name. Readers will be much more interested in your page when they see their names in it.

The following is a simple example of how to customize your page with someone's name:

```
<HTML><HEAD>
<TITLE>Prompt Example</TITLE>
<SCRIPT>
function getname(){
    fname = prompt("Enter your name:","")
    return fname
}
</SCRIPT></HEAD><BODY><SCRIPT>
xname = getname()
document.write("<h2>Hi there, " + xname +".</h2>")
</SCRIPT></BODY></HTML>
```

The `getname` function used in this example returns whatever the user enters in the prompt dialog as the entry for the `xname` variable. JavaScript then uses the `write` function to write the variable, and it appears on the Web page. Figures 19-5 and 19-6 show this example in action.

This example introduced an important concept in JavaScript: a function can return a value. Not all functions return values, but those that do are useful in situations when you need to process user responses.

Knowing Where You've Come From

JavaScript can give you the URL of the *referrer* — the page that the user was on when he or she clicked on a link to come to your page. You can do a great deal with this information. Many people who run Web pages want to know how people got to their page. This information enables them to concentrate their marketing efforts on the appropriate audience.

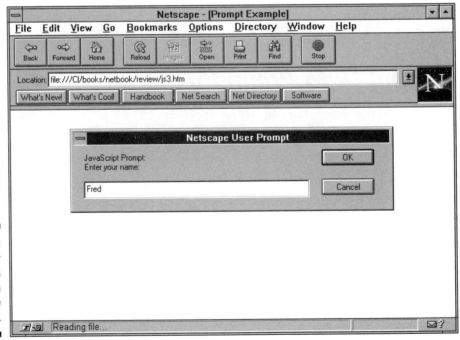

Figure 19-5:
The user enters information in the prompt box.

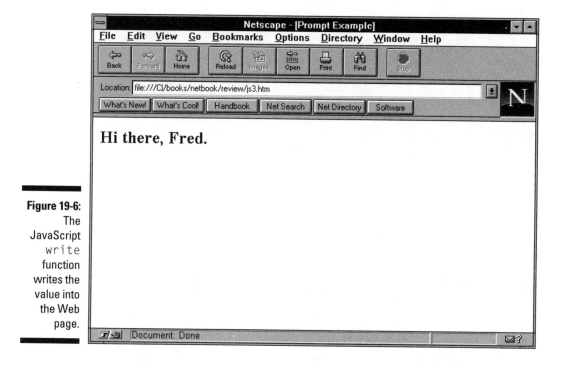

Figure 19-6:
The
JavaScript
`write`
function
writes the
value into
the Web
page.

The following example uses an *attribute* of the Netscape document. Attributes are the informational values stored by a Netscape document such as its background color, foreground color, the URL of the page, and the referrer. The preceding example used the `write` function to write information to the screen. In the following example, the same function writes the value of the referrer attribute to the screen with some pleasant results (see Figure 19-7).

```
<HTML>
<HEAD>
<TITLE>Know Where You've Come From</TITLE>
</HEAD>
<BODY>
<H3>Hi, thanks for visiting from
<SCRIPT>
document.write(document.referrer)
</SCRIPT></H3>
</BODY>
</HTML>
```

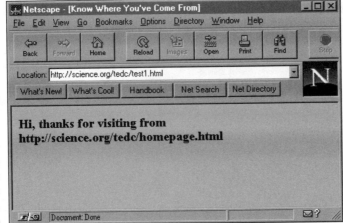

Figure 19-7:
Amaze
users by
showing
them where
they've
come from.

Seeing a Page of a Different Color

Colors make a Web page exciting. Having the colors change, depending on a user's actions on the page, is even more exciting. Two of the colors that we change in this example are the foreground and background colors of the Web page (known to Netscape as the *document*). Remember the onMouseOver event from the first JavaScript example? We'll use the same event to create a lightning effect when someone drags a mouse over a link.

The preceding example displayed the values of the Netscape document's attributes. The following example changes the values of the attributes to produce an interesting effect. We change the values of document.bgColor (background color) and document.fgColor (foreground color). This example includes a function we've named invert, which changes the foreground and background colors back and forth between white (designated by #000000) and black (designated by #ffffff), shown in Figures 19-8 and 19-9.

```
<HTML>
<HEAD>
<TITLE>Fun With Color Changes</TITLE>
<SCRIPT>
function invert(){
    if (document.fgColor == "#000000"){
    document.fgColor="#ffffff"
    document.bgColor="#000000"
    }else
    {document.fgColor="#000000"
    document.bgColor="#ffffff"}

}
```
(continued)

```
</SCRIPT>
</HEAD>
<BODY>
<A HREF="http://science.org/ " onMouseOver="invert()">Moving
   your mouse over this will cause a color change </A>
</BODY>
</HTML>
```

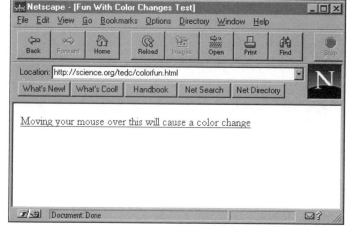

Figure 19-8:
The Web page before a user drags the mouse over the link.

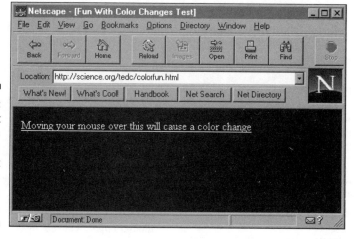

Figure 19-9:
Here's what happens when the invert function changes the colors.

Opening Additional Web Browser Windows

You can use the JavaScript `window.open` function to automatically launch Netscape, enabling you to have more than one copy of Netscape running on your computer at the same time. Use this function when you want to show your viewing public a different page, or image, without having to leave your Web page. Figure 19-10 shows a new copy of Netscape being opened when the mouse passes over a link. You can trigger this in other ways — for example, using a button in a form.

```
<HTML>
<HEAD>
<TITLE>More Netscape Navigators than you know what to do
        with</TITLE>
<SCRIPT>
function pop(){
window.open("ftp://ftp.netscape.com","NetFTP", toolbar=0,
        location=0, directories=0,
status=0, menubar=0)
}
</SCRIPT>
</HEAD>
<BODY>
<a href="http://www.netscape.com" onMouseOver="pop()">Netscape</a>
</BODY>
</HTML>
```

You can mix and match all the examples in this chapter to get your Web page to do exactly what you want. Remember to check out the online JavaScript documentation for extra help.

A powerful JavaScript feature is its capability to customize the way the new copy of Netscape appears. (see Figure 19-10). Table 19-1 shows all the parameters that you can set in the `open` function. Only some of these parameters are set in the preceding example. You can experiment with any of them.

Table 19-1   Parameters Available in the open **Function**

Parameter	Description
`toolbar[=yes|no]|[=1|0]`	If `toolbar` equals `yes`, the Netscape toolbar appears in your new window.
`location[=yes|no]|[=1|0]`	If `location` equals `yes`, the Netscape location bar appears in your new window.

Parameter	Description
directories[=yes|no]|[=1|0]	If directories equals yes, the Directory buttons (such as "What's Cool") appear.
status[=yes|no]|[=1|0]	If status equals yes, the status area appears at the bottom of the window.
menubar[=yes|no]|[=1|0]	If menubar equals yes, the menu bar appears across the top of the window.
scrollbars[=yes|no]|[=1|0]	If scrollbars equal yes, both horizontal and vertical scroll bars appear in your new window.
resizable[=yes|no]|[=1|0]	If you want your new window to be resizable, set this parameter to yes.
copyhistory[=yes|no]|[=1|0]	If you want the history to be copied from the originating window to the new window, set this parameter to yes.
width=pixels	Set the width of your new window by specifying a number.
height=pixels	Set the height of the new window by specifying a number.

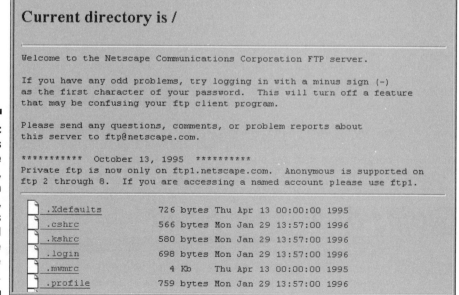

Figure 19-10: This Netscape window, showing an FTP site, was launched from the example JavaScript.

The JavaScript documentation says that you can use the open function for two different purposes: to open a specific type of document and to open a new copy of Netscape (as we did in this example). This function has many parameters. You'll probably want to refer to the documentation when you use this function.

It's a good idea to check the JavaScript documentation once in awhile. You may find changes in the way JavaScript is written that you'll want to reflect in your own JavaScript programs.

Sending a Confirmation

You also use JavaScript to display a Confirm dialog box, which displays your message and asks the user to either confirm or cancel. This type of dialog box is great for messages such as "Are you sure you want to submit this form?"

The following example asks users if they are sure that they want to leave your page whenever they try to close Netscape or enter a new location (see Figure 19-11):

```
<HTML>
<HEAD>
<TITLE>My Adventure</TITLE>
<SCRIPT>
function check(){
    confirm("Do you really want to leave my page?")
    }
</SCRIPT>
</HEAD>
<body onUnload="check()">
<A HREF="http://www.netscape.com">Netscape Home Page</A>
</BODY>
</HTML>
```

As you become more comfortable with JavaScript programming, you will learn how to choose what you want Netscape to do, depending on whether someone clicked on the OK or Cancel button in the Confirm dialog box.

Getting Back to the Future

This section presents a simple way to create a link that takes the user back to the preceding page. Most Back buttons or links are hard-coded — in other words, when you click on them, you go back to the link that is written in the

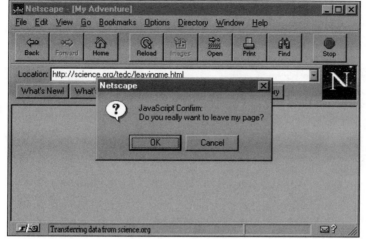

Figure 19-11:
When your user's Web page tries to unload, this confirmation appears.

HTML code, not really back where you came from. This example creates a simple link that allows people to go back one page as though they had clicked on the Back button in their Web browser.

In JavaScript, the history object keeps track of the pages that the user has visited. Using `history.go -1` takes the person back one place in history. Likewise, if you change `-1` to a positive number, you cause the user to go forward.

The following is a script for an example page, shown in Figure 19-12, that contains a simple Back button. Notice that we defined a form on which the button is the only object.

```
<HTML>
<HEAD>
<TITLE>Go Back Test</TITLE>
<SCRIPT>
function goback(){
    history.go(-1)
}
</SCRIPT>
</HEAD>
<BODY>
<A HREF="http://www.netscape.com">Netscape Home Page</A>
<FORM>
<INPUT TYPE="button" VALUE="BACK"  NAME="backbutton"
            onClick="goback()">
</FORM>
</BODY>
</HTML>
```

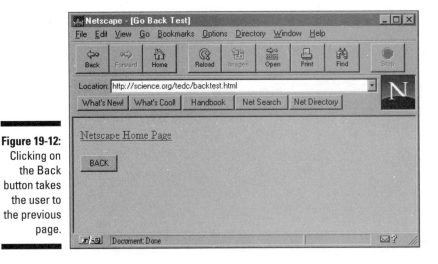

Figure 19-12:
Clicking on
the Back
button takes
the user to
the previous
page.

Proving There's No Place Like Home

In the preceding section, "Getting Back to the Future," we showed how you to create a Back button that takes a user to the page from which he or she just came. What if you want to take the user to your home page instead? This section presents some JavaScript that changes the message that users see in the link that takes them home. If users have come from one of your pages, the message tells them that they can go back to your home page; if they came from somewhere else, the message invites them to visit your home page (see Figure 19-13).

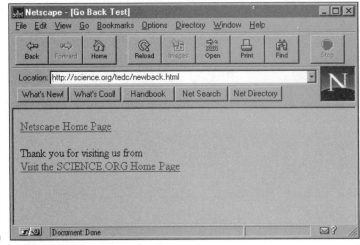

Figure 19-13:
Change the
message
that appears,
depending
on where
the user
came from.

```
<HTML>
<HEAD>
<TITLE>Go Back Test</TITLE>
</HEAD>
<BODY>
<A HREF="http://www.netscape.com/">Netscape Home Page</A><P>
<SCRIPT>
    TheURL=document.referrer
    TheHost=TheURL.substring(7,22)
    if (TheHost == "www.science.org"){
    goplace = "Back to Previous SCIENCE.ORG Page"
    document.write(goplace.link(TheURL))
    }else
    {
    document.write("Thank you for visiting us from " + TheURL
            + "<br>")
    goplace = "Visit the SCIENCE.ORG Home Page"
    document.write(goplace.link("http://www.science.org/"))
    }
</SCRIPT>
</BODY>
</HTML>
```

JavaScripting an Interactive Web Page

If your company wants to sell products but can't run a point-of-sale program over the Internet, you may be interested in this JavaScript example, which is a little more advanced. Figuring out what everything does in this example can be fun.

```
<HTML>
<HEAD>
<TITLE>Point of Sale System</TITLE>
<SCRIPT>
function order(){
    this.amount = 0;
    this.item = "";
    this.totitems = 0;
    this.addamt = addamt;
    this.additem = additem;
    this.CreateInvoice = CreateInvoice;

    }
```

(continued)

```
function addamt(amt){
    this.amount += amt
    }
function additem(thing,amt){
    this.totitems += 1
    this.item[this.totitems] = thing
    this.addamt(amt)
    }
function CreateInvoice(){
document.clear()
    PrintString = "<H1>INVOICE</H1><H3>Items</H3>"
    for (i=1;i <= this.totitems;i++){
        PrintString += this.item[i] + "<BR>"
    }
    PrintString += "<h3>Total: $"+this.amount+"</h3>"
    PrintString += "<h4>Send us money and we'll send you the
            stuff</h4>"
    document.write(PrintString)
    }
gear = new order()
</SCRIPT>
</HEAD>
<BODY>
<H1>Virtual Corporation's Shopping Page</H1>
Click on the items you'd like to purchase and then click the
            Done button.
<FORM>
<INPUT TYPE="button" VALUE="Tennis Shoes"
            onClick="gear.additem('Tennis Shoes',6
5.00);form.OrderTotal.value='$'+gear.amount">
<INPUT TYPE="button" VALUE="Digital Camera"
            onClick="gear.additem('Digital Camer
a',985.00);form.OrderTotal.value='$'+gear.amount">
<INPUT TYPE="button" VALUE="Mountain Bike"
            onClick="gear.additem('Mountain Bike'
,428.00);form.OrderTotal.value='$'+gear.amount">
<P>
Total:
<INPUT Type="text" NAME="OrderTotal">
<INPUT TYPE="button" VALUE="Done"
            onClick="gear.CreateInvoice()">
</FORM>
</BODY>
</HTML>
```

This example creates the form shown in Figure 19-14. Clicking on a product button adds the price of the product to the total. You can watch this figure increment as you click on the buttons. Clicking on the form's Done button creates the invoice shown in Figure 19-15.

This JavaScript example introduces some advanced topics, such as creating new objects. These advanced features are explained in more detail within the JavaScript documentation.

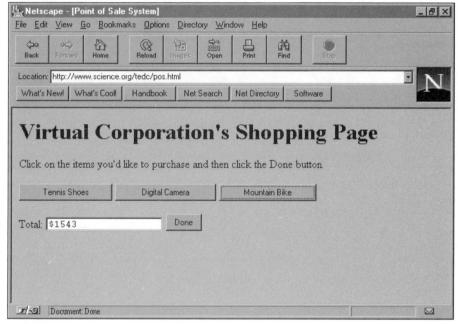

Figure 19-14:
The Virtual
Corporation
Point of Sale
System.

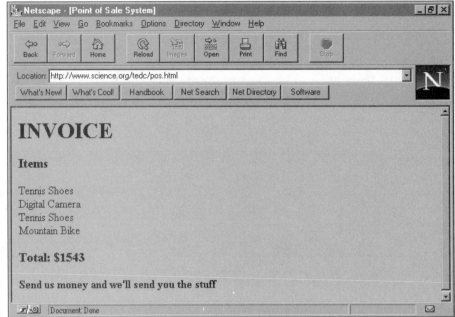

Index